BRITISH POETRY 1964 TO 1984

BRITISH POETRY
1964 TO 1984

Driving through the barricades

MARTIN BOOTH

ROUTLEDGE & KEGAN PAUL

London, Boston, Melbourne and Henley

First published in 1985
by Routledge & Kegan Paul plc

14 Leicester Square, London WC2H 7PH, England

9 Park Street, Boston, Mass. 02108, USA

464 St Kilda Road, Melbourne,
Victoria 3004, Australia and

Broadway House, Newtown Road,
Henley-on-Thames, Oxon RG9 1EN, England

Set in 10 on 11 point Palatino
by Fontwise
and printed in Great Britain
by
Thetford Press Limited
Thetford, Norfolk

Library of Congress Cataloging in Publication Data
Booth, Martin.
British poetry 1964 to 1984.

Includes index.
1. English poetry--20th century--History and criticism. I. Title.
PR611.B6   1985   821'.914'09   84–13425

British Library CIP data available

ISBN 0–7100–9606–2

CONTENTS

v

PREFACE

This book is written from a closely personal viewpoint and does not seek to be an academic text. As will become apparent, it is hoping to react against the academicism which has, in its own ways, more than assisted towards the ruination of British verse since the end of the exciting era from approximately 1964 to 1974, when such atrociously narrowing values were put aside for a newer sense of creative energy, truth and expertise. Similarly, the book tries not to be dogmatic, but that is less easily accomplished for, if it is a personal document then it must, at times, take on the prejudices of the individual. However, much of the comment in the book comes from others who were and are involved in the act of keeping British poetry going.

Poetry seems, more than any of the other branches of literature, to engender cliques, hard factions, groups, entrenched attitudes and general animosity. This is to its detriment and its eventual downfall. It is the function of this book not to sweep these aside, but to point them out and comment upon them, their harm and, fair to say, occasional use.

Above all, the book hopes to give a sense of direction to poetry, that it might avoid some of its pitfalls, at the same time acting as an introduction or guide to the poetry road and why it has reached as far as it has. It might also be taken as an object lesson by those who look to joining it, or leaving it, or standing by it and watching the (often) benighted travellers pass.

In Britain, poetry has gone from being largely sterile to immensely virile and has returned to sterility within a decade and a half. The causes are fundamental to the art of poetry writing and, where they are bad, they should be cast out.

PART ONE

How it is and was. . . .

1

British poetry is a mess: it has lost itself in a bog of indifference, apathy and artlessness such as it has never seen before. Despite the prevailing attitudes of the public towards verse these days the poets, by and large, simply aren't matching up to the demands of, as a trader would put it, the market pressures. It's as if a new vegetable market has been set up, with clamorous crowds longing to purchase aubergines, cabbages, lettuces, peppers, carrots, artichokes and all manner of common and exotic vegetables only to discover that the farmers are determined to grow tulips, lupins, hybrid roses and, as a sop to the market masses, asparagus that can also be used as a foodstuff as well as its more important and vital role as a decorative fern in flower arrangements. Especially wreaths.

Sound education in the schools has brought about in the last two decades an awareness for poetry in the public that has been largely missing since Anglo-Saxon times. Teachers bring to their pupils the delights, fun and intellectual prowess of poets. Poetry lessons these days are not the boredom-hour of listening to Masefield's superb, but endlessly repeated 'Cargoes' or 'Sea Fever' with homework set to learn the work off by heart for Thursday's lesson when someone is going to have to recite it. A whole generation or two of British schoolchildren, now in their thirties or forties, can recall parrot-fashion some fragments of those two poems, possibly mixed in with shards of de la Mare's 'The Listeners' and Auden's poem about the night mail taking the post north through wartime Britain. Those with somewhat more enlightened teachers might have come across Crabbe's 'Peter Grimes' or near-indecipherable bits of Wordsworth's The Prelude. Certainly Shelley, Keats, Tennyson and Byron (who was Bad) were shovelled into minds that were either deliberately apathetic to all this fairy nonsense, or innocently ignorant, or genuinely confused or a mixture of all three. From time to time, a bit of Kipling was thrown in to keep the humour going and to show that poetry was not all merely an assemblage of beautiful thoughts. Sometimes it was patriotic and moving.

For the best part, though, poetry was seen as an art that was elevated above the common man. To introduce children to poetry was rather like taking them through the Tate Gallery: here the idea was not to explain some of Turner's more complicated paintings, but to say that this is a Turner and isn't it lovely and you must see that this is genius in paint. The attitude was take it or leave it. Most left it.

Art, for many centuries, has been the province of the rich and fortunate elite. This is not a matter of class division or elitist advantage so much as a matter of historical fact. The wealthy with power had time to enjoy the arts and the rest had to spend most of their time making money to live by, their profits being shared by those with responsibility for organisation rather than tillage or weaving.

Most people simply didn't have time for it. Their hours were employed on other, earthier matters. Art did not enter into their lives except, perhaps, when in church where they were surrounded by it.

Today, if ever an art form, after a period of tremendous success, was to be seen to actively and almost purposefully seek to destroy itself, then this is it. Poetry is killing itself. And, as poetry is but the abstraction of poets, it must follow that British poets are in the process of killing themselves off. The dodo syndrome: the stupidity to fail to learn from good times past brought about the bird's demise. Poets in Britain are doing more than a fair imitation of the luckless bird. The irony is that the dodo couldn't fly and it wasn't too good at running, either. Poets can fly and they can run. But they won't.

2

WHEN WAS BRITISH POETRY REALLY ALIVE TO THE PEOPLE?

It was alive to a huge section of the British population at times in the period roughly covered by this book. That is, 1964 to 1984. Admittedly, those dates seem arbitrary, but there is reason for setting the boundaries so for, within that time, poetry in Britain has gone through a complete cycle, one that has in its passing shown just how powerful it can be when the mood takes the writers. Simultaneously, it also shows what a load of rubbish is foisted off from time to time upon an unsuspecting and misguided reading public.

This cycle – from incomprehensible poetry to incomprehensible poetry by way of understandable, enjoyable, enlightening

4

and enriching poetry – has in the past taken yawning eras to slip by, rather than one generation and a half.

Perhaps it is the speed with which this has gone streaking along that has confused poets and writers and readers alike. They can recall, 'within living memory' as it were, what things were like in the good old days. That means, for the sake of this argument, the second half of the 1960s. However, this facility for speedy recognition has not aided judgment, for those who have seen through the whole pack of the cards still do not appear to appreciate when they are holding a strong hand. Perhaps poetry people are like those in the rest of the world who still find it hard to come to grips with the fast communication of satellite phone links and Ceefax television. They live in a wriggling environment where continual bombardment by information and emotion simply befuddles the brain.

To see the cycle more accurately might be to see it in slow motion. Early on in English poetry, the same thing came to pass, but it did so over centuries, not decades. This particular wheel started to spin with the invention of English poetry.

There was a time, thirteen hundred years ago or so, when British verse belonged to the people. It was not protected by an elite who hoarded it but was shared by all and sundry, for it concerned itself with the common experience and the public historical background. Admittedly, it did elaborate upon or twist this a bit at the whim of the bard or those who paid his keep and to whom it was advantageous to see that his poetry remained culturally and politically in the blue. Even then, poetry was manipulated. This was not done necessarily with the guile of the present understanding of the meaning of propaganda but simply as a means of keeping tribal units together. To the Anglo-Saxon ear, even resounding defeats at the hands of the Norseman could be turned into epic victories of human struggle and glorification of what were, in the context of the age, military and political blunders of almost Suez and Falklands proportions. Whoever it was who wrote 'The Battle of Maldon' did it in grandiose terms, despite the fact that the encounter was merely a minor skirmish and defeat was brought about by high pride in Byrhtnoth's character. The leader of the English force made a fundamental error that caused his men to be massacred. Poetic licence was born into the English language. Yet the point is that this form of the tale was what the people hearing the poem wanted.

That audience, in what should be the true spirit of poetry, was sitting around the fire in the longhouse waiting for the bard to entertain them at a level at which they could appreciate his verse, his presentation, his subject matter and his skill with words. They did not appear as many British poetry audiences do these days, as one poet recently put it, as a group of folk attending merely in order to keep out of the rain.

The bardic entertainment did more than the narrow interpretation of the word might imply these days: poetry was education, information, opinion, retention of tradition or history, group identification and sheer abstract joy as might come from any art form, as well as entertainment. Poetry was much, much more than a stylistic putting-out of language, narrowed by the individual, as it has now tended to become. It was a major part of the verve and expression of the artistic and intellectual life of an entire appreciative community. Poetry was held dear.

So it was that the earliest British poets, writing in the vernacular, fulfilled an accepted and required demand and a distinct social role. The poet was to his listeners and very occasional readers accepted as a vital part of common cultural life. What he said was taken to heart, often learned by heart and it became a part of the public consciousness. People paid the poet attention. They thought about what he said. Poetry was not limited – as it often is today – to an art form only for those with a vested interest in it. It was everyone's, and it is not stretching the metaphor too far to suggest that poetry and its relations were the Anglo-Saxon's television set, covering his existence in its scope.

Reading some of the Old English poems today, we can enter into the true spirit of poetry, one that has been recaptured in recent years and is now lost again.

Poetry at its best reflects the world from which it comes. This may be the narrow horizons of the poet's mind, in which case the poetry might be good but hardly far-reaching for it is, under such a constraint, unable to comment on the wider life. If the poet extends his horizons, or writes about something that is personal yet common to many – say, an emotion known to all: love or hate – and portrays it in more than a limited viewpoint, then the poetry takes on a grander theme and is considerably more successful.

When poetry speaks for people (not just a person or two) it is doing its main job. It becomes a poetry for people that goes beyond the narrow bounds of the poetry specialists, be they scholars or poets themselves, or those who abound on the fringes of poetry and are on the increase.

To an Anglo-Saxon, poetry was an extension of life: one look at a fragment from 'The Battle of Maldon' shows poetry at its best, achieving success that might well be imitated or striven for by modern poets, and was for a while in the last two decades or so:

And then those heathens hacked him down
Alongside the two who were supporting him.
Ælfnoth and Wulfmær collapsed to the dust,
Both dying in defence of their lord.
It was then that cowards fled in retreat.
Godric fled, abandoning Byrhtnoth.
Choosing to forget his lord's gift of a horse,
He vaulted into his saddle,
His lord's own saddle, ignoring the law,
. . . .
And they fled into battle
Saving their own lives in the still forest.
More men followed them than should
Had they thought of their rewards
Formerly given by their lord, his generous gifts.
It was just as Offa told Bryhtnoth one day
At a council meeting at the meeting place.
Many spoke as men of their courage
Who would prove to lack it on the battle's face.

Poetry past was not just a means of retaining history and entertaining. It was concerned with the spiritual as well: religious poetry was abundant. Partly, this indicates the start of the rot in British verse, for this type of poetry was controlled by an elite for a set aim. The monks and priests, who could read and write, had obvious advantages over those who relied upon memory for their poetry. Yet the point is that poetry was used so much by the church because it knew the power of poetry. Christianity still existed in a superstitious land and had borrowed – and continued to borrow – a good deal from the pagan worshippers. This included verse. Poetry was magic. The poet was more than a member of the literati: he was a sage-like character, a wizard, a witch-doctor or shamanic figure who used words instead of (or as well as) concoctions and herbs. Whoever it was who wrote 'The Dream of The Rood' knew of this control that words in poetic form could have:

High upon that hill I suffered
Great grief. I saw the Lord of Hosts
Pulled on the rack. Blackness deeper than night
Hovered over our Lord's glowing corpse.
Shadows flashed across the land,
Dark shapes under low clouds. Creation wept,
Howled for the King's death. Christ was crucified.

7

From far and near, nobles travelled
To the Lonely Prince. I saw all that.

And two lines of verse from a silver strip on the Brussels Cross additionally show the magic associations that poetry bore. The lines are talismanic:

My name's Rood. Once, shivering,
Wet with blood, I held the Mighty King

Yet again, the entertainment value of poetry was often married to the magical and, in this, one sees the start of the widening of poetry's possibilities. The Anglo-Saxon riddles were aimed at a number of levels of understanding. They were entertainments, but also charms, spells, tricks of acrostics, sometimes repositories of learning. 'Riddle 83' might be about iron or ore, but other interpretations are possible:

I began way back and have outlasted winters,
living in towns after the fire-master
let go the lives of men ringed by flame,
purged by heat. Now the earth-brother,
who is my enemy, who first gave me ill-luck,
has me locked up. I remember well
who pulled me and my kin from our first place.
I can do him no harm yet, sometimes,
I am an instrument of imprisonment
throughout the wide world. I've many skills;
in middle-earth I have vast strength;
yet I am bound to conceal from men
the magical origins of my precious abilities
and my drawing forth. Guess at my name.

This was a time then when poetry was in a magnificent golden age. Since then, other golden ages have come and passed, when poetry has broadened out into a huge landscape of possibilities. The cycles have passed by – 'The Age of Chaucer' was one, where poetry was for anyone who could read and thereby see the oblique social and human comments the poet was making in his work of the human condition; Shakespeare and his contemporaries did it, albeit in the theatre, with plays that contained much poetry, or the controls of poetic language, and were aimed at the various levels of education and social standing in the audience; Milton, to some extent, reflected the upheaval of his times but was beyond the reach of the carter or ploughman or miller; the

Romantics struck at the sensibilities of their times, but again, they weren't writing for the general public, but the embryonic middle class of well-to-do folk.

John Milton, in some basic ways, shows the fault that British poetry has often slipped into. He wrote of matters that were of substance to his times. He wrote of his times in such a way that, reading him now and with education on our side, we can see so much of his world. But he was beyond his own people and, for that, his poetry was a failure and still is – few London cab drivers or Leeds lorry drivers or West Country farmers bother to read him.

3

What has gone before is generalisation: its aim is to outline rather than dogmatically indicate trends. But that is not to state that it is mostly untrue.

It can be argued that it is only in the twentieth century that poetry has had the opportunity once more to reach through to the common man from the mists of the privileged, as it did on long nights in Anglo-Saxon halls.

This widening came about in a number of ways, not in any order of preference, but as an unconscious addition of different elements towards a whole. The fragments that join together are those such as the rise of the middle classes, broadening education, mass production of books and simplifications of printing processes (which, in another boom after the Second World War, helped poetry achieve its rapid increase in the 1960s), a desire to read or be educated or be entertained, an increasing thirst for knowledge in an age in which the arts became truly accessible through reproduction techniques, an impinging upon the masses of simplistic poetry (as in advertising, for example), an interest in art as a recoiling away from modern technologies, and a series of events which fortuitously brought poetry into the public eye as a purveyor of mass emotion, thought and, resultingly, literary involvement. Just as had been the case in pre-Norman Conquest centuries. . . .

The first, and most important of these events, was the Great War: an event that shook the nation and held it hideously spellbound for over half a decade.

For the first time, war – always an emotive subject in the

extreme – was no longer a battle of armies conducted on a foreign patch of soil or, if nearer home, just as distant from the public by way of the divisions between the common man and the military. It was a conflict of nations and all that that implies: doggedly loyal patriotism, jingoistic pride and belligerent prejudice, all of them gut-level emotions. Tens of thousands were swept up by the call to arms and, at last, the whole nation could take part in something of national importance, either by wielding a bayonet or by following the action closely in the by now highly efficient mass medium of the newspapers. As the conflict was so dear and so close to so many, it meant that poetry written by the troops, as it were, reached a wider audience than letters home to loved ones. At first, that poetry fitted the mould of what one was used to expect of it in military terms – that is, the patriotic clatter of words such as those the likes of Rupert Brooke shovelled out. These were often shallow pieces intended for the fooled or the foolish:

> If I should die, think only this of me:
>   That there's some corner of a foreign field
> That is for ever England. There shall be
>   In that rich earth a richer dust concealed;
> A dust whom England bore, shaped, made aware. . . .

The emotiveness is wishy-washy and the soldier is reduced to the level of Brooke's other poem, 'The Little Dog's Day':

> When the blood-red sun had gone burning down,
> And the lights were lit in the little town,
> Outside, in the gloom of the twilight grey,
> The little dog died when he'd had his day.

Less poetising, more poetasting. . . .

As the war developed into a mud- and blood-bath of attrition, and the truths of the front line were known, poetry changed too and, for the first time, it had a force which it was to discover really could move mountains as well as men and genuinely aid the forging of swords into ploughshares. Poetry now did more than educate or entertain. It could direct and it took on a political importance such as it had not previously had in Britain. Blunden, Sassoon, Owen, Rosenberg, Graves: these were the men who were widely read and not just by the well-educated. Sassoon created a furore not only by returning his medals, but by publishing his verses. What was more, he was of the landed upper class and they were not expected to work against the status quo: that he did, and with poetry, set things awry.

His poetry is famous and it pulled no punches:

> If I were fierce, and bald, and short of breath,
> I'd live with scarlet Majors at the Base,
> And speed glum heroes up the line to death.

He was not alone. Blunden followed suit:

> Just see what's happening, Worley. – Worley rose
> And round the angled doorway thrust his nose,
> And Sergeant Hoad went too, to snuff the air.
> Then war brought down his fist, and missed the pair!
> Yet Hoad was scratched by a splinter, the blood came,
> And out burst terrors that he'd striven to tame,
> A good man, Hoad, for weeks. *I'm blown to bits.*

So did Owen with lines like:

> Gas! Gas! Quick boys! – An ecstasy of fumbling,
> Fitting the clumsy helmets just in time,
> But someone was still yelling out and stumbling
> And floundering like a man in fire or lime. –
> Dim through the misty panes and thick green light,
> As under a green sea, I saw him drowning.

Such were to tear hearts for years and still do.

This was poetry for people, if of a somewhat vile subject matter.

Subconsciously, this writing for people was to have an effect upon other poets than those spawned of the war's horror and this sense of awareness has continued through to the end of the 1970s.

Most of the Georgian poets, which classification held most of the war poets too, were published by Harold Munro in his Georgian poetry anthologies which issued from his The Poetry Bookshop in literary-fashionable Bloomsbury. There were five different books in the years 1911–22, edited by Edward Marsh, which took the 'poetry for people' lesson to heart and were deliberately aimed at the public. The books were certainly popular: the first ran to over eleven editions in three years and the second sold nearly fifteen thousand copies in the space of a year. In recent times, few anthologies can better such a publishing track record, except the Oxford University Press collections such as *The Oxford Book of Contemporary Verse* (ed. Enright) or

Penguin Modern Poets 10: The Mersey Sound, containing the earlier work of Adrian Henri, Roger McGough and Brian Patten.

Munro's books were not published patronisingly nor did the poets compromise themselves of their artistic integrity. They plumbed what the public wanted, which was what they were feeling, and this is important: poetry was relating directly to the mood of the masses.

Some of the greatest poets of the century appeared in the Georgian anthologies, even though, as we can see with hindsight, they weren't Georgians. They took their object lesson from what the war had done. Poetry for people.

D. H. Lawrence was one of these. Walter de la Mare was another. Names long since lost followed suit – Ralph Hodgson, James Stephens, Martin Armstrong. . . .

Poets discovered another important fact in those times: they are not precious. They belong to the world and occasionally they become a part of it. Indeed, for the ten years from 1964, they came nearer to the common body of humanity than at any time since Shakespeare's day, bar the Great War, perhaps. And, in Shakespeare's day, he himself was probably not widely known outside London and its social hinterland and ramifications.

It is strange, ironic and sad that today, in a world of satellite links, advantage isn't taken of this. For literature, with a few exceptions that will become apparent later, is still governed by London and those who live there, whether they are publishers, publishers' editors, writers or the literary hangers-on. The popular expansion of the Great War and the 1960s has contracted once more into narrowness and cliquery. Too much is spent these days in artistic effort, editorial argey-bargeying, paper, energy and cash on making poetry just for poets.

Poetry is no longer for people. It is increasingly only for those in the know. And those are the poets.

4

WHAT IS POETIC SUCCESS?

For the poet, success can be recognised in terms of sales figures, reputation, attendance at readings, critical notice in the 'right' journals, publication outside main volumes (for example, in magazines, on the radio and so on) and inclusion in major anthologies.

Yet to what extent is this real success? With the exception of major poets, those with enormous, superstar positions such as Ted Hughes, Seamus Heaney or Philip Larkin, few others sell their books in excess of one thousand copies. Established London publishers, with well-known, long-standing poetry lists, seldom print as many as a thousand copies in the first place. The books are very rarely reprinted. One can hardly base success upon book sales.

Reputation is another matter altogether. How well-known a poet is does not relate to any degree of artistic success, but simply the efficiency of the publicity machine, often related to being well reviewed in the press – the *Times Literary Supplement, New Statesman, Stand, Poetry Review*. These are hardly popular reading with the general public. Fame comes about in other ways where the public are concerned. Andrew Motion became famous not for his books, but for the fact that he won £5000 for a single poem in a poetry competition that was co-sponsored by ITV, which networked the results to every TV set in Britain. This gave him a reputation and importance out of proportion to his actual achievement. James Kirkup, in the mid-1970s, became famous for the publication of a poem suggesting that Jesus Christ was a homosexual: court cases followed, he was found 'not guilty' of blasphemy under an archaic law and that was that. But the fame was there. In Kirkup's case, it was cruel, for he was a fine poet long before he became famous, and his fame grew upon such a little thing. D. M. Thomas is now famous as a poet, but only because of the smash success of his novel *The White Hotel*. So reputation is an unreliable gauge.

Attendance at readings: hardly a yardstick towards success. Audiences will come on reputation alone, regardless of the poetic standards. This is well illustrated by words overheard at a reading by W. H. Auden in Oxford, within a year of his death.

'I've come to see the great poet . . . haven't read much except for A Levels. . . .'

'He can't read. Sounds like he's got a mouthful of plumstones. But he's a fine poet, so I've come to listen to him.'

'I'm curious. Heard a lot about him. And there's this court case of his. . . .' (Auden was, at the time, involved with a somewhat scandalous prosecution in Oxford that embarrassed the university authorities and variously shocked or amused the student corpus.)

The reading was packed out, standing room only. But in artistic terms, it was a failure. Auden did not read well or clearly, he did not project his poetry. Hundreds heard just an articulate mumbling. More recently, in 1982, at the Ilkley Literature Festival, hundreds reportedly turned up to hear Craig Raine and

13

Andrew Motion reading their own works. Their reading was said to be nothing out of the ordinary and yet they apparently commanded a listening audience the size of those usually drawn together by Ted Hughes or Seamus Heaney, who are superb poets and readers of their own work. Gate money is no measure of success.

Critical notice hardly makes success. Many critics will only review the work of their friends. In the mid- to late 1960s, this wasn't always the case: Ian Hamilton, who was hated by many for his vitriolic notices of their books, nevertheless gave sound if personally biased comment on a wide range of poets. Alan Brownjohn, writing in the *New Statesman*, achieved a high point in objective, sound literary criticism. But few members of the real public read these notices. Poetry reviewing is not like fiction reviewing: a fiction editor knows that a review sells books, regardless of what the critic says. But with poetry, that is not the case. Poetry reviews written by poets in the same introverted style as their poetry are unreadable by the general public.

Publication in magazines does lead towards a degree of success. Magazine editors have to accept only what they think will be read by their subscribers: if they publish otherwise, they lose subscriptions, income and sales and, consequently, their magazine. Publication in small presses can lead to some success, and broadcasting too. I will deal with these later.

Strangely, anthologies often bring success. Here the book is often more widely purchased by the public and, of course, with each poet contributing only a few poems at the most, only his or her best work appears. Reputations and success have often been based upon such slim evidence. Sometimes it holds good for the rest of the poet's output and sometimes it doesn't.

A good example of a poet who did, in the 1960s, build a solid and justified reputation on one poem is Alan Brownjohn. In his first book, a privately printed slim volume of fifty-five pages entitled *The Railings*, published in 1961, he included 'Two Poems after Prévert'. The book was a thin success in that poets and poetry lovers bought it, read it and enjoyed it, but the list of subscribers to the book, printed in the back, shows the calibre of those who supported this 30-year-old poet: Bergonzi, Kirkup, C. B. Cox, Roy Fuller, Redgrove, Norman Nicholson and others. The success of the poet grew from the second of the Prévert poems. Known as 'the rabbit poem', it is about a child going to visit the last rabbit left alive in England,

Nibbling grass
On the only patch of grass

In England, in England
(Except the grass by the hoardings
Which doesn't count.)

This poem rapidly appeared in schools anthologies and adult anthologies and was picked up by the mood of conservation that began as a ground swell in the mid-1960s. The poem was set to music, recited in hundreds of schools and even had a sculpture based upon it. It caused Brownjohn to become very well-known indeed. This was a stroke of good fortune for him and for poetry, for he is a fine writer. But his success is based upon the slightest of things. The last rabbit!

More fundamental than the risky business of popular recognition is artistic success. Art, to be successful, must reach through to mankind. It fails if it appeals to but a few, or if it is so esoteric as to be beyond the comprehension of all but the chosen. To be a success, it must do something, fill a need, spur thought in the masses. Of poetry, this cannot be sufficiently heavily stressed, for poetry is one of the art forms most readily accessible to the public. It is the easiest to write, though not necessarily well, and can be the easiest understood. If this accessibility isn't tapped, the poem fails.

A successful poem is, therefore, one that can be understood and appreciated – *felt* – by many. How this is achieved is up to the individual poet, but the fault with modern British verse is that it often ignores this basic premise. Of course, success comes by degrees and one can't expect all poems to work on all levels, but the fact remains that the foundation has to be in feeling.

Poetry that is locked up in itself, or plays such games as to be obscure, fails and adversely affects the rest of the art. And there is too much of that sort about these days, as will be shown.

5

WHAT IS A POEM?

That facile question, so often thrown at poets whilst visiting schools or reading to small audiences in pubs, is not as foolish as it may seem, for in the last fifty years the poem has undergone a good deal of change, particularly in the 1960s. Poetry was, until the turn of the century, an ordered business with structural demands that were dependent upon what the poem did and how it appeared when it was committed to paper. With the advent of sound broadcasting and a change in artistic attitudes towards traditions, poetry took a leap.

Compare a poem by, say, Swinburne with one that was written well within thirty years of his death at a time when the world still moved comparatively slowly. Compare it with one of Pound's Cantos. The opening lines of 'Canto II' from *A Draft of XXX Cantos* shows only too well how and to what a great extent poetics had altered in a very short timespan. Had Swinburne – or any of his contemporaries – been around to see Pound's work, they would have been speechless at what was passing itself off as poetry, as they might put it. (Quite what Swinburne would have made of the late 1960s would have been worth hearing!) Taking Pound's 'Canto II', let us look at it alongside the opening lines of Swinburne's 'The Triumph of Time':

> Before our lives divide for ever,
>   While time is with us and hands are free,
> (Time, swift to fasten and swift to sever
>   Hand from hand, as we stand by the sea)
> I will say no word that a man might say
> Whose whole life's love goes down in a day;
> For this could never have been; and never,
>   Though the gods and the years relent, shall be.

And an even better comparison, and one that is striking, is the parallel between Pound's 'Difference of Opinion with Lygdamus'

> And the other woman 'has not enticed me
>   by her pretty manners,
> 'She has caught me with herbaceous poison,
>   she twiddles the spiked wheel of a rhombus,
> 'She stews puffed frogs, snake's bones, the moulted
>   feathers of screech owls,
> 'She binds me with ravvles of shrouds,
>   Black spiders in her bed!
> Let her lovers snore at her in the morning!

and Swinburne's opening lines to 'Dolores':

> Cold eyelids that hide like a jewel
>   Hard eyes that grow soft for an hour;
> The heavy white limbs, and the cruel
>   Red mouth like a venomous flower;
> When these are gone by with their glories,
>   What shall rest of thee then, what remain,

O mystic and sombre Dolores,
Our Lady of Pain?

Poetry had travelled a long road between those two pieces. In the period from 1964, poetry was to undergo even more massive change in terms of structure, content and conception.

New divisions came into being, some harking back to earlier days, others arriving fresh to the times. Whereas poetry had once been 'pastoral' or 'lyrical' or 'romantic' and written as a sestina or a sonnet or a ballad, now it was breaking other boundaries – concrete poetry, sound poetry, visual poetry, and poetry that was categorised because of its subject matter – to love poetry was added sci-fi poetry, underground poetry, 'pop' poetry and, more recently, punk poetry. And so on. To some extent, this was but to split up poetry that had existed previously into yet more definitions. In other cases, it was to break genuinely new ground.

Form was changing and technology allowed new advances – some might call them retreats.

The one that made the biggest impact was concrete poetry and this will be dealt with later, but sound poetry grew too and became quite popular for a while. Free verse, blank verse and an apparent abandonment of controlled form flourished. One says apparent, for actually there was considerable awareness of shape and structure, but it followed no set and strictly defined course. It was this freedom from control that was to be a major factor in the development of British (and English language) verse.

But the question remains: what is a poem? Successful or otherwise? People, both poets and others, were faced with this problem in the 1960s. Until then, more or less, one knew what a poem was. It was a set of words that rhymed (or not), had a metre (that was measured in feet, just to confuse the issue) and was written in verses (some called them stanzas) and they were about high-flown emotions or rhetorical ideas. They were beautiful. Or they were about manly emotions. Or love.

Poets became, in the 1960s, thanks to the influence of popular music, the new troubadours. Anything became a poem if the creator called it one. Bob Cobbing, the leading light of the concrete/sound poetry world in Britain, gave 'readings' or 'recitals' – one is hard put to state exactly what they were, for both words are inadequate – at which he performed strange noises either by mouth or by a large tape recorder. The poems, for they were called so, were very effective at times. They reached the heights of creative ingenuity and, to Cobbing's credit, he was doing five years or more ahead of Samuel Beckett what the latter did in his 'sound' play, in which a voice, much amplified, breathed through the life of a man from birth to death-hush in about forty-five seconds. Cobbing called it poetry. At times, it verged on music and certainly Cobbing's voice was that of a singer rather than a reader. Whether it *has* music or not is debatable. (At a reading in Farnham in the late 1960s, an enterprising member of the audience handed out aspirin to those who had attended and received splitting headaches at the speakers of Cobbing's tape recorder.)

This 'anything-is-a-poem' definition went to ridiculous extremes, on the way going through some interesting developments which are touched on later, culminating in one poet printing

and calling it the ultimate poem. It is a full stop. Argument developed around this and one faction decided that this was not so. The ultimate poem is:

If that passes muster, then truly anything is a poem, from Wordsworth's daffodils to a slug crawling on a rock leaving its trail of slime. That is bunkum. Not anything is a poem.

Poetry has almost as many definitions as there are poets. Coleridge called poetry 'the best words in the best order' and Flaubert said it was as 'exact a science as geometry': likewise Wordsworth with 'poetry is the breath and finer spirit of all knowledge', the 'impassioned expression which is in the countenance of all Science'; and he also stated it was 'the spontaneous overflow of powerful feelings' taking its 'origin from emotion recollected in tranquillity'. Of course, there were other opinions; George Farquhar said it was a mere drug and Dickens's Mr. Weller said, 'Poetry's unnat'ral; no man ever talked poetry 'cept a beadle on boxin' day.' When Boswell asked Johnson, 'Then, Sir, what is poetry?' he received the reply, 'Why, Sir, it is much easier to say what it is not. We all *know* what light is; but it is not easy to *tell* what it is.' Keats, who spent a good deal of time in February, 1818 thinking about the meaning and place of poetry, stated that it should be 'great and unobtrusive, a thing which enters into one's soul, and does not startle or amaze it with itself, but with its subject.' Later in that month he wrote to John Taylor that poetry should 'strike the reader as a wording of his own highest thoughts. . . .'

Clearly, there are contradictions here. What has to be done is to draw a norm somewhere, adding those lessons learnt in the post-1960 period when poetry boomed and spread itself very wide over its own catchment area, soaking up everything from the full stop (or blank space) to taut, ordered, controlled poems.

Some definition must be reached for the trends these days seem to dictate that anything goes. And a definition sets boundaries so that understanding can take place within a context. And understanding is essential for artistic success. At the same instant, our definition must be as catholic as possible to allow for the wider framework of poetry now evidently a major part of its shape and appeal.

A poem must use words (with or without the structure of language at times) with some consciousness of deliberate placing, and must be able to be understood by more than just the poet writing it. The words used must convey a meaning in themselves – they may also simultaneously make a pattern that appeals to the eye for response – and this meaning must be something that seeks to attract an emotional response. What Keats referred to as 'highest thoughts' is really a distillation of emotion. Traditionally, poetry has been involved at its very core with emotion and that is the key to it all. A poem is an emotional piece of writing that reaches through to the soul in its own way, possibly doing, at its best, what Coleridge stated – doing it with the best words in the best order. For 'best' one might say 'most appropriate'. This allows for a wide spectrum of analysis.

'Drinka Pinta Milka Day', one of the Milk Marketing Board's most successful advertising slogans, becomes a poem. So does the more current milk plug, 'Gotta Lotta Bottle'. It uses the best words in the best order and it appeals to the emotions in that it brings about a laugh (if you like milk or own a dairy) or a groan (if you hate milk, see the slogan as an overworked cliché or are an alcoholic). It's easily understood. It's not great and unobtrusive (Keats), but then poetry needn't seek always to be high-powered, that overflowing of spontaneous feelings. But, again, Keats was correct to an extent when he thought poetry should startle and amaze but it can do it with itself, not just with its subject. Of course, what he failed to mention was that the poem startles and amazes with a conjoining of itself and its subject: his most effective poem, *The Eve of St. Agnes*, succeeds for that reason, as far as it does succeed.

So a good poem, in short, emotively uses words to express intelligent or emotional thought from one human being to the other. That seems to be the basis of it all and it is the criterion, however unconsciously it might have been adhered to, that governed the flowering and popularity of verse in the 1960s. The more the poem was understood, the better it was. The more successful.

6

ANYONE CAN WRITE A POEM

This premise was, in many ways, at the core of the poetry revival of the 1960s. Until then, with a few exceptions, poets were considered to come from a specific group of humans with one or more of the following attributes – well (that is, university) educated, upper-middle- or upper-class, preferably immoral (thanks to Byron) or uninterested in morality and living by loose codes of conduct, poor (the ivory tower syndrome) but with secure financial backing for when the muses ran off with someone else, over-emotional or over-sensitive (or both in the case of Shelley), romantic, occasionally addicted to either narcotic drugs or booze (thanks to Coleridge and Dylan Thomas) and, sometimes, just a little outrageous. Many were considered namby-pamby (thanks to Keats, perhaps): indeed, my own father, discovering that I was published as a poet and being not too keen on the prospect for the association with the above points that that might imply, questioned if I might become a homosexual next.

Of course, this is not a little amusing looked at from the perspective of the 1980s, or beyond, when attitudes and understandings have altered considerably. The point is, though, that my father's attitude was that of a very large percentage of the population. It came to him from his own education which was coloured by the Romantics. As in modern times, poetry came from just the sort of people as those that fit the set of guides above, and it follows that that was what the poet would be known by – the yardstick was cut, as it were. Shelley, Keats, Byron, Coleridge, Tennyson, Wordsworth, Southey – the whole gamut fitted like a key in a lock. Poetry had been gripped by a certain class of person.

Those who did not fit the mould were occasionally still popular, but somehow they rode to their position not as poets but because they were otherwise known: or their poetry was known for a particular popular stance that it took. Kipling, for example, was not university educated and came from outside the class system for he fitted into a category apart from it – the Indian raj. He was well-known as a novelist, worked for a while as a journalist and, as a poet, was famous because his name was already well-travelled to the public and he was known for his jingoistic or 'Indian' poems. He was stereotyped as *the* Anglo-Indian poet. His poem, 'Gunga Din', encapsulated all the British wanted to think of India where they saw themselves as benevolent tyrants, understanding overseers and fair and just governors of a heathen bunch. High up the ladder in the public's eye sat Kipling, speaking for this. How sad! This was not the case at all. He did not sympathise with the cruelty of the British in India, did not like what he saw and Gunga Din did not carry water out of friendship, regardless of the soldiers' boorishness. The supposed sympathetic ending to the poem is not acceptance of Gunga Din being 'a better man', but a patronising aside. Poor Kipling! He is remembered for this: forgotten are his moving poems about the British foot-soldier's lot, his Masonic poems and religiously inclined verses, his poems of England and his tremendous and brilliant attacks on colonialism and snobbery – 'We and They' is one of the most powerful poems of disgust and reproving hatred ever written.

Other 'non-poets' who became poets were, of course, soldiers in the First World War. Many were educated upper-classers or the like – Blunden (Christ's Hospital then Oxford), Sassoon (Anglo-Indian millionaire family background), Graves (Charterhouse and Oxford) – but others were not: Isaac Rosenberg came from poverty in the Jewish East End of London and Wilfrid Owen, though from a family once wealthy, had a father who was, at the time of his poet son's birth, a railway clerk. It is interesting to see other directions poets took that might suggest that they were unsuited to the literary ranks. Keats was apprenticed to a surgeon, Thomas Hardy (born of peasant stock but with a father who subsequently 'did well') was an apprentice architect and repaired church masonry, George Crabbe (and a few others) were priests and T. S. Eliot, after an academic career as a student of some brilliance in Smith Academy, St. Louis, Harvard and Merton College, Oxford (his father was wealthy as an executive of the Hydraulic Press Brick Company, in Missouri – hardly a poetically inclined background!) became a junior school teacher and bank clerk for Lloyds Bank. Thus come the famous.

Yet it remains: most poets – note even Eliot, for all his writing of poverty in such poems as 'Rhapsody on a Windy Night', had a secure financial back-up in a steady job, if not his father's accrued dollars – came from a certain type. The exceptions were rare although they gradually grew to be more numerous until, in the early 1960s, they started to flourish.

The myth that poets are born, not bred, went out of the window. Poets were writing well, becoming published and read and remembered – and, importantly, were being considered and recognised as poets – who came from a wide range of social and educational backgrounds. These will become apparent later, in sections on individual poets.

Poetry was in the reach of those who could write and think. Not necessarily in that order, nor with any degree of skill with regard to spelling (editors could correct genuine mistakes and query any deliberate new spellings or attitudes towards it) and punctuation (where it was used) and grammar. . . . This widening of skill, for want of a better term, did lead to a good deal of charlatan activity. The full stop as a poem, for example. Interesting gimmickry but hardly poetry. A necessary part of the process of the art in a state of flux and change, but not one that could be expanded upon – merely reduced, to the blank space. For it *is* important that these phases of innovative thought take place, to prevent the art becoming static. The trouble is that they were seen by many as art itself.

In the schoolroom, where most poetic activity traditionally goes on, changes were taking place through the first half of the 1960s that set an atmosphere going that was to explode later. Under the influence of such people as Robert Druce, poetry became not a rote learning of the famous lines but an activity of forming and making poems from living language. His *The Eye of Innocence*, published in 1965, was an extension of his work as a schoolmaster and it had a front seat in the drive towards using language innovatively rather than simply as a means of factual communication. Poems written by children and quoted in Druce's book show the efficacy of his methods: the results were certainly as good as much that was appearing – and was to appear – in small magazines over the next decade. The work was mostly conducted by 11- to 14-year-olds and they speak for themselves:

> The changing cit,
> Growing, being disfigured into an interplanetary sleeping
> station,
> From damp, low, tenant houses,
> Slate grey and homely,
> And quaint little corner shops,
> Selling tea fingers and marmalade,
> Overlooked by gasometers

At the time Druce's book appeared, he was a lecturer in a teacher training college and his influence was spreading. However, others had had the same desire to extend the ranges of language from a skill process to a creative, emotional one. Two such men were the poets John Moat and John Fairfax. What they did has, in a subtle but no small way, already altered much of the extension of poetics and the literary arts in general and it is no understatement to say that their ideas and dreams – for that was all they were at first – have solidly and beneficially affected British poetry since the late 1960s.

Between them, Moat and Fairfax had a good deal of educational experience ranging from, as Moat puts it, 'private and state, junior and senior, D-stream and university'. They realised that the teaching of literature was a sterile process and they saw that this was ultimately going to affect poetry and the arts in general, once the vitality of the 1960s began to thin and ghost away. (It has and they are at the barricades fighting this, though by proxy now, as will be explained. . . .)

In 1969, at Beaford Centre in Devon – a small, local arts centre – they ran an experimental course with fourteen 16- to 18-year-olds deliberately drawn from a wide range of school and home backgrounds, from all over that county. The course lasted five days and was residential. Nothing was deliberately expected of the students and nothing was structured around them in an obvious way. They did their own cooking, and lived together. What they had in common was not an expertise in literature but simply a curiosity as to what literature was at. Primarily, they all had an interest in poetry. During the five days, they each followed their own direction of interest. This was not a course leading to GCE examinations or university entrance. It was education in its purest sense, for its own sake. It was the widening of the mind.

The outcome amazed Moat and Fairfax. This random group of teenagers – to a person – produced at least one finished, polished piece of imaginative writing. Their encounter with Moat and Fairfax, both published poets, opened the students' inner eyes, as it were, and something 'intangible, and, as far as we can judge from our follow-ups, indelible has been engendered for each student'. Moat saw this as a major leap forward. Poetry could be communicated and – dare one use the verb, but what else is there? – *taught*. Not as an academic discipline harking back to the sterile days of poetry, but as an intellectual one. Accepting this, poetry is an intellectual exercise and one that is central to everyday human living. . . .

In 1971, Moat and Fairfax obtained the first permanent centre

23

for what was now called the Arvon Foundation. They obtained an eleventh-century farmhouse in the very rural heart of Devon, with a thatched roof, a priest's hole, what estate agents call 'inglenook' fireplaces, an orchard, a derelict barn and a goose house. Totleigh Barton – a barton is a cow-house – was renovated, for it had not been occupied for some time, heated and had modern plumbing installed. It was approached by a mile of unmetalled track (subsequently and thankfully concreted) which tore off the exhaust pipe of Peter Redgrove's car when first he drove it there, stands near to the river Torridge and an ancient, magical well is hidden in nearby woods – St Mary's Well. The kitchen-cum-dining room, with a massive refectory table built in solid oak, is haunted by a sixteenth-century monk or priest. He's seen elsewhere in the house, but especially installs himself in the kitchen. Meadows surround the house and living there is like stepping back into the Middle Ages.

It is fanciful to think that this time machine of a house is linked in to the years of the last great public boost of British poetry but it might be so. Totleigh Barton, with an atmosphere that is simultaneously magical and real, mystical and plainly obvious, makes for creative thought. The actions of the sage or wizard that are involved in the making of poetry are alive in this extraordinary place.

In 1975, the Arvon Foundation, now rapidly expanding its reputation, obtained from the poet Ted Hughes the use of Lumb Bank, an equally wonderful place in a valley cut by Colden Water above Hebden Bridge in West Yorkshire. The house, once a millowner's mansion dating from the heydays of the Industrial Revolution, looks out over a wooded coombe with sparse cottages in it. In the beech trees hide the moss-wild remains of the factories that once filled the valley: higher up is where Wesley preached to the mill-workers, in a natural amphitheatre of hillside and, much higher up still, is the pub, blasted even in summer by winds and rain that rob breath. Nearby is the village of Heptonstall with its grave buildings, its narrow and treacherously steep streets and the tomb of Sylvia Plath.

This is not a travelogue for the sake of poetic prose. It is important to understand what these two Arvon places mean. They mean that there is somewhere that, for a modest fee, people – that is, the public – can come to live for a five-day span in the company of two creative artists with whom they work, from whom they learn and, equally important, to whom they give feedback in the literary game. To 'tutor' an Arvon course is probably as valuable for the writer as it is for the student. And these two places, because of their in-built wonderment and unique environments, bring together all the forces needed for creative thought. These are teacher, talents, setting, atmosphere, enjoyment, seriousness and – above all – active participation in the job of thinking outside oneself.

Moat has written that

> We live in a society conditioned to accepting the imagination as extraneous, as an adjunct to life, as at worst a subversive pastime and at best a teacher's aid. But it is now, for a thousand reasons, a matter of real urgency that we explode the heresy that education and the arts are exclusive concerns.

He might have added that poetry is not an exclusive concern either. And so Arvon set about linking people to creativity.

The majority of courses at either of the two Arvon centres are literary – 'Starting to write', 'Making people', Poetry and prose', 'Fiction and the wider public', 'Scriptwriting', etc. Yet some are linked marginally away from literature, such as the courses in recent years entitled 'Songwriting', 'Television playwriting', 'Word and image in the theatre' and 'Imagination and gender'. The Totleigh Barton barton is adapted as a theatre workshop, the barn at Lumb Bank likewise. Both places have quiet rooms, libraries and informal sitting rooms. They are made as un-institutionalised as possible. After all, the students are meant to live with the tutors, not exist with them.

So what is an Arvon course all about? How does it shape itself, make itself work in merely five days? The answers to these two questions are at the core of what British poetry ought to be doing these days, instead of shilly-shallying and backfiring about, making a lot of noise and precious little valuable art.

The Arvon course enlightens and awakes. It introduces emotion, experience and assimilation of these into the distilled alcohol of art.

Best, perhaps, to go through a diary of a course, albeit somewhat shortened. Appropriately, take a poetry course at Lumb Bank in late autumn. Students: seventeen sixth-formers, mixed sexes, about equal in both. Tutors: two poets with a third, as is customary, coming on the middle day of the course just to read and talk in the evening. One teacher in charge, sent from the school plus a former pupil of the school now a university undergraduate who is skiving lectures for a week because he wanted to attend the course, even if it does mean mucking in with the former juniors over whom he was a senior prefect. And even if it means returning to 'school discipline' after the liberties of university. Which it doesn't.

Everyone arrives on Monday evening about 6.00: it is drizzling and cold. The centre directors – John and Nadia – are there with a main evening meal lined up: after that, the students take it in turns to do the evening meal each day – breakfasts are self-catering and lunch usually imbibed in the pub (long, long walk) or carried in a pack made up at breakfast. Baggage is driven up from Hebden Bridge railway station, the students elect to walk up the valley. It takes forty-five minutes if you don't get lost. The road to Lumb Bank is just passable by vehicles: the Arvon vehicle is a four-wheel-drive Jeep affair. After dinner and settling in – tutors in single rooms, students in rooms of three or four beds or bunks – the centre directors read out the very barest of rules – fire drill, food rota, swill out the bath: nothing more than a family of four would do for itself at home. Tutors talk, settle in and then walk to the pub. The work starts after breakfast the next day.

At 9 a.m. on the first day, the tutors see each student individually to see what they want – it's a time of sounding out characters and setting the thinking patterns going. A task is set for each student, each different. A girl is told to go and put her head on the fireplate at the base of one of the few factory chimneys left nestling in the woods; a boy is told to go to the highest bit of land inside three miles and sing on it; a girl wearing a rosary is told to sit on the rock where Wesley preached and write her own psalm about what she sees; a boy with a Honda jacket is sent to find a wrecked car at the bottom of a gully up the valley . . . places, of course, the tutors have sniffed out prior to the students' arrival, or that they know of from a previous visit.

Everyone leaves and are not expected back until tea-time. It is suggested that they write of their experiences. The writer/tutors spend the day talking, writing, working on plans for further tasks or going through work presented to them by students on the course who have already written something and want a comment on it. Some tutors don't encourage this as they want their charges to start afresh.

It is a comment upon the form that the course takes when it is noted that the teacher's role is simply one of guarding the morals of his pupils after lights out. At no time during waking hours does he impress school rules or disciplines upon the pupils. The course is there not as an addition to their school work, as a biology field trip might be considered for example, but as a separate intellectual experience. It is rare on an Arvon course that the teacher or minder does not get fully involved, as a student. Those who do hold back simply prove the validity of the course, for they have missed out on such a chance and are now seen to be unable to handle it in personal terms.

At tea-time, the students return in dribs and drabs from their day out. They invariably seek out the tutors and show them what they have written.

This is the astonishing bit. They've all written. These aren't all top GCE A-Level English students: some are far from top, especially in modern schools where the entry requirement into the sixth form is not governed by exam passes alone, but more a matter of keeping some people off the unemployment register.

The tutors see the work, make comments, suggest changes, steer the poem and the poet – for these are now poets! – and possibly outline the next extrapolation from that piece of work.

After supper, the poets read their own work or talk about it – correction, the tutors do. The Poets are now surrounded by other poets. The distinction between them is one only of experience, number of books published, age and expertise. Everyone on the course – everyone in the building – is a poet.

This metamorphosis on the first night is remarkable to watch. There is no ordered instruction, no teaching, no forcing. The tutors act more as mentors than masters. By the end of the first day even the most intransigent or embarrassed or reluctant pupil is fully into the reasons for being there. The transformation has occurred and is complete.

After the tutors have read their work, a party head for the last half-hour of opening time. Now another move seems to have passed. Some of the students stay behind. They opt out of the pub in order to write. And they do. No bedtime is stipulated. Some work until the early hours.

Day 2 has the tutors spending the whole morning with the students, on a one-to-one basis. They rework poems, draw conclusions, praise, damn, encourage and dismiss. They treat the students as fellow workers in verse, not underlings gaining an apprenticeship. Other tasks are set – think you are a cow; climb a tree; be alone; study flames gathering in the beautiful, black-leaded fireplace in the dining room. Anything that is appropriate to the individual and will get that person out of their skin. (One boy, once, wrote a long poem about being his own father and seeing himself as his son – shades of Wordsworth and subsequently published in a reputable magazine.) The second evening, the poets talk with the students after supper, read work by other poets and discuss it, or give more individual attention. Either on this night or the next, the visitor arrives.

The second day is the hard one for the tutors: they have to spend at least ten hours that day working at full blast on all the students' verse. At the end of that day, the tutors are usually exhausted and often sleep early. To write continuously, at beginners' level, all day, is mentally draining. For the students, it is an even more exhausting time for they are now spiked upon the drive of tutors and the energies required to write. They are on a new journey and one strange to them. They have all the excitement of a child discovering his first seaside.

The next day is one in which, usually, the students have found their feet and the tutors help the few behindhand to catch up with their own, self-imposed tasks. Often some students on these courses find the going rough for they have yet to learn the secret of the writer – dogged and determined self-discipline. After lunch on the third day, the visitor arrives. This is always a writer in the same literary field as the tutors – on this course being outlined, a poet. Usually, the visitor is unlike the two tutors. A pop poet visits two serious ones. A rural poet visits two townies. That sort of thing.

The visitor brings in more than him or herself. He brings in a new direction, prevents the others from getting stale, injects new interest and a new face, brings in new ideas – the tutors are rightly getting idea-punch-drunk – and a new set of critical rules. Ideally, and commonly, the visitor looks at work and draws comments. This is the next astonishing thing. Teenagers, wary of themselves at home, suddenly are prepared without self-consciousness or pretentiousness to show their work, often something very close to themselves or even their private lives, to a third party who is a total stranger. The butterfly of poetry is emerging.

That evening, after a special supper, the visitor reads his own work, talks about it and then goes to the nearest hostelry with the students and all.

Teenagers in pubs are animals apart from human beings. Watch them. They are usually 'silly' or 'show-off-ing' or inhibited. But not on these courses: they always drink sensibly, talk a lot about their work that day, discuss literature and matters literary, and take the opportunity of meeting their tutors – sometimes writers whose work they have come across in school – and getting to know them.

On the Friday, the students try to work through their poems to some degree of completeness, with the aid of the tutors. This day is usually concerned with technique. On the last evening, the students read their own work to each other, often the first time any of them have read out their own work in a professional gathering, so to speak. After that, the evening develops into a social one with chat, laughter, sometimes word games and so on. On the following morning, usually with regret, everyone leaves to go their separate ways.

Nothing is forced or predetermined or decided. No set timetables are imposed, no rules appertaining to creation laid down. The teacher has his eyes opened, the students see another world outside themselves and often inside, too. The tutors get to think objectively about their art. Everyone, no matter how tiring they find such work, leaves ennervated and awakened to new possibilities.

And everyone, often including the tutors, has written something with expertise, knowledge and foresight. The Arvon Foundation opens doors that education keeps closed or sometimes puts ajar for a short time.

The point is that ordinary people go in and thinking, intellectually aware, creative persons come out the other end without having had to suffer an educationalist's treadmill or force-feeding programme.

This shows that anyone, *in the right environment*, can make poetry. Adult Arvon courses are even more widely distributed by way of students than school-orientated ones: this makes for interaction as well as creation, a swapping of experience. (I 'taught' a course in 1981 the student body of which consisted of a town crier-cum-builder, a Liverpool barmaid, an Australian student, a nurse, two retired ladies, a young man and a young woman novelist: the latter subsequently published a novel and was taken on, a few weeks later, by a major literary agent. The young man subsequently published a booklet of his own work – he was a teacher who went back re-fired for the classroom furnace – and the nurse wrote a published short story.)

These people, those who were 'successful', had talent latent in themselves. They added this, after it was allowed to blossom, to ordinary language skills and became writers. They reached a point of acceptable standards – acceptable to editors and the like, that is: to the two tutors on the course, they had reached that well before.

What Moat and Fairfax started – and which continues now as a trust – was a means of getting people to create, of not so much removing the mystique of writing as widening its accessibility. The Arvon Foundation carries on what the 1960s started; that is, the awareness that poetry exists in everyone. And the foundation continues to evolve this ethos today, when the mood is against it. Ironically, it sometimes uses as tutors those very writers who seek once more to keep poetry exclusive. One wonders what some of those individuals are like on a course.

Since the mid-1960s, then, poetry has been opened out at the creation end of the game. It has spread to others than the traditional custodians, and its ease of construction, with a laxity of strict techniques, has made it belong to everyman.

Twenty years later, the tide is surging the other way again. Only the Arvon Foundation and a few of the more enlightened literature officers of the regional arts associations react against this appalling trend, at adult level. The Poetry Society, in association with a major chain store, do likewise at school level with a writers-in-schools scheme that is particularly effective and successful. Otherwise, things aren't so rosy for the would-be poet and the art in general.

7

There was something abroad in the 1960s that set a tone or mood for the burgeoning of poetry which was quite apart from the changes taking place in education.

To understand this, it is essential to consider what those times were like and to realise that they followed on from a period of austerity and greyness. Britain was left after the war with a legacy of damage, run-down cities and industries and a war debt of enormous proportions. This took the better part of fifteen years to be overcome and, when it was finally shifted, it left the way clear for fun once more.

It's not the place of this book to write a social history or to study the causes of the social changes that occurred. It is enough to accept that they happened and to see that these changes went so far towards building up a vibrant atmosphere in which poetry could take off.

Taking 1960 as an arbitrary year, consider what was happening in the arts so far as that extraordinary figure, the ordinary man, was concerned.

Television had taken a firm hold; education was universal and improving its standards; universities were expanding and many newer ones opening; books were cheap and paperbacks booming as never before; photography (the non-painter's medium) was becoming sophisticated but within the reach of everyone; advertising was bringing colour to drab environments, including those in the mind that had grown dull from the harder years; the economy was heading for a boom; there were no major wars going on – Korea was over and Vietnam hadn't really gathered momentum; music was expanding rapidly.

Music, plus the education of the arts, allowed everyone an entry into creating. Making art is a longing many have, but, until then, few could seriously hope to achieve.

Musicians were not born, they were trained. Either they enrolled in university music courses, or they joined colleges of music, or they learned their art from travelling the road and the halls for years before stepping the boards for the first time. Some came from musical – or music hall – families and had a leg up, but most did not. Many gained their art through gruelling poverty and determined effort to succeed. And many of them died of alcoholism, drugs or failure along the way. Only the lucky, very talented and strong survived the apprenticeship years.

As a result of the long period of training, as it were, the musicians turned out had their roots firmly embedded in traditions. Jazz musicians of the 1940s, for all their big band sounds and lines of trombone players, were still harking back solidly to the 1920s music they had known and, through that, to the embryonic 'jass' of the negro South. Classical music was even more rigidly traditionalised with even the most up-to-date composers acknowledging in their work the debts due to the Great Masters of Bach, Beethoven and Chopin and Company. They had music sewn up at their level. (As will be seen, poetry operates that way now – one group has the 'real' market and the rest have their own, almost separate market at a different level.) The two halves of music seldom met.

So music was exclusive because in both halves, it required a set criterion of skills before one could perform it acceptably in the eyes of others.

Then, in the 1950s, diverging from jazz, came skiffle. It was still played by trained musicians, but they used loose forms and unusual instruments, particularly the guitar. This most accessible of instruments was cheap to buy, not difficult to learn to a simple, but *performable*, standard and was becoming fashionable. Drums (substituted by empty suitcases) and washboards took on the rhythm section and a bass guitar, not a common instrument, became a part of the line-up. Music could be made by virtually untrained musicians, certainly by comparison with their elders. Skiffle groups had their day and faded. But they left their mark and this was soon to be enlarged by the importation of the American rock-'n'-roll bands. Here Britain's youth saw the chance to rise to fame and money and expression without the previously required education. Presley had worked as a truck driver and came from hill-billy backgrounds: that he could sing was aided by the biggest hype in show-biz history to that time.

He was an image of the working class made good and with working-class music, at that. Others followed with 'ordinary folk' as their roots or ordinary music as their sound – the ordinary meaning of the everyman: the Everly Brothers, Paul Anka, Bobby Darin and others.

In England, rock-'n'-roll bands were forming and the first and most successful of the earlier appearances was Cliff Richard and the Shadows. Richards, born Harry Webb, had left school for a clerking job, and played in his spare time with a local band in Cheshunt. This was what a lot of youngsters were doing. Cliff Richard was one of those lucky ones, though: he met up with two astoundingly talented musicians and, with them, set up in a coffee bar in Soho. He emulated Elvis Presley, even copying the American's style and looks. Before long, he made a record which rode high in the pop charts – the new, everyman sign of musical success which worked against or, rather, had nothing to do with mainstream music – in late 1958. Six months later, he became the best-selling musical pop artist in Britain and dominated sales for the next six months. A local clerk had made it. If he could, anyone could. What was more, his first hit was written by one of his band – a rare but significant event.

For five years, until 1963, rock-'n'-roll proliferated as no art form had ever done. Music with a beat linked to simplistic rhymes and words became an important part of a 'sub'-culture.

Sub-culture is a rude word. It was not a *sub*-culture, but simply *another* culture. The prefix implying 'under' was tagged on it by those who controlled what was being put about as the genuine culture, this definition based upon the reliance of the art embraced as having aesthetic expertise in it. The point that was lost and which caused the arts to polarise was the refusal of the high-brows to accept that the low-brows had as great, if different, an expertise of their own. Snobbery has long been the scourge of the arts and, where poetry is concerned, it is still.

Then came the Beatles. Whatever the publicists insisted, the band was made of four 'ordinary working-class' lads from an industrial seaport who had a flair for music and an ability to write the words to the notes. The early songs were meagre poems by comparison with what was to come. 'She loves you! Yeah! Yeah! Yeaaaaah!' is hardly Wordsworth.

Or is it?

It was an expression of the time, of an emotion and it reached millions upon millions. In poetic terms, the Beatles were *hugely* successful. It was their poetry that made them famous, not their music. There were other groups about at the time that were musically more accomplished and who had the right sort of publicity machine behind them. What they lacked were the words that people could know, understand emotionally and assimilate.

From 1964 onwards, the Beatles developed with their public and, indeed, *the* public. Occasionally they set up trends in poetry, as in other things, but mostly they rode with the changing arts.

And so education, music and the arts of literary creation built up, in collaboration with the increased evolution of the hi-fi system and television, an atmosphere of vitality and motion.

The western world was simultaneously growing in affluence. After the harder, post-war years came the 'money years' and money to be spent on luxuries and enjoyment. And the release from grey years gave way to new social attitudes, liberties and excitements. Society put on a new face of life and permissiveness. Anything went. Personal liberty reached strange and new ends. And with this liberty came a freedom to do as you would. This manifested itself in the hippy flower-child, the drug usage of the times (especially the softer drugs, but later those that harm and kill – the excesses grew out of all proportion, as they always will), the emergence of the sub-culture into the pop culture and the seeking for new boundaries.

Culminating in the arrival on the moon, the 1960s were a time of extending boundaries. Everywhere the accepted was being racked to its limits. Some sought peace against the wart of war that was growing (safely distant) in the Far East: some sought technological breakthroughs and attained them; some sought medical advances and got them; some sought new horizons for themselves, reached for them and arrived there in the tourist explosion. Others, wanting to try a new art and one that had been especially elitist in the past, took to poetry and made it great. For a while, at least.

Freedoms permitted by the new social atmosphere of the 1960s also allowed for changes to traditions and the accepted norm. In the world at large appeared mini-skirts, bikinis, junk foods, plastic in place of wood . . . the list goes on and on.

In poetry, this freedom allowed an escape from the tight controls of form and content. Blank and free verse flourished and poems could now be written about anything. A glance ahead to the subject matter of poets writing in the period illustrates this.

The world, between 1956 and 1966, had changed so much that it was, in many ways, unrecognisable. And, as it changed, so did poetry for poetry reflects its times.

No one's work shows this more readily than does Bob Dylan's. His influence upon music and the emotional attitudes of the last twenty years is beyond counting. In his songs lies the kernel of the poetic nut in modern times for he fits perfectly the shape of the 1960s poet – one who disregarded tradition and what others had done before him, yet drew upon it for what he needed only when his own originality required a little bolstering or anchoring. His poetry was new, but related to the whole. He did not pander to the past but used it and continues to do so unlike many British poets who have fallen upon tradition as a one-legged man does upon a crutch.

Look at the words (which the modern musical world continues to this day to call the *lyrics* of the song, thereby accepting the debt to poetry) of many of Bob Dylan's songs and you see the new poetry as it was then in all its force:

> While preachers preach of evil fates
> Teachers teach that knowledge waits
>
> Can lead to hundred-dollar plates
> Goodness hides behind its gates
> But even the president of the United States
> Sometimes must have
> To stand naked.

This is the nub. Poetry in form, poetry in emotion, understood by all, emotional at several levels. When this was performed on tour in 1974, these lines brought the audience to fever pitch for they reflected the current attitudes towards the American administration at the awful end of the Vietnam War and the Watergate scandals. Here was poetry doing its job. And superbly.

Yet, similarly, look at the early poetry of Peter Porter and the work of George MacBeth, Brian Patten, Ted Hughes, Edwin Morgan . . . and literally hundreds of others. There is the same thing happening. The desire to innovate and create with poetry and poetic emotion umbrellas the lot of them. Nowhere can this be seen better than in the parallels one can draw between Bob Dylan's songs and T. S. Eliot's work, and Paul Simon (of Simon and Garfunkel), on the sleeve of his 1975 album, *Still Crazy After All These Years*, acknowledges that the song, 'My Little Town', grew from a quotation from Ted Hughes's poem, 'Two Legends', published in *Crow* in 1971.

8

Nothing is going to succeed, be it the spread of poetry or the sale of pop-rivet guns, unless it has a means of mass distribution with the strength to penetrate outside the immediate circle of potential users. Poetry has historically been the cinderella art in that it has not had this opportunity to extend its reach. (Needless to say, part of the trouble for this art being left behind on the evening of the ball was that it spent much of its time not only accepting the job of sweeping the floor, but actually enjoying it and not really wanting to meet a prince. Poets have a notorious and justified reputation for being outsiders with an almost manic pleasure in inflicting upon themselves the pain of the outcast exile. It's part of the selfishness of poetry that, now that it has permeated as far as the cliques that vie in the present day, is bringing the whole thing down.)

Prior to the 1960s, poetry distribution lay in the hands of the London publishers and a few, very select, literary magazines that operated on the narrowest of lines and outlooks, selling largely to the literary world itself or what might, somewhat inaccurately, be termed the intelligensia. Poetry also appeared in university student literary magazines and it was here that much good work was discovered and much more lost, along with a dross of adolescent garbage, but seldom did any of this reach beyond the precincts of the universities or the university towns. Students were still something of an elite group and so were seen as set apart from humanity.

Gradually, however, during the 1950s, things became ready for change. This change was encouraged or fostered by a number of very important factors, which were to prove far-reaching.

This first was the invention of the small press. Poetry has traditionally appeared in small runs of just a few hundred copies. A look at a bibliography of Victorian poetry shows that hundreds of books appeared – even thousands – written by 'A Country Lady' or 'Miss Anastasia Double-Barrelled Name' who had the books published and who either sold them herself to friends or to a wider circle of peers, or paid for the publication (a particularly nasty business that carries on to this day), or could assure sales in some way or another to a publisher who, not at all unlike his modern counterparts, was predisposed towards poetry being an instant loss-maker and was therefore eager to accept anything that swelled his lists but for which he didn't have to exert much energy in order to cover his outlay. Other small editions were likewise published, but these were often the work of established poets who already had a public following (or a clan of backers in universities and the like) and the titles were handsomely (that is, also expensively) made and sold at a classy price as potential collectors' items. There is no harm in this, it just keeps the verse only in the reach of those who love it and can afford it. These types of books were the caviar of the poetry meal.

Printing was a costly business. It was labour-intensive, time-consuming and the materials were not cheap. Large editions of thousands of copies were needed for a substantial profit: smaller runs could make money, but not a lot, despite the superlative purchasing orders from the British public library system. Novels could scratch along on a run of, say, two thousand copies, but poetry could not. Two thousand copies sold was a rare event except with the Big Names' books and, even then, they didn't often match the sale of even a mediocre novel. Poetry was not over-borrowed from libraries, either. Most of the public only saw poetry in anthologies where a minute selection (often spanning centuries as in the highly sold and popular *Palgrave's Golden Treasury*) appeared, or in school. Traditionally, poetry has been a financial wash-out.

Publishers, accepting this, refused and refuse to put their sales machines behind verse. Poets, believing this, fall short of the potential their art could achieve and so the vicious circle turns. It was difficult for poets to break into publication unless they had the entry card that consisted of a university education or a friendship with the publisher and/or his editors or a substantial supply of exceptional good fortune.

At the end of the 1950s, however, poets who were reacting against the in-breeding of verse were appearing and required print. They got it. The small presses, hitherto restricting themselves to the production of costly limited editions, underwent a metamorphosis that was to change the face of poetry and set up the atmosphere for the living years ahead.

A major factor in making this possible was that printing became cheaper because of new technology. Print reproduction until the early 1960s was restricted to letterpress printing where much of the type was still set by hand in the myriad of small printers' shops all over the country. Apprentices spent hours placing letter after letter into a text which was then set up, aligned, proofed, altered, changed, re-set and justified and then, on fairly slow machinery, printed. Then came collation and binding and so on and so on and so on. It was laborious and expensive. The only alternative was the duplicator such as one sees in schools these days being used to run off a couple of hundred parents' letters about uniform or circulars about school meals. The standard of print was poor and the typeface restricted to the one on the nearest typewriter.

Then, over but a few years, there came into general use automatic setting machines of one sort or another that cut out the costly handsetting of type. Next came the sophisticated offset lithography machines that allowed photoplates to print books. And the duplicators became more sophisticated and people with no or little skill could now print a page that looked acceptable. By 1971, booklets and books of verse could be produced that looked well designed, were well printed and attained a high standard of manufactured production. Suddenly, verse had the ability to make itself available at a reasonable price. And it did. Small presses appeared like ants at a picnic in the second half of the 1960s. Some already existed and carried on, going from strength to strength.

It seems appropriate at this point to name a few and state their owners' ideas. Yet it must be realised that it is no falsehood to state that, for every press mentioned below there are ten not given a look in. Perhaps the longest standing at the time, and still continuing to operate, is Howard Sergeant's Outposts Publications. This has published between twenty and forty booklets per annum since it evolved from *Outposts* magazine in 1956: the magazine had been operating for twelve years before the new venture was embarked upon. Authors' work is accepted on merit, but the press does stipulate that each author must be able to ensure a certain number of sales for his or her title, thus making the process not quite as much of a risk for the editor/publisher as most small presses are wont to be. From the extensive author list, many of whom, it is fair to point out, have since sunk without trace, one can see the first poetic publications of such poets as made good – or big – in the period from 1960 onwards – Alan Sillitoe, Harry Guest, Ruth Fainlight, D. M. Thomas, Peter Reading amongst them. The magazine that fathered the press published the first poetic attempts of greater still – Kingsley Amis, Muriel Spark, Vernon Scannell and Elizabeth Jennings.

Sergeant's aim was in common with most of the better small presses. He sought to publish the best poetry available, with particular bias towards the newcomers and the unestablished. Apart from an entrepreneurial kick, he was rewarded by the feeling that he was contributing towards a liveliness in the art, giving through this an opportunity to many who would otherwise have stood little chance of becoming published. The *Outpost* booklets were not exceptionally made: they were – and remain

37

today, for the enterprise continues – adequately printed and bound in card covers, with a uniform and somewhat dated design, but this helped the price to remain low.

The mother magazine flourishes still: Sergeant's print-run steadily increases and he does publish a wide variety of poets, but he tends to keep to the safe ones, not looking too hard at the more experimentally alert. This ensures a safe readership, but the point remains that he and his little concern have survived so long by appealing particularly to poetry lovers and not just to the poets themselves. In more recent years, say from 1976, his booklets have sometimes verged upon vanity publications, of which more will be said at the end of this section, and this has weakened his standing with poets. The magazine continues to be a power in the land of British verse.

In the earlier days of the small press era, and the period from 1964 certainly can be classed as such, many presses were (unlike Sergeant's) not just published by one man, but also printed by the same person. The men best known and most deserving of admiration in this direction were Roy Lewis (Keepsake Press), Alan Tarling (Poet & Printer Press) and John Cotton (Priapus Press and accompanying magazine of the same ubiquitous name).

Roy Lewis started his operation in 1958, subsidising it from his earnings as a journalist (later specialist) on the staff of *The Times*. His aim was 'just to publish interesting poetry and some prose, contemporary or otherwise'. After a while, the press became a little more financially self-supportive, but never totally so. One hundred titles appeared by 1981, almost all of them printed by Lewis on a hand letterpress that was set up either in his garage or a garden shed. He published booklets, what he called poemcards, which were boldly printed broadsheets bound in card covers and individually illustrated by well-known, contemporary artists and a few thin volumes. It was he who first published the work of, for example, Peter Porter but it was not just verse he kept to, bringing out Charles Wesley's *The American War* and a collection of Victorian, political handbills.

Similar in that the publications were truly home-made on a small, cheap handpress in Alan Tarling's Poet & Printer. Like Lewis's work, the booklets were well designed and published the work of established and unknown poets although, in both publishers' cases, they did not take first-timers, but concentrated on at least those poets already acceptably noticed in the small magazines. Tarling financed his venture from his own earnings in a 'proper job' and also saw his printing as, as Lewis puts it, a process that was 'one of the small tributaries of a great river'.

A headmaster in Berkhampstead, John Cotton has built up a fair reputation as a small press and magazine editor and publisher as well as establishing for himself his own niche as a poet. He is one of the many small owners (Lewis and Tarling are uncharacteristic) who are simultaneously poets themselves of greater or lesser extent. Priapus Press rose from the ashes of the magazine which ran from 1962 to 1972. Once more, Cotton follows the pattern of those others already mentioned – publish what they consider good, regardless of position in the poetic hierarchy. However, this does mean a mix of famous and lesser-known poets. Cotton's list includes D. M. Thomas, Peter Redgrove, Sally Purcell, George Szirtes and Emma Rose: for Purcell and Rose, since much more widely published, this was a first appearance.

All three of these latter men, Lewis, Tarling and Cotton, have made similar comments about their presses; Cotton states he wanted to 'give a platform to new, unpublished poets (which commercial publishers have irresponsibly abandoned as a policy) – we include some established poets in order to set them alongside their peers'. It is also fair to say that the known poets serve another purpose for the small press in that they boost sales and thereby earn that additional finance which might be spent on lesser-knowns. Most, if not all, the better small press publishers bear this in mind as does any large London firm.

From Cotton's comments, one can see that he does not consider himself a commercial publisher at all, but again, it is the aim (if not the result) of many small press people to make at least some profit in order to plough this back in and to give some sense of credibility to their concerns and their authors.

Small presses kept verse alive, and continue to do so, in the face of enormous impossibilities and adverse conditions: the pun is intentional. In 1975, there were well over 200 small press publishers in Britain, many of them members of the Association of Little Presses that was set up by Bob Cobbing and others at the end of the 1960s. The ALP served little function for its members save giving them a voice in the literary jungle and an identity and fort from which to let fly barbs at the establishment world. Grandiose schemes of marketing and distribution networks failed, not through antipathy or bad organisation, but through the fact that many presses wanted to keep their individuality (and closely guarded customer lists) and many more were just too disorganised to carry on the responsibilities involved in joining in the ALP plans. More recently, Ian Robinson has established Independent Press Distribution in London, offshooting this from his considerable involvement in the small press scene where he was the founder and mover of Oasis Books. This looks as if it might survive and succeed where ALP did not.

The presses maintained breath in the poetic body by publishers accepting a wide variety of manuscripts and bringing these out regardless of possible financial bombing or flying. With smallish print runs, but not smallish production costs, it was feasible and it was not long before the better-selling authors (not necessarily the famous ones) were produced in larger editions and incomes improved.

Yet where the presses really made a major contribution was in maintaining a high output of titles, thus engendering and causing a specific field of literary activity to stay at boiling point. Oasis Books published fifty-seven books in ten years; Sceptre Press published over 400 booklets, broadsheets and books in thirteen years; Second Aeon Publications, who get a better mention later in the section on magazines in the period, produced over a hundred books and broadsheets in eight years; Enitharmon Press, founded in 1969 and still going strong, has published over eighty-five books (some of them substantial hardbacks); Peterloo Poets/Harry Chambers, a champion small presser, has published forty-eight books in nine years. These presses built up a corpus of poetry, making it available at a time when it was wanted, and are now retaining it in print.

What is more, and it is a long-standing state of affairs but not one that should necessarily change, the bigger publishing houses tend to overlook the fact that most of their poets began in small, if not tiny, presses. They should, therefore, encourage such tiny set-ups as publishers were wont to do in, for example, Victorian times when they supported and uplifted short story and fiction magazines from the pages of which they took their mainstay authors – Hardy for instance started just so, Dickens likewise. But no! Quite the opposite occurs. The big publishers ignore those doing their groundwork for them and give distinct distance to them. Not only that, but the Publishers' Association is more than reluctant to include small press publishers in its ranks. And further, those in power see to it that small presses are not seriously considered when, for example, the Poetry Book Society makes its quarterly choice and recommendation.

The small press has given rise to a particularly unsavoury business angle on publishing which must be mentioned. It is the vanity press. Often run so as to look like a Big Firm, it is a company that advertises that it wants poems to publish and, when it receives submissions, almost invariably accepts them for inclusion in a book which has a grandiose title like 'Top Poems of 19XX'. As soon as the submitter is told that the work is accepted, he is also told that he has to pay towards production of the book.

Most real poets know better: never pay to be published. But many would-be poets in the public do not know this and are conned. The books appear and can usually be found within a twelve-month in a remainder shop, assuming the remainder buyer has let his judgment slip. Quite often, the books are subsequently pulped after the contributors have bought a few copies for themselves and their friends. The desire to write poetry became so strong – and still is, for these companies still exist – that anyone thought they'd make it to the big time via such roads. They didn't. The conmen moved in. To their shame, they even advertised in *The Times Educational Supplement* and unknowing teachers pointed their pupils in the direction of the editors. (When I taught in a grammar school in the early 1970s, I had several pupils who fell foul of the net of vanity publishing. I guided them clear and quickly: a letter to *The Times Educational Supplement* about such publishers was printed but although many must have listened, many others didn't. At the same time, to prove these publishers valueless, I submitted two poems to them, both consisting of the first lines of all of Dylan Thomas's poems in the collected works, jumbled up. Both were pleasantly and enthusiastically accepted. The fee for publication was, I seem to recall, £12.50 for the two.) Wherever a man has vanity, there is someone ready to make loot out of him. How sad that poetry, which holds men's hearts as dear, should be so used.

It is pertinent to end this section with some comments from small press publishers:

> Harry Chambers: 'So far, none of my volumes has been made a Poetry Book Society Choice, though one of my authors – passed on to Oxford University Press (Peter Scupham) – has received this honour and John Mole, now with Secker & Warburg, has been a Recommendation.' (Scupham's first book, *The Snowing Globe*, was outstanding and considerably better than his subsequent volume.)

> Howard Sergeant: 'One might think that such literary journals as *The Times Literary Supplement* would be sympathetic and helpful – but they seem to be more antagonistic than otherwise . . . [they] might well have recognised the difficulties in running a magazine and a small press, and been more supportive. As it is they have been destructive and negative. One succeeds in spite of them.'

> John Cotton: '. . . We have helped to launch some very talented and worthwhile poets . . . to keep, with others

doing the same thing, literary standards going which commercial publishers have abandoned in pursuit of mass markets.'

These comments speak for themselves.

But why is it so? The commercial publishers, as Cotton terms them (and, in doing so, frankly insults himself for he is as commercial as the biggest) cannot see the value of small presses. They do not have their own book runs affected at all. They forget that many of their authors have their sales increased by small press firms which send out their little books and the like throughout the vast network of poetry readers and writers and, thereby, inadvertently advertise for the London houses.

Of course, some small presses are much more insular and keep themselves to themselves: Mandeville Press (run by Peter Scupham) publishes but a few poets and caters for a somewhat select readership, albeit a catholic one; Sycamore Press (founded in 1968 by the poet and Oxford don, John Fuller) has kept a low profile but is a sound concern with a powerful list including Auden, Redgrove and Larkin; Greylag Press, a later addition to the press circles and organised by Jim Vollmar, has a short list but a good turnover.

Generally speaking, though, small presses don't shout about what they do. They sell their wares successfully through knowing their markets and exploiting them as any good businessman would. Some have sold their titles in thousands, which is a good deal greater a turnover than many a Secker & Warburg poetry book. This is despite all the contacts such a huge firm has through its representatives travelling the country to every bookshop and its ramifications overseas.

John Fuller has said, in respect of his press but it applies to all, that, 'we've contributed the *right* dab of colour in one corner of the canvas in a way that may have influenced other dabs. . . . But, of course, the whole picture is quite beyond our influence.'

With due respect to Fuller, for his Sycamore Press has been an inspiration to others (including Sceptre Press which, in its early days, emulated it), as has Lewis's Keepsake Press for another, he is very wrong. Small presses don't dab the canvas, they outline it the whole damn picture and colour a good bit of it, too. The establishment publishers simply stick in a few more features and – sadly, for they don't deserve it – provide the frame.

9

Not all small presses have remained small. Some have expanded with considerable verve and are now out of the league, so to speak, having grown so big as to either set themselves up as a class apart or, worse, join the establishment publishers.

By definition, a small press is small not because of the size of its staff or the number of its titles produced per annum, but by its own decision to call itself so. Some small presses have out-published everyone else. It might be argued that small presses are small because (i) they publish small books, with few pages, (ii) they have small capital backing, (iii) they run a small list or publish in small print runs of not more than, say, 150 copies of each title, (iv) they deal with small printing machines or small printers (though one printer who has more than made his mark in the years from 1970 in poetry production in Britain is Christopher Skelton, of Skelton's Press, Ltd: he began by producing just Sceptre Press titles from a small, back-alley works and now prints for quite a number of the better small presses from a fine printery in a superb, Victorian former factory), (v) they sell in small numbers, (vi) they have a small distribution structure or they simply see themselves as small and select.

So how do 'small' presses become so 'big'? They do so by publishing important titles and gaining in artistic stature; or by publishing the famous and gaining in reputation; or by selling vast numbers of books – and by vast, one is talking of thou-sands, not the hundreds the big publishers aim at.

Enitharmon Press is a good example of the small press grown big. The press was founded in 1969 by Alan Clodd, a bibliophile of considerable expertise and drive. Like most of his peers, he has another job as well as publisher and, from this, he has financed his list, bolstering this with increasing sales and, on occasion, Arts Council of Great Britain grants, one of the few small presses to be so honoured. Clodd is characteristically modest about his achievements, but amongst them he has chalked up the publi-cation of the highpoint of John Heath-Stubbs's poetic career, *Artorius*, he published David Gascoyne's *Journals* and started a revival (long overdue) of interest in this poet's work and he brought out the well-known two collections of the late Frances Bellerby's work. These are some of the older names in the poetry world: Clodd hasn't kept to them. He brought out the work of Frances Horovitz, the best female poetry reader in Britain, John

Moat, Richard Burns and Jeremy Reed, poets not well known until Clodd gave them print in book form. Enitharmon Press has almost always published books, not booklets. Some of his books have been prose works (Gascoyne's one, for example), but they have all had a link to verse and so deserve the mention even if out of the province of this book: someone's whose work he produced in proliferation was that of the late Hugo Manning, one of the great and ignored poets of the middle part of this century.

Enitharmon Press's story is over a decade old. Others are rising up to join in and it is in these that the future of British poetry rests. Consider three of them as typical of the two dozen of their ilk: Bloodaxe Books (founded 1978), Ceolfrith Press (founded 1970) and Harry Chambers and his Peterloo Poets, touched upon in the last section.

Chambers began publishing in 1972, somewhat by proxy. His first four books were financed by E. J. Morten, but edited by Chambers himself. He commenced in earnest as a lone editor/publisher in 1976, financially surviving on his sales and an Arts Council guarantee against loss. He set out from the start producing pamphlets and books, and the size of his list and the obviously high quality of his authors has set him up as a major publishing house for poetry, the main aim being to publish 'poetry of quality by new and neglected poets'.

He has succeeded, as has Coelfrith Press which has been heavily subsidised from the start by Northern Arts, one of the regional arts associations, the Arts Council and the Borough of Sunderland, the only such to support by direct means a small publisher. The list has stretched to over seventy titles including work by R. S. Thomas, Glyn Hughes, Richard Kell and Nicki Jackowska. Some of the titles have been collaborative ventures between poet and artist, Jon Silkin, John Heath-Stubbs and Thomas amongst them.

Michael Farley, who administered the press and ran its affairs in every detail, is best quoted in full on the matters of the small press making big (or good). His comments are as follows. The questions in italics were those asked which elicited the responses. Several points come up here that are dealt with shortly, but they can be included here, early, in order not to disrupt the pattern. (Since the following questions were asked, in mid-1982, Ceolfrith Press has considerably drawn in its publishing horns and Farley has quit to start his own firm, Taxvs Press. This is a sad move as it reduces further the established names in the small press world, but at least this pruning has caused a new company to form.)

What editorial policy existed?

From the very beginning there has been a policy of a balance between the publication of poetry and of books of the visual arts. . . . The Poet and Artist series of books and pamphlets combines the work of contemporary poets, such as R. S. Thomas, Jon Silkin and John Heath-Stubbs with the work of artists such as Barry Hirst, David Gormley and Edwin Easydorchik.

However, the central concern of the press remains the publication of contemporary poetry of outstanding merit. A certain emphasis is placed on the work of new and neglected poets and, while Ceolfrith has no intention of confining its function to those of a regional publisher, a new series entitled Ceolfrith Northern Poets . . . ensures that the press meets its commitments to writers working in the north of England.

What disasters were there – or problems?

Apart from one or two seriously ill-judged publications in the early days, Ceolfrith has been remarkably lucky in avoiding real disasters. One perennial problem is that, being dependent upon annually re-applied-for grant aid, we find it difficult to plan our publishing programme with any accuracy further ahead than the end of each financial year. In consequence, we have sometimes had to go to press in too much of a rush; usually we have managed to avoid doing too much harm to our standards of book production, but we have occasionally had to accept uneconomic printing costs as the price of getting things done quickly.

Another annoyance is that for the same reason we find it impossible to give authors firm publication dates further ahead than six to nine months, and that it becomes very hard to know how far ahead in time one dares to accept a MS for publication. A little misplaced enthusiasm would have the press booked up for the next decade . . . or possibly two, depending upon the funding available.

Northern Arts (the Ceolfrith regional arts association) has been and remains very generous though, and it would be churlish to complain too bitterly about problems which arise from the very means of funding that keeps us alive.

What do you feel the press has contributed to the general poetry scene?

During the life of Ceolfrith Press several of the most important imprints for the publication of poetry ceased publication or reduced production to a dribble – Fulcrum and Trigram spring to mind. Another thing was that a number of the major houses publishing poetry as part of a larger literary programme dropped it altogether, or cut right back to the safest, most firmly established names – Penguin, Macmillan et al. Of course generally speaking the really small presses, the fine printers on the one hand and the duplicator boys on the other, have simply kept going, or at least have been replaced by others as daring and industrious. Money, I suppose, is partly to blame: the less you have the less you risk losing and a flopped book with a run of 150 copies on the trusty Roneo machine will hardly break even the poorest publisher. But the well-produced permanent book, containing a reasonable number of pages and selling at a price affordable by people other than wealthy book collectors, has taken a terrible knock. It is left to a comparatively small number of presses, one of them Ceolfrith, to pick up the pieces. A fair bit of our recent publishing has been, almost literally, that. In the last couple of years or so Ceolfrith has published, for instance, full-length collections from Glyn Hughes (ex-Macmillan) and Richard Kell (ex-Chatto & Windus), both excellent poets dropped in the cutbacks. We have collections in preparation from, among others, William Martin and Richard Caddell, both important poets who have been around for quite a time now, yet have failed to have full-length collections published because of the lack of publishers like Fulcrum Press, willing and able to take risks with the publication of experimental work of a high order.

Altogether Ceolfrith has had a not dishonourable twelve years of it, but I can't help feeling that, God willing, our time is only beginning. There is a very great deal of excellent work looking for homes and the only imprints capable of, or willing to do it justice are the smaller, usually grant-aided operations like ourselves. We can produce sizeable, permanent collections at prices slightly below the average publisher's for similarly sized books, but to a significantly higher standard of design and workmanship than is usual among the large houses. We can take far more risks with experimental or original work and with righting wrongs done to unjustly neglected poets who once had access to full-scale publication.

Our real weakness is distribution. In the present economic climate, it is difficult to persuade booksellers' buyers to take risks with the stocking of work by poets they've never heard of, even with nationwide teams of professional reps; perhaps this is the main reason for the big publishers' cutbacks.

Bloodaxe Books is Neil Astley's dream come true and that is not to be journalistically flippant. As Astley was so forthcoming – and deliberate and truthful and, above all, accurate – in his response to research for this book, his responses (with the questions) are also given below.

How was it financed?

I had a bale of paper and not very much money. I managed to persuade a few people to lend me small amounts. I raised a little from the first few months' sales of the pamphlet (the first, Ken Smith's *Tristan Crazy*). But my bank manager wouldn't lend me £60 to help with what he termed my 'speculative venture' – that was National Westminster Bank. The Bloodaxe account is now with Lloyds who are much more understanding. Somehow I managed to pay the printers' bill for 750 copies of the pamphlet. The first six months were a case of struggling on with that one pamphlet and then I managed to get Northern Arts to make the first of their grants to the press to fund the publication of the next pamphlets. Between 1978 and 1982 I ran Bloodaxe part-time – firstly whilst working for Dove Cottage, then whilst doing postgraduate research, and most recently while working in a bookshop. I'm now the press's full-time editor. I've also managed to get grants from other sources for specific books. In terms of analysing the grant aid, the best thing would probably be for me to give a short list and this should be self-explanatory:

1979–80	Northern Arts £1000 + £250 Basil Bunting long-playing record promotion grant
1980–81	Northern Arts £1000: Welsh Arts Council £500 (for Nigel Wells's book): West Midlands Arts £500 (Tony Flynn's book)
1981–82	Northern Arts £1000: Arts Council of Northern Ireland £400 (Tom Paulin/ Noel Connor book)
1982–83	Northern Arts £10,000

Sales have always exceeded grant aid and I'm trying to increase the sales proportion of the income all the time; but grants are still essential. It should be noted that Bloodaxe benefits from the imaginative and generous funding policies of Northern Arts and that all the funding in the north of England is devolved to Northern Arts by The Arts Council, who have made an additional grant to Northern Arts to enable them to fund Bloodaxe as a major client.

How many titles have been published?

1978	1 pamphlet
1979	4 pamphlets
1980	6 books: 1 long-playing record
1981	1 book: 4 pamphlets: 1 pamphlet reprint
1982	10 books: 5 pamphlets: 1 pamphlet reprint (some of these as yet projected)

What editorial policy have you?

Initially to publish a number of fine poets who'd either not been published or whose work had received erratic or inadequate publication – in contrast to better-known poets of inferior quality. To reflect the wide range of contemporary British poetry. To be flexible, open-minded, catholic while maintaining high standards, looking for craft and truth. To support the poets by publishing their work in well-produced editions. Also to produce other kinds of titles where the need exists – for example, the long-player of Basil Bunting reading *Briggflatts*. To run a coherent publishing programme which includes pamphlets as well as books, poetry in translation as well as contemporary British poetry (as from 1982) and from 1983 a modern fiction list, basically of reissued novels which ought to be available in trade paperback. To show the reading public an alternative to the dull, unimaginative, gimmicky, arid, mechanical, egotistical, manic, propagandist, effete, pointless kinds of so-called poetry put out by the established publishing houses and greeted enthusiastically by their lackeys in the reviewing establishment. To give consistent publication to some of the best poets now writing in Britain. To compete with the commercial publishers on their own ground, *not* to remain in the backwaters of small press publishing.

What major successes do you feel you have achieved?

It is probably too early to assess this. I hope I'm making some headway in establishing or consolidating the reputations of poets like Ken Smith and David Constantine. Most of the books are getting reviewed and they're getting into the shops. The press's next move will be to improve shop sales – with a distributor now handling the orders and with repping coming. Many shops have found that some of the Bloodaxe titles do sell, whereas they get stuck with books from the established houses. There is a moral there and it has to do with the poetry itself, with presentation and pricing policy. I'm writing an article now which makes the point that there are many books published by small or independent presses which actually sell better than the products of the commercial publishers . . . small firms . . . publish poets with a readership and to order just from well-known publishers because they have the name and the prestige is short-sighted and loses money. What *Bloodaxe* must succeed in doing as much as possible is to break the stranglehold that the large poetry publishers have on the shops.

What disasters have there been?

Disasters and problems have existed all the time. Cash flow is always the main problem – selling enough books to pay the printers and to cover the authors' royalties and many other things. This was almost a disaster in 1980/1, when expenditure far exceeded income and a slump in sales in which the recession was a contributory factor nearly killed the press just as it was beginning to achieve something. But one learns from such close shaves and the programme and budget are now better planned. You have to be forceful and ambitious, but cautious as well.

From the above two lengthy quoted passages, one can see only too well the problems of the small presses that seek to be larger and, subsequently, richer in artistic drive, integrity and serious-mindedness.

Before looking at the problems, one should look at the small presses who have 'gone over', to use spy slang, to the other side, the side of the London publisher and the likes. Top of the list here is Carcanet Press. Carcanet Press was founded in Oxford in 1968 by Michael Schmidt, having developed organically from a literary magazine started in Cambridge around 1964. Schmidt took on the magazine in his second week as an undergraduate fresh in from Harvard and, in what he terms a grand last gesture for the journal in which there appeared to be little future, he published (with the aid of two co-editors) after two years eight pamphlets of poetry by poets he had come to admire through the pages of his dying publication. That was in 1968, when small presses were starting their boom years. To everyone's astonishment, including Schmidt's, the pamphlets sold well and 600 copies of each (with one coming more as a book than a booklet) went reasonably quickly. The publishing bacterium, the disease of all small press people, was in their systems and more publications swiftly followed. Carcanet Press (today known as Carcanet New Press Ltd) built up a quick list of poetry and soon extended this until it now publishes verse, verse-related books, memoirs, past poets' work republished, a substantial translation list and biography followed (bravely, considering the times) by fiction.

From time to time, Carcanet faced financial problems and has been near to liquidation and official receivership, only to be baled out by the Arts Council, a rare privilege not afforded to many small presses.

Schmidt was lucky in his timing. He set up shop at the height of the poetry years and kept going when the larger publishers brought in their cost accountants and sub-standard editors and began to trim or execute their poetry lines. To date, over 400 books have appeared, some of these becoming award-winners. One might ask why the Carcanet list is a particularly uneven one, publishing not only some of the best (and, in some cases, most neglected poets of the century – Edmund Blunden, Edgell Rickworth and Charlotte Mew, for example) but also more than a fair sprinkling of the most mundane poets.

The answer lies in the fact that, firstly, Schmidt has more than cornered the poetry market and, secondly, he has become so big as to no longer be an independent small press but simply one of the giants, with power, influence and a position of strength from which to dictate the directions of British verse. He is generally too modest to agree with one, but it might well be false modesty. He must know the throne from which he controls so much.

The situation now is that Schmidt has, in many ways, become one of the arbiters of poetic taste, as much as an editor for a London publishers, and he must be wary of becoming one: unfortunately, he is slightly bending that way in that, although he does publish a good many younger poets, his list is narrowed by a thin definition of verse and the books he publishes are very much of a muchness or pandering to the 'new scene' of pseudo-intellectual wafflery. It is as if his small press ideals of bringing out the new and unknown have become somehow corrupted and lost in the mêlée of having to make a profit and justify himself to the Arts Council doyens who in turn only want to see publishers in the established mould.

As with most arbiters who tend to publish only their own sort of verse, Schmidt is now doing just that. It is a pity that this sometimes means bringing out books by those with little talent, especially where he is discovering new poets as opposed to producing books by those dropped or axed from the London publisher lists for whatever reason. It is indeed a shame to see how this valiant small press has turned into one of the multinationals as it were of poetry, to the exclusion of catholicity.

Not all the small presses have gone this way; at least, not quite so far. Anvil Press, founded and run by Peter Jay with an assortment of financial backers over the years, has kept going a small and yet select list of poets with both reputation and talent on their sides, often being those who have been successful in other fields of poetic activity apart from volume publication. Anvil is a small press in the common sense of the word: short runs, but sound production; good poets if not highly famous ones; catholic tastes and an avoidance of sheer gimickry but not an ignoring of the new.

A press handout prepared by Peter Jay gives an interesting insight into the background of such a company. It was written at the time when Anvil Press, now known as Anvil Press Poetry, moved into the co-activity of Wildwood House, a joining since severed. The hand-out is quoted more or less intact below and it gives sound indicators of the concepts and ideals behind the typical small press that has expanded but not gone overboard. Jay himself is, for a poet and poetry man, remarkably low-profiled and a modest figure who gets on with it rather than using his energies for the establishment of a power base within the art or the construction of a coterie. In the blurb for Anvil he wrote:

> Like many small presses set up in recent years Anvil Press Poetry descends directly from a poetry magazine. Anvil's source of energy was the magazine *New Measure* which ran for ten issues between 1965 and 1969, which was a magazine concentrating exclusively on printing new poetry and translations rather than articles and reviews. This 'anthology' format allowed the magazine's editor to assemble a body of writers he believed deserved more extensive publication and whom he believed were not likely to be published by anyone else. This initial impetus has remained unflinchingly consist-

ent since Anvil Press Poetry was formed on this basis in 1968. Of sixteen poets published in issue 9 of *New Measure* (summer, 1968), which announced the press's formation, thirteen of them still figure in the 1982 Anvil list. . . . The initial years saw Peter Jay concentrating upon the group of good quality writers arising from the ashes of *New Measure*. With this investment the press survived its formative years and withstood the economic pressures of the mid-1970s which saw many independent presses absorbed or destroyed. Since then the publication perspective of Anvil has been considerably broadened and a wide-ranging list has now been assembled. . . . The focus is on contemporary English poetry and this is broadened by many translations of contemporary European poets, and interest fostered upon Peter Jay when he was assistant to the Poetry International festivals from 1969 to 1972. Apart from one novel, one book of criticism, one book of Shelley's prose writings and a series known as 'Poetica', which is devoted to foreign poetry 'of classical status' (e.g. Persius, Petrarch) the Anvil list is entirely devoted to contemporary poetry. . . . The open quest for the excellent and the fresh, Peter Jay's apparent indicators, cannot always prove ultimately successful. The wide-ranging catchment nets some first rate work but, inevitably, this does not always remain consistent. This imbalance aside, it is a welcome sight to see such an impetus injected into contemporary poetry publishing. . . . Anvil Press Poetry as an entity sometimes verges upon the anonymous, a centralising unity and coherence seemingly absent. The advantage of this unobtrusive anonymity is that the poetry is forced to declare itself on its own terms . . . each volume is an individual volume. But the disadvantage is that within Anvil the two bodies of contemporary English writing and contemporary European writing sit uneasily next to each other, the diffuseness and variety of the one overshadowed by the relative solidity of the other. They should be shown to inhabit one corpus.

The above shows an imaginative, catholic but discerning editorial mind at work and this has led to the creation of one of the best of the small presses and certainly one of the longer running.

Before leaving Anvil, one might consider the following phrases from Jay's potted history: 'writers . . . whom he believed were not likely to be published by anyone else'; 'the press therefore commits itself to a special responsibility towards new writing in this country.' Not one establishment publisher can claim either of these quotations for himself and it is true that Jay receives a comfortable, but not overly generous, Arts Council grant, but nevertheless he survives in the all-important market place and his books do sell. Given the sales resources of a big publisher such as Macmillan, for example, the grant would, one feels sure, be unrequired.

Small presses are plentiful and a guide to them all would be exhaustive and exhausting. But it seems right to end this chapter with a list and potted commentary on a few apart from those already mentioned. It should show that poetry is being kept healthily alive despite the overwhelming forces acting against it from the direction of the big publishers.

Another small press is Rivelin Press, run by David Tipton, a not-well-known poet and novelist, without grant aid except for some support from his regional arts association. Publications are usually from sixteen to thirty-six pages long and well printed by offset-litho. His list includes a good deal of translated poetry by authors generally unobtainable from anyone else as well as titles by Jeff Nuttall, Cal Clothier, Allan Burgis, Philip Callow and Jim Burns. Few titles exceed £1.50 per copy and some sell very well indeed.

Fuller d'Arch Smith, Ltd is a publishing house run as offshoot from a rare book dealing firm of the same name, founded in the late 1960s by Timothy d'Arch Smith (formerly *The Times* Rare Bookshop organiser) and Jean Overton Fuller, the poet and well-known biographer. The company has had some very successful books from a short list, not seeking just to publish poetry by poets but also, for example, John Snow, the famous cricketer. Other authors include Susan Musgrave (her first book outside Canada and one that established her reputation in Britain), Peter Redgrove and Penelope Shuttle working together on an award-winning co-written volume, George MacBeth, Randle Manwaring, Howard Sergeant and Brian Hill.

Scorpion Press appeared at the end of the 1950s and published poetry titles for about ten years. Production consisted of hardback books and substantial pamphlets, all of which are now collectors' items. The press existed before the real 'small press' emerged and it was really living in a vacuum, neither attacking the big publishers' lists nor threatening them: in fact, it was paving the way for many of them for Scorpion Press produced some of the first books of those who were to become very famous indeed – George MacBeth, Peter Porter, Christopher Logue, David Gascoyne (a reprint of an Editions Poetry London book, the author already famous, to say the least), Robert Nye (famous later as a novelist) and Jenny Joseph. MacBeth's reputation was made by this publisher; so was Porter's. Some of the poets published have since vanished from poetry making which is sad for, in keeping with this publisher's list, they were all of very high standard – Roger Hobdell and Shirley Toulson, to name but a pair. The books, though superbly made, seldom exceeded £1 in cost even in the late 1960s.

Fulcrum Press was founded by Stuart Montgomery, a poet and doctor. It came into being in the mid-1960s and, by the end of the decade, was publishing a large number of books. The list was similar in some ways to Scorpion Press in that it produced hardbacks and slimmer paperbacks by poets who were up-and-coming and the press sought to establish reputations, which it did. It re-established some, too: Basil Bunting, long ignored and unjustly so – he was perhaps the best (or worst) example of how the big publishers trample on poets of real and proven merit – was brought back to print and success by Fulcrum. Others on the list included Christopher Middleton, Pete Brown (to be world-famous as a rock music writer for Cream), Roy Fisher and Lee Harwood. Montgomery and his press were additionally very important for another activity, that of publishing new American poets in Britain – Gary Snyder, Ed Dorn and Lorine Niedecker, not to mention Ginsberg – whose influence was soon felt in no slight way.

Menard Press is the invention of Anthony Rudolf who started the seed of his press going in the mid-1960s, whilst a student at Cambridge. Himself a translator of some note, he has been keen to bring out translation material but has not ignored British verse. His best books are those written by Nicki Jackowska (whom he first published in book form) and George Buchanan, for whom Menard did as Fulcrum had for Bunting. Rudolf works at times in collaboration with other poetry publishers (Sceptre Press, Carcanet and Anvil Press have been his co-publishers) and, since 1980, has started to run down his poetry list in favour of anti-nuclear weapon and peace publications. What peace gains, poetry loses.

Writers' Forum was started in 1963 by Bob Cobbing and is the country's most important concrete poetry publisher. Standards of production of titles vary from the grim to the superb but all are pacesetters in their field. Over 300 titles have appeared including work by Eric Mottram, Jeff Nuttall (his first book), Lee Harwood, Bob Cobbing and Bill Griffiths. The seminal *Concerning Concrete Poetry* was published by this press and set a way for the future, being part manifesto and part guide. Despite 'cheap' if not 'nasty' production, many of the titles have sold in their thousands due to the expertise and drive of the one-man publisher.

Northern House which grew out of the School of English at the University of Leeds, is now run by associates of *Stand* magazine. Authors include Jon Silkin, Jon Glover and Jeffrey Wainwright (the editors of the press) plus Roy Fisher, Ted Walker, Ken Smith, Sorley Maclean, Tony Harrison, Geoffrey Hill and others. Print runs reach the thousands.

Blackstaff Press was founded in 1971 and began as a deliberate commercial undertaking assisted by the Arts Council for Northern Ireland – the press is centred in Belfast. It has published three dozen titles or so, all of them full-length books and most of them related to Northern Ireland although the editors claim that this is not company policy. It is true that they have published English work – Wes Magee's books of verse are the best examples – but their finest work has been Ulster-orientated, culminating in the extraordinary poetry of Paul Durcan. In addition, they have given voice and print to the likes of Frank Ormsby and James Simmons, Medbh McGuckian and John Hewitt, thereby encouraging not just the young writers but also those long established whom time has passed by or pressed into the background. Like Carcanet Press, Blackstaff have taken in poets who have been axed by the big London houses and it is ironic that they now make a profit from the sales of such authors' books. This immediately begs the obvious question: why were they axed in the first place, when they were potential profit-earners for their publishers? What is more, Blackstaff draw even nearer to the ideals of poetry (as they should be) by publishing work that is what they term, somewhat inaccurately, 'folk' poetry: there is in their list a book of dockers' poems. In their environment of Ulster, the press staff can (and do) rightly claim that they kept the poetry of their region alive through times that worked against literature. They are continuing and it is just as well, for the times are still against the central vitality of literature.

Those few mentioned above, and many others, have the potential to be great, both in size and in influence. They are running in a world that is contrary to them and would see them flounder as many have before.

Why have the small presses that are defunct passed on? The answer is complex, but it can be divided into roughly defined areas that touch on the central issues.

Most small presses were (and are) one-man operations, originally established through personal interest in the art and built up as a hobby. Here lies the crux. A hobby is a pastime, not an occupation, and many small presses collapsed because they did not see themselves as businesses. They failed to advertise well, to distribute properly, to design intelligently and to market. Those that saw themselves as business concerns have done well, remaining in operation and serving the literary and wider communities well.

Others that closed down did so for a variety of reasons: Second Aeon stopped because Peter Finch, the publisher, felt that the magazine had run its course and their financial security, the literary philanthropist Cyril Hodges, died, leaving a large hole in the bank account; contributory factors were also that Finch obtained a job managing the Welsh Arts Council bookshop in Cardiff and, as an employee, it would have been hard for him to get a grant which, significantly, equalled the amount Hodges put up. It should be mentioned here that, through Second Aeon, Hodges probably did more for the emergence of poetry in the period, especially from new poets, than any other single man and the debt to him must be finally acknowledged. With the end of the magazine, so also the press that brought out parallel booklets. Asa Benveniste's Trigram Press stopped publishing because the publisher grew bored with poetry, although he admits that the press isn't actually dead yet. Like many bitten by the bug, he is reluctant to admit he's quit. Fulcrum Press, run by Stuart Montgomery and with a hefty initial list that brought to prominence such poets as Basil Bunting, Pete Brown and Roy Fisher, stopped under financial and personal pressures: Montgomery is a full-time medical doctor and running a publishing concern on top of that is a heavy undertaking, to say the least. Fantasy Press has vanished. Digby Press, run by John Digby, seems to have produced but one book – *The Railings*, Alan Brownjohn's first – then disappeared.

These few had the opportunity to take over the poetry world. Why did they not? They had problems in getting into the bookshops, without representatives. They had to fight the lethargy of the reading public that was engendered by the establishment publishers and their output of poets' poetry. They had to fit their activities into the working lives of the publishers – Montgomery, as we have said, is a doctor; the other small pressmen hold in their ranks headmasters, schoolteachers, university lecturers, journalists, poets and writers, a postman, a computer analyst, a bus driver, students, a nurse, printers, etc. They had to face rising material costs, not to mention printing costs, despite the ease of production methods. (The price of paper rose 600 per cent between 1972 and 1980.) They had to face astronomical postage rates which hit distribution because the mail is the main way small presses get their work about. Finally, they had to face the gradual collapse or monopolisation of public readings of verse which grew smaller from the mid-1970s onward. Interest in poetry was flagging due to the rise of inflation, the cutting back of literary societies that were having their grants slashed (or losing clients that paid at the gate who would rather eat than hear verse), the increasing takeover of the reading circuit by a few who were either good value to hear or were becoming hyped.

Unlike any other business, poetry can hype itself with ease. It has built into itself such an old-boy network now that anyone in the know with those in power can be promoted beyond their value. The Poetry Book Society, the literary awards schemes, the National Poetry Centre – all these are controlled not by those writing good verse or publishing it, but by those who have succeeded in getting to the positions of power not through merit but through connections. When you own the phone company, as the saying goes, you listen to the talk and when you own the wires, you can add your own lines.

Consider the aforementioned Ian Robinson. He is a typical small press man and a look at him and his operations over the years since 1968 shows just what small pressery is all about. He made mistakes and he had considerable successes.

In 1968, Robinson was a lecturer in the then Kingston College of Art in London. As a student, he'd tried to start a literary magazine after trying earlier to do the same as a schoolboy. (It is interesting to think how many small pressers have done likewise for the number is substantial: perhaps it is a hereditary disease rather than an acquired addition.) In that year, he wandered into Better Books, in London. This was an avant-garde bookshop that stocked a large number of small press publications which it displayed on a big table in the basement. (Better Books was to go to receivership several years later. Always hard to get payment from, when it went it badly affected the finances of a number of small presses which had outstanding debts and who eventually received only a small portion of what was owed. Being unworld-ly-wise, the small publishers had not foreseen the collapse of the firm. There is no record of the closure shutting down any small presses, but some, with shoestring budgets backed by private as opposed to book earnings, were very badly burned.)

What Robinson saw fired his imagination and his enthusiasm. He was also upset by the atrocious standards of production. Knowing nothing about publishing, editing, small presses, modern poetry or much else, he set up his magazine, *Oasis*, which came out first in November 1969. Like many of his peers, he came into the game blind as a mole and learned from there the ways through the tunnels of the literary lawn.

He made mistakes. His printing wasn't superb, but it was far better than others'. The magazine is mentioned here in Chapter 10. From the magazine, which started to publish single-author issues, Robinson set up Oasis Books. In this, he met with success. He found that the books he published eventually covered their costs, and the profits (as with so many small presses) were fed into more books. Only two grants were ever made, totalling £400 (a pittance), but the firm carried on without Robinson having to pump private money into it. He was lucky, of course, for the college paid for the paper and supplied the printing machinery, Robinson working it with others. It is rare indeed in this country for any educational establishment to back such a venture. Even sound journals of the 'university variety' are seldom so financially or practically supported.

Oasis Books sold not through the fame of their authors, but through the tenacity and alacrity of Robinson who knows his market place better than most. Reviews gained sales, especially those in small magazines as well as the accepted journals. At readings, the poets often sold their own books and this was a major source of income for all small presses: Lee Harwood, one of Oasis's authors, achieved Robinson's bestsellers in this way. Word of mouth sold copies. Libraries bought copies by ordering through the British National Bibliography where librarians automatically ordered all poetry titles (as they did all fiction, all crime, all reference books and so on; those heydays are now but pleasant dreams). Some bookshops like Compendium Books in London bought copies to line their shelves and fill their mail order catalogues. Other bookshops like Bertram Rota Ltd bought for the overseas university markets (especially in North America) which are always interested, unlike our own country's universities, in keeping abreast of artistic development and as an investment for collectors, who have historically followed poetry as avidly, if on not such a large scale as they have art. Robinson has seldom advertised and yet his sales were sufficient to keep him going, if not to make him publishing's Freddie Laker. A thought: if Robinson could do so much with so little knowledge and know-how, why can't the big publishers follow suit and do superbly, with all their marketing resources? Answer: lack of commitment.

Throughout his time, though, Robinson has been constantly aware that, to really do poetry justice, he had to get into the high street bookshops. Some – very few – stocked small press verse and they were usually those who knew that their public wanted such things. Those to the fore in that were Heffers in Cambridge and Blackwell's in Oxford. Both had captive and keen customers – the students. But Robinson wanted to get into the

W. H. Smiths of this world. Interestingly, he never succeeded. Although they support poetry through the writers-in-schools schemes, they will not support it on their shelves.

Robinson has built up, it must be remembered, Independent Press Distribution (IPD), which has gathered momentum, but just how successful it will be in a time of recession and increased apathy from both public and book-buyers alike – those in shops, libraries and so on – remains to be seen.

So, small presses remain small through some belief that small is beautiful; some stay small because they haven't the resources (often counted in hours in a day) to expand; some stay small because that gives them autonomy; some grow larger and hold their integrity and some seek to be powerful names on a par with the Faber & Fabers and Secker & Warburgs.

Yet for most, Robinson is the ideal. Producing small and well-made (but commercially priced) books across a wide field (in recent years no longer limited to verse), he sells through limited but successful channels to afficianados of the art. He reaches bookshops who have the foresight to buy literature and who can sell it. He aims to improve the lot of his trade fellows and, simultaneously, himself. He is what the bigger small presses should be. He is dedicated, anxious to serve art and its followers, a skilled editor and judge of literary merits. Like all of his ilk he survives in spite of the attitudes in poetry today which seek to riddle the art with factions, cliques and schools and to adversely affect and sour everything that was achieved in the 1960s. The major publishers are primarily at fault for this.

10

In 1964, a far greater number of London publishers had poetry lists than there were around a decade later. Most of the boom years had come and gone without any major investment in poetry by the big publishers. A lack-lustre approach towards poetry, linked to the historically proven adage that money comes from prose and reputation from poetry, caused a veritable stagnation to well up in the confines of Mayfair and Bloomsbury.

Part of the trouble lies in the fact that, until recently, the British attitude towards publishing was that it was a gentleman's pastime rather than an industry. Publishers were seen to be and often were upper-crust men with sound family and financial pasts who indulged in the bringing out of books in much the same light as they would purchasing a vineyard in the Dordogne to supply their own dinner tables with good clarets. It was not until Allen Lane and the invention of the paperback that publishing reached a wider audience. Yet the patronising, often semi-philanthropic attitudes of the publishers remained and remains to this day so far as poetry is concerned. Publishing verse was and is seen as a sop to the intellectuals or an act of charity on the part of 'benevolent' publishers. Authors traditionally were seen not as the prime makers of literature, but as underlings who provided what the publishers could make money out of. With such atrocious conceits and ideals at heart, what hope had poetry? Certainly, poetry for the people, as opposed to the top bracket, had virtually no chance at all where the London publishing houses held sway.

The main firms that had poetry were Macmillan, Faber & Faber, J. M. Dent, Routledge & Kegan Paul, Oxford University Press and some others. Of these, Faber was the biggest and most prestigious and the best.

It had the past that many envied – Walter de la Mare, Eliot, Auden, these were the names associated with Faber and, in the early 1960s, they extended their list by taking in new poets that were forging new ground in both British and American verse. The company brought to prominence Ted Hughes, Sylvia Plath, Thom Gunn and others of certain and massive talent who were to have considerable influence upon British verse and continued to do so throughout the period in question. Faber's was a list that rang of the good old days and it was a poetry list that was self-supportive both artistically and financially. Certainly, it did not make its directors wealthy men, but it certainly did not detract from their income and it set a standard that others looked up to and attempted to emulate. In 1966, a new poet was added to the phalanx – Seamus Heaney, an Irish poet of power such as hadn't been seen since Yeats. This seemed to cap the pyramid. Faber & Faber *were* poetry publishing.

The others had small and select lists that come nowhere near that of the market leaders. J. M. Dent had Dylan Thomas as their leading poet but tended not to bother with the others on their list to whom they did not give equal push and drive. Routledge & Kegan Paul had Peter Redgrove, another important poet whose influence has echoed through the subsequent years, but Redgrove was not, until the late 1970s, a major source of income on the poetic scales. Oxford University Press ran what was at best a discreet list of academic or semi-academic poets, many of them related in one way or another to the university itself.

Macmillan, who saw themselves very much as a 'gentleman publisher', or certainly gave that impression, had a good list that carried such eminent names as Charles Causley and R. S. Thomas, not to mention W. B. Yeats, but they were not to expand this until later in the 1960s under the editorship of Kevin Crossley-Holland. They were to prove for a while to be as important in the dissemination of modern British poetry as Faber was.

What Macmillan did ought to be an ongoing process. Crossley-Holland saw the potential of the new verse and went out to construct a list that contained the front runners of the new directions the art was taking. He signed up Alan Brownjohn who had previously published just one small press volume. He took on George MacBeth who was already published by Scorpion Press and had a large readership. He retained Causley and Thomas. He added to these the poets Elizabeth Jennings, Patricia Beer, Ruth Fainlight, Alan Sillitoe (not just a fine prose writer) and Michael Longley with others. The list was entitled Macmillan Poets and it was advertised to the literary world in block-booked space in the best of the literary journals and with publicity leaflets. In 1969, the front page of the leaflet promised great things. It read:

> This leaflet features those poets published by Macmillan in the last twelve months. The most important development during that time has been the innovation of *Macmillan Poets*. This is a paperback series, and publication generally coincides with the hardback edition of the same volume. By the end of the year, at least ten volumes will have appeared in the series, evidence of the continuing success of the Macmillan poetry list.

Blurbs on the poets and comments on their new books, along with an order form that covered the whole list, was included in the pink and black foldout. It was a publisher gearing up to sell verse. (The entire list on offer shows how the publishers saw poetry as a continuing process of tradition: in that leaflet they offered – in addition to those above – the work of Thomas Hardy, Martin Bell, Keith Harrison, Philip Hobsbaum, Muriel Spark, Tagore, David Wevill (who cuts across the verse of several countries in his stand), John Wain and Yeats. Also present was the Canadian poet, Tom Marshall, the American poet Louis Simpson and two of the Sitwells.)

The heyday was here. Macmillan got the ball rolling that Faber had pushed off and others joined in. Several years later, the list was abruptly closed and the poets were publisher-less. Crossley-Holland went to Gollancz to try the same thing over, but a combination of events, not to mention the fact that the steam was just beginning to leak from the poetry engine, made this a brief reappearance of the list. Today, Macmillan mainly publish just Causley and R. S. Thomas who, without colleagues present, look sadly forlorn outside a list in which ideal-situation poets aid poets in the eyes of the capturing of readers.

The poetry list, as a publishing concept, is essential. It is valueless to publish a single book in a void for that book will simply disappear (or receive less sales impetus) in a wedge of dissociated material – a novel published by a firm known mainly for scientific textbooks will be lost without trace, even if the book is relevant to the science aspects of the company. Few publishers kept to verse books, or carried them on once started.

Some publishers did produce the occasional book of verse in a general list. Often those books wallowed, and equally often and undeservedly did none too well for publisher and author alike. This was not true, of course, if the author was already famous in either another field or as a writer with another house.

John Murray, for example, publish with considerable success the poetry of Sir John Betjeman. He is known to the public not only as a poet (and Poet Laureate) but as a lover and champion of architecture and the finer points of national heritage. He became very widely known through television exposure and through his early, wistful and appealing poems that recapture like time capsules the 1920s and 1930s. But he is a loner, like Causley and R. S. Thomas; there is no list around him, no poets who ride with him. The publishers are content to hold on to a gilt-edged poet and not to spread their investment. This is a waste of such an investment for the public would soon become aware of any connection therefore buying the work of anyone who was deemed good enough to appear alongside such a figure. What is more, a poet's position as Poet Laureate – the country's top poet, so to speak, at least as far as the nation as a whole is concerned – should now be used as a furthering-step for the art in general. Here is the instance of a publisher believing that poetry is but a gentleman's hobby, an elitist activity in the artistic world. How else can it be construed? If the publishers of Betjeman were interested in poetry then they would realise the opportunity they have to build a list around such a fine writer. But they don't.

Of course, John Murray are not alone, by a long chalk. In 1962, admittedly just out of the period this book is mainly concerned with but still of relevance, Collins published *Hong Kong House* by Edmund Blunden. They had previously (in 1957) published *Poems of Many Years* in a large edition of 3000 copies: the 1962 collection was produced in 1500 hardback copies. Shortly afterwards, in 1964, Blunden returned to England from his long life abroad and was honoured in a number of ways, the most obvious being his election to the Professor of Poetry chair in the University of Oxford. And here was an ideal opportunity to bring out a new book (Blunden had new poems available) or a collected works. It would have sold. It did not appear. Instead, Carcanet Press brought out an adequate but hardly far-reaching selection of work in 1982: Blunden died in 1974, lost to his readers for the last ten years of his life. Why? It would seem that his publishers had left him out. Blunden, sadly, was another one-off. And the lesson is still not learned. Hutchinson are still doing this: in 1980, they published Ruth Fainlight's book *Sibyls*, having published two previous collections in 1973 and 1975. However, their list is minute, and so the poets disappear, the books don't get sufficient promotion, they are not lifted along on the awareness that a list provides. What a shame! Of their few poets Ruth Fainlight is an extraordinarily gifted one, Dannie Abse has a sound following as a prose writer and Kingsley Amis is practically a household name with *Lucky Jim* in his curriculum vitae.

And this is a point to be laboured: who thinks of Amis as a poet? He is one, and a good one, but his verse is lost because he is not seen to be in a swim, in a current of poetry publishing.

There are some publishers who do do the right thing or have the right idea. Secker & Warburg, for all their cliqueyness, have a sound and thriving list which has in many ways sopped up the blood from the murders of past lists. Poets who have been wounded when Macmillan and Gollancz shut down have been taken in – George MacBeth and Alan Brownjohn, to name two – and around this nucleus has been constructed a gathering that does all good. Young poets are brought in, older ones who were ignored are published (with some American poets who deserve the merit of an English audience) and an atmosphere of poetic strength is obtained. At the same time, money is made because the publishers are associated with poetry and therefore people turn to them to see what's going on in the field. Here is a list doing what it is supposed to do. One may not like all the poets and there is a certain amount of old-boy-networking necessary for one to be accepted on to the list, but putting that aside, this is what should be going on. Through such a framework, the art builds, holds and gains a following. If the list was more open to a diversity of poetry – say, if it published the likes of Gavin Ewart (hidden in the Hutchinson set-up with the likes of the poetry of the novelist Elaine Feinstein) – it would become a major and important movement in poetry publishing.

In 1962, there appeared a paperback book of verse that came out under a new series heading, Penguin Modern Poets. The first title contained the work of Lawrence Durrell, Elizabeth Jennings and R. S. Thomas. Although Penguin Books had published verse in the past, this was their first venture into contemporary poetry and it was a brave and important move for it placed introductory samplers of modern verse into the hands of the public at a cheap price: most if not all poetry in those days was produced in expensive hardback. The first Penguin book sold for 3s 6d (17½p) and it is interesting to see that the book went into three more printings in the next five years. The success of the list and the risk had paid off for the books were being bought. The Penguin Modern Poets grew, became nicknamed PMP (pronounced p'mp) and thrived, evolving into a major input into modern poetry and its publishing. The popularity of these books gradually exceeded all others, especially on the publication of *PMP 10* (all the books were numbered), which contained the poetry of Brian Patten, Adrian Henri and Roger McGough. Still priced 3s 6d in 1967, this book consolidated three poetic reputations and gave the new poetry – the Liverpool Poets – a boost beyond their wildest dreams, one suspects. It was not a case of hype, but of publisher meeting demand and by doing so, creating more. This book reprinted eight times in seven years and reprinting for Penguin does not mean an extra few hundred copies. The last book in the series, *PMP 27*, appeared in 1979. The recession linked to a new drive within the publishers to accept only books that would satisfy the minds of cost accountants and their ilk put paid to the list. This was a body blow that still hurts poetry. At a time when just such a list was needed, it was stopped. Had it continued, the books might today be saving verse from slipping away for, if it published the trash, people would see it and say what they thought with their wallets and if it published the good material. . . . Penguin have published other verse since then, but in tiny quantities, and their only verse books now are anthologies, some of them outstandingly good (like *The Penguin Book of Homosexual Verse*, ed. Stephen Coote, 1983) and some of them notable for their lack of comprehensive study and shallow editing (*The Penguin Book of Contemporary British Poetry*, ed. Motion and Morrison, 1983). However, despite these, when PMP stopped a pillar was dismantled in the temple.

The saddest departure from poetry publishing, having once had a good list in the making, is Jonathan Cape. In the poetry heydays, that company developed an exciting list of poets, the range being wide and the appeal popular and artistically (but not weakly) trendy. The poetry of Ted Walker springs mostly to mind as being at the top of the list there, but there were others who were of great importance in their time and are still widely read – Adrian Henri, Roger McGough, Jeni Couzyn and Adrian Mitchell. The two Adrians and McGough were kingpins of poetry in the boom years. But the list, as with others, has contracted.

Only one publisher has carried on through the years – Chatto & Windus. Prodded and supported by C. Day-Lewis, that company have steadily, though on a small scale, published verse throughout the years that this study spans. Their list is long if not regular in its production. Over forty poets stand on it and the list is awe-inspiring and, interestingly, given in most of the books, as a kind-of come-on to readers, setting the Chatto poets in a context. Few of the other publishers attempt to advertise the fact that they are a poetry producer in their volumes: yet another chance to spread wings and earn reputation and money is lost. Consider this: George Mackay Brown, Phillip Callow, John Cotton, Patric Dickinson, John Fuller, P. J. Kavanagh, Laurie Lee, Laurence Lerner, Edward Lowbury, James Merril, Leslie Norris, Rodney Pybus, Anne Sexton, Jon Silkin . . . all Chatto poets. Or, more accurately, Phoenix Living Poets (PLP), the name and identity of the list. In the latter half of the 1970s, the list quietened down under the editorship of D. J. Enright. The list has the potential to explode once more if it can avoid the trap of many of the others – that of becoming centred around one school. This, unfortunately, seems to be occurring.

But in many ways poetry publishing is a microcosm of the British industrial climate as a whole. Leaders in a certain field innovate, discover, invent and produce and those who could sell and spread the inventions fail to do so, or take a part in it in a haphazard manner and only do a half-job on it. With not a lot of expertise, some consideration, a modicum of common sense and business sense, poetry could become a major side show to the big acts in publishing. After all, the small presses have done, pro rata, extraordinarily well. They have outstripped their huge competitors or fellows and some have become big themselves. Carcanet is a good example. So why, with all their expertise, are the big publishers not joining in? Whatever the reason, the big publishers with all their resources to sell still don't try to expand a market that could be much bigger and more profitable.

11

This section could be the biggest in the book if it was to document its topic fully: indeed, it could make a book on its own for it deals with the phenomenon that largely made the poetry boom – the rise and demise of the small magazine. In order to keep things to a sensible length, only a handful of magazines will be covered here, but that is but expediency.

In the period 1964 to 1972, there appeared in Britain over 600 small magazines devoted to either poetry alone or poetry and visuals or poetry and other branches of literature. Some had a run of one issue, some had a run of three or four and just a few, with sound editorship or financial backing provided from either an enterprising philanthropist or a good subscriber list, ran for a good number of years.

What enabled these small publications to thrive was, in part, what helped the small press to get off the ground: the cheap, new methods of printing. Duplicated magazines appeared at the bottom of the list so far as production standard was concerned. Offset litho-ed publications came higher up. Above them came the very few letterpress-produced issues.

The magazines can be split into two rough groups, the first being of magazines that existed prior to 1964 and kept going through the whole time span, and the second those that appeared for the first time during those post-1964 years. Before embarking upon a look at the various magazines, it is important to say that many are left out not because of their insignificance or poor standards (either of production or content) but simply because there is no room to list them. The editors of those magazines – for example *Scribe*, *Expression*, *Volt*, *Edge*, *Tracks*, *Candelabrum*, *Leaves*, *Pink Peace*, *Last Fly*, *Glass Onion*, *Scrip* and *Flame* – were the unsung heroes of the day who set up a climate in which poetry could be published, read, circulated, discussed, criticised, understood and assimilated. Without them, I believe, nothing like what was achieved would have been even approached. Working from a variety of backgrounds, the editors ranged from keen students to social workers to lecturers to others on the fringe of the rock or pop music fraternity. Few were writers and virtually none were trained in anything remotely near editorial journalism or printing production. They learned by trial and error and those that were successful became so not by counting their subscription lists and bank incomes but by judging how widely catholic their output was in style, taste and intention. Those who lasted longest did so because of the interest that their publications aroused and this did not necessarily mean controversial interest but genuine fascination with an art form that was, suddenly, a popular sub-culture and seen as such by many. It is an historical fact that any underground – be it Polish and anti-Nazi in the Second World War or culturally subversive – promotes its own publication system and that the issues produced circulate widely through those in the know. So it was, in a way, with poetry except that the poetry was not so much an underground as an alternative that became accepted. And, like all such systems, it contained its own personages who became, within that context, very well-known indeed. These people were to be loosely grouped as the small magazine poets. A few, very few, subsequently became known through their trade work to a larger, general public following: most did not, not because of the poor standards of their art but because they were frowned upon by the bigger establishment publishers who, with a training of academic backgrounds and a repugnance towards 'folk art' – an expression used by one in 1979 when speaking of the punk poets who were, at the time, drawing in audiences that could not hope to be summoned by any other poet except perhaps Ted Hughes or Seamus Heaney – rejected them automatically as alternative and, therefore, lesser by achievement and design. (The process continues: at the time of writing, no publisher has taken on a collection by a punk poet, apart from John Cooper Clarke who was more an innovator than a developer of the genre, and those who draw in considerable audiences – Attila the Stockbroker, for example – are ignored.) Even the biggest of them all, the entrepreneurial and mercurial Mike Horovitz, has yet to have a major collection of his work published by one of the traditional publishers; once again, 'tradition' steps in to ruin the future heedlessly, upsetting the process of tradition working with the present to form the future. Perhaps this is why the post-1979 accepted poets are such a boring lot, as a general rule.

The small magazines were never boring. They were anything but. Charismatic, odd-ball, self-conscious, precocious and determined, they reflected the considered whims and talents of their editors and contributors, people for whom poetry was more a way of life than a way of passing time. A look through an archive of such publications, if such a collection exists, would be an exciting exercise for therein will be hidden or smudged and sometimes atrociously printed, silk-screened or duplicated, the foundation upon which the poetry boom rested or the boom against which it washed up not as flotsam and jetsam but as pearls or seaglass upon the beach. What impresses one most is the vitality of the publications.

How did one set up a magazine in those days? It might be worthwhile briefly mentioning this for it seems that the return of such an expansion of publication is far off, if indeed it will come again. What generally happened was something like this: someone became interested in poetry. Simple. The interest might have come from recent days at school and the widening of the curriculum in English to include more modern verse, from hearing a poet read on the radio (or, very rarely, TV), from attending a reading or from simply starting to write oneself. Whatever stimulus was at work, the desire to create seems to have been overwhelming in some people. Not satisfied with writing their own work, they desired to read and communicate with others. Little magazines began as a kind of literary chain letter.

Duplicating machines are cheap and common. Secondhand models came on to the market quite readily in the 1960s as the developments in these machines soon made them redundant and they were shed by shops and offices who bought the later refinements. Individuals could easily obtain them at knock-down prices. Until the mid-1970s, in the years immediately following the oil crisis, paper was comparatively cheap. Art materials – silk-screens, paints and the like – were available and advanced.

The would-be editor had no problem in getting plant or equipment. Those who did not have their own utilised that of their employers – with or without their express permission or knowledge. Students often used their student union machines and some of the best magazines, though the most short-lived by nature of the impermanence of student life, came from art colleges, universities and colleges of education. In those days, students had time to work so: jobs were plentiful and the pressures were off the examination slog routine. Far from laze about smoking dope, many took to creating and the psychedelic explosion gave wind to the tide.

Once equipped with his printing works on the kitchen table or in the garage or the office basement, the editor was ready. His next task was not to get subscribers, as one might suppose, but contributors. This was not difficult. He simply wrote to those poets whom he had heard of or read and asked if they would consider sending something new to him. Most usually, they did. Payment was non-existent. Poets received payment of sorts in copies and some, those who either hold to shrewd business sense or a magpie-like reluctance to throw material away, have recouped financially since by selling the rarer magazines off to collectors or libraries. No one made money from the process.

Contributors seemed to generate subscribers. Word spread that such-and-such a poet was in such-and-such a new magazine and orders came in. The grapevine was at work aided by a few magazines that carried lists of their fellow publications. The scene was organically developed from there and that was that. The editor charged a small sum per copy, usually hardly enough to cover his production costs, and added postage. Subsidy came from other directions for some.

The magazine network thereby came about almost spontaneously from a variety of sources and stood alongside the ranks of the few establishment literary journals which were and are closed shops as far as the up-and-comer is concerned.

After a while, the magazines did not so much close down as fade away, the demise caused by a change of job, a loss of finance for whatever reason, an encroaching boredom or desire to escape the inevitable hard work involved in turning the pages out, stapling them and collating them and licking them into envelopes, or simply the breaking down of the secondhand duplicator.

This is, of course, a vague outline, but it is a typical one and many a publication that forged a way for poets started this way. Without these publications, the poetry years could not have happened. They were vital and came along at just the right moment, a convergence of factors that made it all possible.

Those which seem worth remembering are chosen for mention here for their impact and long standing, not just because they were superior in content or numbers printed. They are given in following pages in no set order, but as they come to mind, those that span the period coming first. They are on occasion borne of the literary establishment or its fringes, but no harm for that. That they helped to build the scene is the important part of their place.

There were, of course, magazines that were literary but which took little part in the development of poetry or simply stood alongside and took aboard the odd poet. These magazines are hardly worth a mention in this context, for they were really observers. Ironically, some of them have since died a death – *Blackwood's Magazine* comes to mind. Others carry on, but are still so narrow as to be discountable – for example, *Encounter*.

The longest-standing magazine to cover the period was *Poetry Review*, the official organ of the Poetry Society. Started well over fifty years before, it saw the change in poetry come about and, to some extent, reflected this. It had a number of editors between 1964 and 1982, the most notable being Derek Parker, Roger Garfitt and the ubiquitous Eric Mottram. Parker found the new poetry

somewhat hard to digest, one feels. He had held the editorship
from the earlier 1960s when the society, which appointed the
editor of the magazine, was a little-old-lady organisation with an
executive council prone to in-fighting, back-biting and generally
hating each other in a most gentlemanly manner, only occasionally allowing the professional animosity to draw near to actual
bodily contact over the discussion table. However, in the
circumstances, Parker did well for he brought the magazine into
the new age of poetry and he did not ignore the rising stars. He
set a standard that his successors built upon. By the turn of the
1960s, the magazine had gained such a position in the eyes of the
public that when Mottram took over there was considerable
uproar at his contributors' list – he was including poets who
were exceptionally avant-garde – or so it seemed – and the
readership revolted, though noticeably not for long. That the
controversy made the national newspapers was sign enough that
poetry was more of a big deal than it had been in the cosier years
of the pre-uprising. Whatever harm Mottram might or might not
have done to the *Poetry Review*, its parent body of the society or
the art itself is lost now. That he created such a stir was good
enough. It added to the world of literature. One can hardly see
the press taking much notice of such a thing nowadays. Poetry
has now lost its credibility because it has been weakened by
forces already discussed. Besides, the next editor, Roger Garfitt,
swung the pendulum the other way and studied his contributors,
publishing new and known alike.

Poetry Review was never as important a magazine as the name
and position might suggest. It was not a magazine which
published all of the new poetry, only a time-capsule-sized piece
of it mingled with exceptionally traditional work: it is a not
altogether fair indication, but it does show something, that when
the magazine started to publish what some old retainers considered to be outrageous and outlandish work, many wrote in
complaining that 'this is not poetry' and that the magazine should
contain more middle-of-the-road work with a smattering of
subscribers' poetry. However, the magazine was important as a
kind of central axis around which both establishment and fringe
and small magazine publications revolved or evolved. If it acted
only as an example to be avoided, at least the magazine served a
solid function. After some time, the magazine became a weird
hybrid. It was no longer an establishment publication run by the
mandarins of the Poetry Society, for the mandarins were extinct
and new forces were afoot that brought the *Poetry Review* into line
somewhat. Younger poets appeared, younger critics wrote
reviews, younger poets won or contested the various awards held

in the society's province. The structure of the society altered: it became the National Poetry Centre housing the Poetry Society and it opened a bookshop, a bar and, later, a print-room that could be used or loaned to small magazine and press editors. This would have been previously unheard of. Reading programmes expanded. Life was coming to the old place and *Poetry Review* metamorphosed into, if not a butterfly, a goodly moth. But the changes wrought in the magazine took it away from being what it was, the old guard journal, but it did not make it a new, up-and-coming bombshell. It fell between the stools. Looking back at the issues since 1964, one would expect to see a barometer of taste and development but what one does see is either a strange mix of talents (and non-talents) or a house journal to certain cliques. The magazine therefore has no true position as what it always sought to be – the magazine of British poetry.

Where *Poetry Review* is generally unrepresentative of the real small magazine, *Outposts*, *Stand* and *New Departures* are not. They are the sort that make literature in their own ways, and did so right through the 1960s and 1970s. Others came and went, as shall be seen, but these three soldiered on to great effect.

Howard Sergeant started thinking of *Outposts* in October 1943. He began by collecting poems together to make up the first issues and this has made him the grandfather of the little magazine. The first issue of the magazine appeared in February 1944 and, for the rest of the war years it appeared spasmodically, the editor facing the twin problems of being on military service and having a hard time finding the necessary supplies of paper. However, after the stringent years were passed, the magazine appeared – and so continues – as a quarterly.

For a typical small magazine, *Outposts* is near the centre of the breed. It is a small-format publication with about forty pages of poetry, poetry reviews and a few poetry-related advertisements. It is stapled and has a somewhat outmoded but well-known cover design and it looks hideously conservative. It is not. Sergeant's catholicity of taste makes for a well-rounded magazine although he does steer clear of the borderlines of poetry where it verges upon sound or concrete forms. The magazine, very unlike its contemporaries, is largely self-financing. It does, from time to time, receive grant aid from arts associations and the like, but it is not dependent upon these, the editor accepting them as a bonus rather than a staple diet. (The pun would not go amiss with him.) The print-run is around 1800 copies per issue, which means that it outsells many of the other literary magazines, larger and smaller in reputation and artistic value.

As it has been around for so long, *Outposts* magazine can claim some major coups. The work of many well-known poets has appeared in its pages long before they had their first collections placed with publishers. Seamus Heaney, Vernon Scannell and Dannie Abse fit this category. Even more of an achievement is the fact that Sergeant published the very first verse of Anthony Thwaite, Kingsley Amis and Elizabeth Jennings, to list but three. Equally remarkable is the fact that Sergeant pays his contributors. Admittedly, the fee per poem is small but it is a fee nevertheless and it boosts the poetic ego and gives the art some pride. To receive a voucher copy and a cheque is rare indeed. (It has been mentioned already that the magazine spawned a small press and this, like its parent, continues but it has by no means retained its standard of good poetry publishing. What is more, whereas the magazine contributors are paid, the small press ones have to pay – not in hard cash but by guaranteeing a certain number of sales of their booklet or chapbook – and there are those who feel that this smacks of vanity publishing, albeit at arm's length. Whichever way one takes the point, it has to be argued that Sergeant has done a considerable amount for poetry.)

Another magazine that saw the era through is *Stand*, edited by the poet Jon Silkin. A quarterly, *Stand* is financed by its subscribers, advertising revenue and by the editor who, from time to time, has shared his editorial load with others, notably the poet Ken Smith. Since its foundation in February 1952, *Stand* has sought to bring to readers what Silkin outlines as a 'record of new verse and fiction both in the original, translation and through criticism' with an editorial policy bluntly stated 'to be sensitive to new work and the society that nurtured it'. The social aspects of literature are close to Silkin's heart and this concern is presented at depth in his anthology *Poetry of the Committed Individual*, published by Penguin and Gollancz in association. The contribution the magazine has made is one of longevity and commitment, although Silkin has often avoided publishing the whole range of contemporary poetry and large chunks are not in the scope of his editorial taste. He says that the magazine has offered a radical alternative to the 'received' scene, but really this is not so, or the radicality is slight. What *Stand* has done is to give a consistent standard of new verse, bending with the breezes of change when these have mustered enough force.

The last of the publications that cover the period, and without a mention of which any book on the subject would be lapsing badly, is *New Departures*. Started in June 1959, it has been all along the vehicle of Michael Horovitz, a poet and editor. He calls himself a ringmaster, Anglo-Saxophonist and jazz poet, and was founder, in the 1980s, of the Poetry Olympics, of which more in

Chapter 12. Others call him a variety of names ranging from those indicating awe and respect to those expressing downright hatred.

New Departures is not a quarterly: it comes when it comes, with only fourteen issues in twenty-three years brought about, in part, by the fact that the whole venture is financed by Horovitz himself and is put together in a somewhat haphazard manner. (Contributions often vanish into the works of the editorial grinder; irregular publication makes it hard to attract subscribers; the whim of Horovitz and the heavy pressures upon his time from other directions steal effort from the magazine.) Other income derives from donations from friends, slim cheques from arts associations and, rarely, advertising. Subscribers in the generally accepted meaning of the word are very few indeed. Despite all this, the magazine has given a lively and energetic boost to the poetry world, leading to Horovitz's editing of a major Penguin anthology, *Children of Albion*, virtually a manifesto of *New Departures* doctrine and dogma.

Horovitz goes the other way from Silkin, Sergeant and *Poetry Review*, publishing largely work that won't get in elsewhere because of its oral aspects. *New Departures* is words and noises on paper, rather than poetry to be read. As such, it is closely related to the basic ideas behind Horovitz's poetry shows of which the latest is the aforementioned Poetry Olympics. As editor, he has tried to internationalise poetry, too, to fight the vacuum of understanding of or interest in poetry, and to 'deflate the ghastly glum fog of "Movement"/New Criticism/elitist atmosphere my friends and allies were heir to, and fought to dispel'. Poetry, to Horovitz, needs cheering up and injecting with adrenalin. He has tried his best and his best has been good enough.

It must be mentioned, though, that he could have done better. Despite the fact that his 1982 edition of *New Departures* was a phone book-sized tome and included the poetry of (amongst others) McGough, Patten, Ginsberg, Elizabeth Smart, Heathcote Williams, Yevtushenko and Voznesensky, it did not give a true picture of British verse or even international verse. In his own way, Horovitz has established an elite of his own sort: many poets cannot get a look in, and these need not necessarily be those of the glum fog. The irregularity of the magazine detracts from its purpose as well, making it seem somehow to be a sort of school magazine, not from children but from a certain kind of poetic climate.

The trouble is that all high editors, like high priests, see only their own religions in the game. Horovitz sees the oral tradition and the left wing of the poetry parliament: Silkin sees the intellectuals and middle-of-the-roaders: Sergeant looks at the right wing, the poetic Tories who don't actually play safe, but look to be doing so. (With Horovitz, often the far left look to be raging revolutionaries but are actually poetic conservatives under it all.)

What is needed is a magazine that includes the lot. *Poetry Review*, the 'national journal', should do this. It doesn't and fails. To get a good view of the whole panorama, one needs to read all these. And, doing this, one has a solid view too for the editors have been consistent in the better three of this quartet, have remained in control all through and give a continuity that most publications soon lose. Because Sergeant, Silkin and Horovitz have well defined and rigidly adhered to policies and ideas, they have provided not only a foundation for judging the whole poetry of their times but have also established a norm against which to set others.

Movements in poetry are best viewed through magazines which are more spontaneous than collections or anthologies, all of which have received publishers' editors' restrictions of one sort or another. It is therefore essential that a thriving magazine system be in existence. Whether or not this has a core publication is irrelevant, so long as the readers are aware that such-and-such an issue is slanted so-and-so a way. Often, because of the personality of the editor, this is not immediately obvious and the readers are bemused or confused into thinking that what they are holding in their hands is *the* poetry.

Other magazines have run the course of the period. *Ambit*, edited by Martin Bax, started in 1959 and continues with private and Arts Council funding, but it is very much a magazine of a clique and restricts its contents to those who are of a set type. (Where it has succeeded is in bringing in good art work beside poems, Hockney and Steadman amongst the artists contributing.) The fault of narrowing the poetic vision rises again. It is inevitable with editorship: only one man can make the final choice.

Or is it? There was one magazine that did the lot, publishing Edwin Morgan's visual and sound poetry beside Peter Porter's densely academic work, Wes Magee with Clayton Eshleman, Philip Ward with George MacBeth, Peter Redgrove, Frances (wife of Mike) Horovitz, and adding, in translation, Dutch, German, French, Eastern European and Scandinavian poetry. Pictures, visuals, abstract doodles, traditional poems, way-out rubbish and way-in rubbish, superb verse, experimental verse, prose poems, straight prose all appeared in it, in issues that could be 250 pages thick, in paperback book format. It was called *Second Aeon*.

The most important magazine of the period, *Second Aeon* was founded and edited by Peter Finch and its publication years, late 1966 to early 1974, coincide with the main poetic years of growth, excitement and state of well-being. Finch did what no one else either could or would. He saw the weaknesses of a system and exploited them to overcome them and try to give some balance and direction to what was a very loose state of affairs, riddled with sub-groups, groups, bands of friends and enemies.

Much of what follows is drawn from Finch's own account of the years of *Second Aeon*. Characteristically frank and forthright, Finch set about his redress of poetry's ills.

The magazine ran for twenty-one issues with the first being a foolscap-sized mimeographed slim thing of six pages and 100 copies. This gradually expanded to the last issue which was a 268-page, perfectly bound offset-litho production. Finance for this venture came initially from Finch's own pocket, justifiably so when one considers his editorial 'policy' at the start, but later on the Welsh Arts Council put up 45 per cent of the cost with another 45 per cent coming from the private funds of the Welsh poet Cyril Hodges who, over the years, had been quietly supporting the Welsh arts. The remaining 10 per cent came from Finch's pocket, advertising and subscriptions. The magazine never made a profit that would anything like clear the grants and private subsidisation. Sales were (Finch says) an impossible task for a one-man business. Copies were distributed by subscription, free copies, bookshops and a network of poetry world people who sold copies on commission both in Britain and the USA from where *Second Aeon* drew about a quarter of its material, bringing to British readers, often for the first time, the poetry of North America, where the art was flourishing (and has continued so to do) to an even greater extent than in the old country. Interestingly, part of Finch's concept for the all-round publication came from the example of *Dustbooks*, in the USA, which carried out a similar function of drawing information and work into a central set of pages. Alongside *Second Aeon* went a booklet production process that brought out over 100 slim titles including some that were of great literary merit and importance – Nicki Jackowska's first work, Peter Redgrove's *Love's Journeys* and an anthology called *Typewriter Poems*, the first easily obtained collection of visual poems made from typewriter work rather than art work.

Editorial policy is best outlined by Finch:

Second Aeon began by having no policy, only an idea to publish myself, and then myself and my friends and then to mix local and other poets. With maturity forced on to the magazine by its age, size and circulation the policy, unstated, changed to become a bird's-eye view of poetry, in English and in translation, in the UK (and America) during the late sixties and early seventies. It was an open magazine, wanting to mix experimentalism with tradition, trying to redress the balance implicit in literature perhaps by leaning hard at the avant garde. I also felt it vital to fill the information gap . . . to review and mention *all* that went on in the small press scene. I avoided reviews and critical works wherever possible but did, towards *Second Aeon*'s end, move into fiction . . . started, as I've said, to publish myself. In the end, though, it had nothing to do with my own work. I felt that the extant balance of values in the poetry world was wrong . . . and that much vital and important work was being ignored because it was regarded as too radical and just simply misunderstood. Such work could easily appear within its own genre but what was needed was a common platform for all that was going on. I tried to provide that.

And, certainly, Finch did. Large chunks of the back pages of *Second Aeon* became listings, in tiny print, of everything he could get his hands on with a very brief comment on it. Small press work, magazines, posters, hand-outs, everything went into these lists which became the main (if not only) source of information that bound all aspects of the poetry scene together. At last, there was a man trying to cut across the petty barriers of cliques to show what everyone was doing and, looking back from the 1980s to those issues, one sees an astonishing array and diversity of art. There has never been the like since and nor is there likely to be.

Inevitably, bar the Welsh Arts Council's support – they are noted for spending more on the literary arts than the other national arts councils – albeit backed by a 'perpetual misunderstanding of what I was trying to do', the establishment roundly ignored *Second Aeon*. No national newspaper, not even, for example, *The Times Literary Supplement* which actually wrote about *Poetry Review* in an editorial at a time when it was in a state of flux and under a caretaker set of editors who produced a slightly less moribund issue than usual, gave *Second Aeon* a single line. It was roundly ignored, despite the fact that practically every major poet appeared in it. Perhaps it was, as Finch suggests, that his magazine employed change and the set literary world was not prepared to consider it. In addition, the magazine hit at the self-centredness of the British scene as a whole and that was – and still is – resented.

The magazine ceased partly because, as I have mentioned, Finch took a job with the Welsh Arts Council and that precluded him from accepting money from them: on top of that, Cyril Hodges died and it was not until after this that his patronage became known. He had insisted upon it being anonymous. It must, I feel, be right now to acknowledge what this man did. Through his agent Finch, Cyril Hodges did more for British poetry (and, to some extent, poetry at large) than any other. He financed its main magazine, he gave it moral support, he backed it in every way possible. He gave the new poets credibility and the old a place in the development. Luckily for everyone, he backed the right horse, too. Finch was not a partisan but a cause worker and he did everybody proud.

The most expensive *Second Aeon* cost 60p. Mostly, it cost 25p though it took £1 to produce. It could have survived, selling, even then, at £1. It stopped, though, and it is right to say that the decline and rot set into British verse soon after. It is justified to feel that the demise of Finch's astounding enterprises led to the slowdown of the art. A central cog had seized in the engine.

Before leaving *Second Aeon*, I think it right to look at just one contents page for that tells all. Below is given the list of what issue 15 carried. A quick glance shows poetry from Britain (all corners), Canada, USA, Japan, Holland, Spain, Italy, Hungary, Sweden . . . and the poets read like a catholic contemporary who's who.

contents

poetry

features

visuals

second aeon 15
is published with the support of the welsh arts council, is a participant in the cosmic circuit, and a member of cosmep.

subscriptions

single issue: 20p plus 7p p&p: usa: 80c plus 20c p&p.
subscription for 4 issues: 90p incl p&p: usa: $4.00.
subscription for 8 consecutive publications or equivalent value ie the magazine and all other second aeon publications: £1.50. when subscribing please indicate which issue you wish to start with, and make all monies payable to peter finch rather than to the magazine.

contributions

poems, articles, stories, illustrations, cover designs, concrete, etc., always considered. please send at least six examples of work with sae or irc. contributions without return postage cannot be replied to.

Although *Second Aeon* was the kingpin, there were other magazines that all contributed to the era by publishing work that no one else would touch and yet which, later, became accepted, important poetry by good poets.

These other magazines filled a void which *Second Aeon* went a good way towards backfilling but obviously could not totally flatten.

New Poetry was founded in the late summer of 1967, under the title *Writer's Workshop*, subsequently labelled *Workshop* then *Workshop New Poetry*, finalising as *New Poetry* in 1974. It started as an offshoot of Norman Hidden's poetry workshop sessions that were held in a pub in central London and it ended in January, 1981. During the earlier years, Hidden had been chairman of the Poetry Society, the first one for some time who was dedicated to getting the ship straight and stopping the in-house squabbling, both tasks being ones he was successful over to a considerable degree for, under his captaincy, the society became respectable and useful to poetry. However, with his magazine, he was seeking, in some ways and most likely subconsciously, to overcome the strictures placed upon *Poetry Review*, for the overseeing of which he was now ultimately responsible.

In some ways, Hidden was a strange fish in the pond. He was an ex-teacher and lecturer with little business background, but he set up *New Poetry* as a fully-fledged company, bringing out books, booklets, and research documents that were all entirely self-financing and which survived without any grant aid being sought. The editorial aim was not a little ambitious, being 'to promote a love and appreciation of poetry on the widest possible scale, and to raise the status of poets within our society'. This was going to be limited by the fact that the magazine itself was usually limited to fifty-six pages, with some illustrations, but the idea was there. Many of the poets published were of the establishment mould, some even more so than others – Auden, Kirkup, Porter, Kathleen Raine, R. S. Thomas and William Plomer amongst them – but many were newcomers and Hidden introduced a schools section for children's verse that was unique. He wrote editorials that were conversation pieces and he included articles by poets, unfortunately usually the establishment figures. There were technical articles on verse-writing, competitions and advertisements. What was astonishing was the circulation figures. The first issue sold an estimated 900 copies, which was way above the going rate for first issues. The figures rose, by 1979, to 9450 spread between four issues. The entrepreneurial Mr and Mrs Hidden formed *New Poetry* into a private limited company but received no salaries: another sign of their approach to the art was Hidden's own guide, *How To Be Your Own Publisher*.

In 1978 Hidden published his seminal *The State of Poetry Today*, a survey that drew upon his readership for such answers as they could offer in response to questions that included the listing of the five best living British poets. The replies were mixed and, to some extent, predictable in that Ted Hughes was the top poet with Larkin as his deputy. The surprise was that the next man was Robert Graves. Nearly two hundred poets' names were included in the listing of top five which only showed the wide taste of the 366 respondents. This might seem false, but the answers came from the select poetry audience of the times. In that, the survey had a certain unique validity.

What Norman Hidden achieved was, in a way, odd. He published and encouraged as every magazine editor did, but in a roundabout way, mingling the new with the old and giving poetry in the small press sense a slant that tended towards the academic. The survey had the ring of the university statistician about it, a cold-ish clinicalisation of the art. It seemed rather as if Hidden was pampering to the design of the people who would eventually sterilise poetry. This was not his intention, far from it; Hidden was (and is) a devotee of the live poetry, the one man who did try outwardly to set it on its feet through the chairmanship of the Poetry Society. He gave poetry a certain hippy respectability. This sense of self-conscious well-being was further promoted by the fact that *New Poetry* survived adequately without any outside patronage. It was living proof that poetry could make money or, at worst, break even if it was properly managed. Hidden's lesson has, unluckily, been ignored by most.

Looking through the list of magazines that sprouted their own small press publishing sides, the fact becomes obvious that quite a number did this – *Second Aeon* and *New Poetry*, *Outposts* and, at the end of 1968, *Oasis* was suggested by its founder, as we have seen a lecturer at Kingston College of Art in London, and followed this progression after it began as a quarterly in November 1969.

Ian Robinson began his venture as a reaction against the poor standards he saw in many other publications – printing was atrocious, bindings fell apart, covers were scrappy: he felt he could do better. And he did. Although it never achieved the status of *Second Aeon*, *Oasis* did go a long way towards it and, when the former closed down, *Oasis* was for a while the only effective small magazine going. It was, typically, funded by its editor but he did have a form of assistance that was as good as hard cash – his employers, the college, paid for the basic costs of the first three issues and subsequently paid for the paper used and had the issues printed in the college's own printing unit. This arrangement ceased in 1976 but by then *Oasis* was a force to be reckoned with in no uncertain terms. In 1977 Robinson started doing one-man issues, concentrating on one poet's work only at any one time, and this detracted from the magazine for it now started towards exclusivity, no matter how well-intentioned, and its appeal faltered as a result. Economics drove this out into the open for it was easier to produce a thin, one-man issue than a fat magazine and *Oasis* at its height was a fat book.

In an interview given in 1981, Ian Robinson answers many questions about his publishing experiences and one of his statements is interesting for it outlines how editors obtained their first contributors:

> From the very few people I knew who wrote – one or two friends and some of my students: they were my first contributors. There's a lot that's not very good in those early issues. I wrote and asked one or two people for work, people whose work I'd begun to read round about then in magazines. Like John Hall and John Welch who were both in Issue 1. Word got round, as it does, and contributors came in the mail. For a long time the magazine was entirely dependent upon the mail. But I began to learn and wanted to control things a bit more. I started much more actively to look around for good work. After two or three years a shift of emphasis began. I found I was soliciting much more work, becoming less dependent upon what was sent in the mail. That's a natural development, I think. My tastes were changing and developing. I was reading more and more. In the last days of *Oasis* I actively discouraged the post box.

The contents lists of these magazines grew organically, like mushrooms in a well-tilled field. The small press world had such a vast ramification of contacts that as soon as one magazine began, news of it rapidly spread. (A major contribution to the spore pattern was the small print listings in *Second Aeon*.) However it came to pass, the fact is that it did.

Much of Robinson's success has already been mentioned in the small press context and his contribution as a magazine editor only goes towards enhancing his reputation. After *Oasis* started to fade, he began, in the late 1970s, to publish a new magazine called *Telegram* but this has not been an overall success, not because of any deficiency in itself but in the society around him.

The small magazine has had its day and its passing is to be heavily mourned.

Before leaving, however, there must be mention made of a number of lesser publications that form a major part of the period and its activity.

Little Word Machine was started in 1972 by Nick Toczek and ran to eleven issues and a book; the magazine hasn't ceased to exist, Toczek stating that it is currently resting and he hopes to revive it as and when he can. As always, it was financed out of the founder's wallet with small grants added here and there by West Midlands Arts Association and later, when Toczek moved east, by Yorkshire Arts Association. The Arts Council of Great Britain gave a hefty grant of £1000 towards the cost of the one book produced, *Melanthiko*, the only British anthology of pan-Caribbean writing which was 200 pages thick and of great ethnic interest. (It has since become a standard text on Caribbean literature.) The magazine in later issues turned towards a rock/pop music bias and this is intended for the rebirth. In common with his contemporaries, Toczek saw himself accurately as a publisher of 'the best of a wide variety of styles of writing from new, up-and-coming and established artists: the first issue, which was advertised with a superb, Modigliani-type poster, contained work by George MacBeth, Jeff Nuttall, Michael Horovitz and a poet much ignored, Pete Brown, who, as I have mentioned, made a considerable name for himself as the writer of many of Cream's big hit records. Financial problems including an £8000 overdraft, distribution worries, boredom and disillusionment caused the magazine to cease. Toczek also believes that his magazine lost out and poetry degenerated because poetry increasingly became, in the 1970s, divorced from real life and apolitical. He draws a quaint but truthful graph of the decline and, although one cannot accept the tailing-off to be due simply to a lack of political *raison d'être*, he has a valid point. Certainly, much poetry – most of that which made it through to accepted, establishment publishers and therefore notice through such journals as *The Times Literary Supplement*, and on to the general public via shops and libraries – was written on roads leading away from real life. *Little Word Machine* died because of public apathy, leading to the editor's own apathy. He states as much. The disease of disinterest does more harm to such thinly financed good intentions than anything else, it seems.

In Ipswich, *Samphire* was brought into being by Kemble Williams and Michael Butler. This magazine ran for some years as a successful quarterly which paid its poet contributors and printed reviews of new, small press books. It was, in some ways, akin to *Outposts* in format in that it had a brief editorial, pages of poems, a few advertisements, a couple of reviews and a brief list of new magazines or small press publications that were of interest to the editors. It was a sound little magazine and it added to the atmosphere of general artistic exchange and information.

Palantir was commenced by the poet Jim Burns in 1974 and it is lucky enough to be continuing through the drab years where it represents a torch held up to the light of mediocrity. Again, it was as lucky as *Oasis* was originally in being funded by Preston Polytechnic and North West Arts Association in conjunction with sales. Containing a healthy mixture of poetry, short stories, articles and reviews, *Palantir* is now a mainstay of the magazine world. The editor states that he is 'non-establishment' with a tendency to support what he terms as Bohemian tradition, as opposed to the academic one. He also seeks to be modernist or post-modernist although in this context what he really means is that he tries to be ahead of the slump, searching for the best of the next generation to be and linking through the present day to the best of the golden years of the 1960s. It is important to know that Burns edited another magazine, *Move*, from 1964 until 1968, publishing in that such poets as Roy Fisher, Edwin Morgan, Gael Turnbull and Lee Harwood, all subsequently to break into the big time but avoid the traps of the worse end of the establishment.

Bananas made an impact in the years of decline. Started by Emma Tennant in 1975 and subsequently taken over by Abigail Mozley from 1978 until its death in 1981, this publication sought to be a modern, general arts magazine that included interviews, poems, stories, reviews, art work and sound advertising. It published to twenty-six issues, some of them dedicated to set themes or directions: for example, issue 15 concentrated upon Spanish and Latin American work, issue 18 on German and issue 26 on Irish. It was funded by the editors to a heavy extent and received, in its last year, the last of its Arts Council grants, this running to £20,000. The figure would stagger many a *Palantir*-like editor. But all contributors were paid well and the magazines made it to trade, high street outlets. Yet it failed. The finances were insufficient but one must question this for many other magazines have survived on what must have amounted to the petty cash box at *Bananas*. Possibly it was too big or sought to cut across the big division.

This is an important consideration. *Bananas* did try to bring together both sides of the fence and it might be argued that it failed because of this. Subscribers were in short supply and the polarisation of the literary scene set it somewhat in the outside world, or in the no-man's-land between the poles. Here one sees

the two systems, so adamant to be themselves and hit the oppo-
sition, losing their better possibilities through what amounts to
internecine warfare. Much is suffering – the readers, the art, the
sense of intellectual progress – because of the intransigence of
the participants in poetry.

It was not bad editing or cash flow that killed *Bananas*, but a
sense of apathy, a resistance to change and to any force that
might prove to be innovative in that it covered all areas of the art.
This was linked to the fact that the public at large was not
interested because, by 1975, it was fed up with a poetry that was
altering towards the smart-alec variety. The hefty grant drove
some away with an 'unfair – why should they get it all' attitude.
The New Review, edited by Ian Hamilton, received even greater
grant aid but it did not sell because it was narrow, literary in the
extreme when what people wanted was a wider scope, expensive
and elitist. It ignored many of the younger poets who already had
large followings in the small press world and plumped instead for
the old stalwarts and the new trendies, many of them writing
beyond the interests of the general mass. These two magazines
set themselves up as enemies of the (poetic) people and while
many sought to be published in them, few held them in esteem.
The war kept them out.

What is desperately needed now is a magazine that en-
compasses the lot – a new *Second Aeon* with the new and narrow
poets alongside those proven to the public, so that all aspects of
the game can be seen and assessed and judged and accepted or
rejected. Thereby will poetry progress and be real. The opportunity exists. *Poetry Review* could be this – and should, bearing in
mind its pedigree – but it won't be because it is too concerned
with itself and its own opinions. It does not seek to be a market
place of verse but simply a specialist corner shop. The Arts
Council could set up a grant for an eclectic, well-edited, catholic
journal, a hefty tome admittedly, for poetry is still alive and
kicking, that appeared twice a year, a 350-pager like *Second Aeon*
was with no holds barred. It could be run on the grant of *Bananas*
plus a bit from Hamilton's now defunct enterprise. It could take
on a deliberate policy of publishing all that is new and, if it
avoided one clique for another, but printed them all, it would get
public readership. Poetry has appealed to the public for centuries
but they don't all want to read *The Waste Land*. Some would like
Pete Morgan's lighter verse, Betjeman's nostalgia, MacBeth's
eroticism or new-found rurality, Redgrove's surrealism or Liz
Lochhead's raucous, Glaswegian humour. So much could be
done. But isn't.

Finally, before leaving magazines like this, a mention of two others. The first is *Iron*, which survived nine years as a quarterly, running a parallel small press with twelve books listed, one of which has gone to three printings and outsold, in numbers, many of the London publishers' volumes. The editor fights against cliques, acknowledges diversity and has published over *900* poets. Give the likes of him £20,000 and see what he can do.

It can always be argued that *Iron* in itself is a clique that fights cliques. It depends where you stand. To have a clique is to have an anti-clique. Like missiles, they all cause trouble and one makes another. What must be done is a calling of a truce or at least a ceasefire, so that talks can begin. The trouble is, knowing the mentality of the majority of the poetry lobby, a ceasefire would not lead to a summit but a regrouping of forces. As long as that happens, what hope poetry?

Last of all, Lawrence Upton and *Good Elf*. A magazine and a small press, idiosyncratic and cranky, sound but seriously unsound, enigmatic, crazy. Six issues (1970 to 1977: declared dead 1981: small press 1971 to shared funeral) added to uncountable number of booklets and the like. Publishing the far left, as some would put it – Cobbing, Fencott, Upton himself. Succeeded in 'showing it was possible neither to mystify or be elitist and sell but without bothering too much about lavish production – I've largely bypassed bookshops. . . .' Started to produce tapes.

Is this where we go? Do we no longer have printed magazines but cassettes? Some are already starting to circulate, with the ease of reproduction these days.

But to recap: poetry and poets must get a grip on themselves and join up to write, not continually creep off to their own corners to do their own things regardless of the rest. United we stand, etc.

12

It has already been mentioned that one of the aspects that set poetry up in the period after 1964 was the proliferation of poetry readings and the establishment of an oral presentation.

Such an arrangement was already in force, on a small scale. Very few poets actually read their work in public and, when they did, they became big news: Dylan Thomas's reading tours became famous, his reading style and the oral demands that his poetry made appealing to a wide audience. Other writers also toured, to a lesser extent. (Indeed, this was nothing new for even Dickens travelled to the USA and elsewhere, talking about his novels and reading fragments from them.) The audiences, however, were restricted. Because literature was still seen by many as an art form in the province of the privileged, poetry even more so, the audiences tended to come either from the wealthy of the locality or the nearest set of universities where poetry was accepted as a major part of the student and professorial life. The exclusivity of poetry made for exclusive listeners.

Once poetry started to break away from the polite, 'safe' narrowness it was used to, and spread its words into the people who hitherto had seen poetry as a somewhat effete pastime, it required a new medium in which to operate, especially as, historically, an oral tradition has always come first in the establishment of new major poetic direction and most people in the everyday world category have become orally orientated since the invention of the radio and, later, television. Oral and visual reception of ideas are fast outstripping the printed word. It's lamentable – there should be a happy amalgam of the lot – but it's happening. Oral presentation was the obviously most appropriate medium. Towards this, poetry moved. Something else that helped this shift of direction was the fact that poetry was not keeping itself as 'literary' in the sense that the word had come to be known – that is, something precious and guarded, like the Elgin Marbles in words. It was becoming 'common' though not in any derogatory way. And, as this was the case, it required a common form that anyone could inherit. The spoken word was the best choice.

How this new upsurge in poetry reading and the oral side of it came about is hard to define or accurately trace. The drawback with a purely oral tradition is that there is no record, or certainly hasn't been until the last twenty-five years and the invention of the cheap tape recorder. True, there are books, but they don't give sounds. Where sound came in, it was heard and then absorbed by the walls and that was that. Few people kept records or recordings of events. Where these were kept, they were not publicised but kept as private and therefore secret property.

It is true to say that the reading as a means of poetic output came into expansion through a number of channels. The first was the Dylan Thomas-type reading in a theatre to wealthy theatregoers or academics who were seeking spiritual and academic elevation of the senses and keeping this close to their chests, the sound of Thomas's voice taking the place that had been occupied by the King's Library or the Bishop's Reading Room in the pre-

Caxton era. (It is true to say that Thomas was perhaps the first – towards the end of his tragically short life – to snap this mould, for the public came to hear him and, with the aid of press coverage and a 'poetic reputation' as a heavy drinker and generally outrageous fellow, he may have done more to set the ball rolling on readings than others might realise.) If Thomas had been alive in the 1960s how much of a boost might he have given to the network?

The second channel through which readings came into their own was the development of poetry in the universities and the overspill continuation that this retained after the participants had entered the real world. Several branches fed out from this tree, but the best known and most influential was 'The Group' of which a slim and not wholly accurate account exists in *British Poetry Since 1960* (Carcanet Press, 1972). It is important to look at this group of poets for they were to prove to be the spine of the new poetry and the poetic popularity of the 1960s and 1970s.

The Group began in Cambridge about 1955, originating in Philip Hobsbaum's student coterie. From his graduation until around 1959, Hobsbaum continued operating as chairman of the friends' circle in London with Edward Lucie-Smith taking over from 1959 until 1965 as chairman, with the meetings taking place in his flat in Chelsea. In 1965, Lucie-Smith's chairmanship ceased and the assembly was perpetuated, partly under the initiative of Martin Bell, under the title of Poets' Workshop. In this form it survived through to the 1970s. In the earlier days, the Group had been funded entirely by Hobsbaum and Lucie-Smith but in its later form, it drew a subscription from members. As The Group, it met weekly; as The Poets' Workshop it met fortnightly through the university terms.

Meetings were strictly organised. A poet's work was duplicated and sent round to all members a week or so ahead of that poet's designated Friday, or else copies were provided on the night so that all could see the text. The poet then read his poems to the assembly who criticised them without restraint. He himself was not allowed to comment upon or interrupt the proceedings. This resulted in particularly truthful criticism, even if it hurt, as it frequently was known to do. It was understood that all comments were made objectively and it is a credit to the system that friendships were not smitten in discussions. Alcohol was not consumed during meetings. (In later days, when The Group was developed into Poets' Workshop, some members insisted on bringing in a bottle of wine – notably Frederick Grubb, a particularly astringent but sound critic – and this would draw censure and tutting from others: it was not the done thing.) There was no editorial policy governing the meetings for all had their turn in due course.

It was at these meetings that many poets who were to become the main stars of the skies first had their airings and received their first major criticism – Peter Porter, Martin Bell, Alan Brownjohn, George MacBeth, Peter Redgrove and others. Martin Bell's wit and range of thought, Porter's erudition and Hobsbaum's magnanimous chairing made the meetings memorable for those attending.

The value of these meetings was considerable. They provided encouragement early in literary careers, provided feedback and bounce-off from like minds and, in the views of some members, the criticism toughened them up for the big poetry world. The encouragement was not restricted to puffing up egos. It allowed poets to develop in their own ways and directions for there was no critical orthodoxy in operation. Indeed, some poets developed away from The Group or The Poets' Workshop in time. It is interesting to look at a membership list of Poets' Workshop for the late 1960s when it was at its most full. The following were on the roster along with many others: Dannie Abse, Fleur Adcock, Leo Aylen, Martin Bax (editor of *Ambit* magazine), Roy Bennett, Alan Brownjohn, John Carder Bush, Jeremy Cartland, Jeni Couzyn, Philip Crick, Florence Elon (the American poet), Jean Overton Fuller (the biographer), Padriac Fiacc, Glyn Hughes, Roger Hobdell, Philip Hobsbaum, George MacBeth, Tom Marshall (the Canadian poet), Gerda Mayer, Harold Massingham, William Oxley, Peter Porter, W. G. Shepherd, David Tribe, Alan Tarling (of *Poet & Printer* press), Donald Ward and John Daniels – and 102 lay members, so to speak. All those above published – or continue to publish – extensively.

The actual reading of the poems out loud built into the consciousness of the poets the basis of the oral tradition and, as The Group/Poets' Workshop was to provide a goodly number of the country's poets for the next decade or more, it follows that they had oralcy built into their poetry from the outset, for they heard it as well as saw it in print. Just how important this is has been overlooked but it has been written up by Philip Hobsbaum in his *A Theory of Communication* (Macmillan, 1970). It is not the place here to go into the depth of this study, but it does support another foundation stone for the growth of the oral aspects of poetry that were to give it such public attention.

A third channel was the British Broadcasting Corporation.

The radio and poetry have never been too far apart. Poetry fits into the medium of radio as if one was made for the other and poetry has formed a small part of the radio menu for half a century. It was in the late 1950s and throughout the sixties and first half of the seventies that poetry on the air took off.

Quite a number of producers have, over the years, been responsible for bringing poetry to broadcasting but it was not until the rise of George MacBeth to full producerhood at the BBC that any one person in such a position took upon himself the crusade to expand poetry through radio. MacBeth entered the BBC as a general trainee straight from Oxford in 1955. He was initially involved with the overseas programming department for which he worked upon current affairs but, some few years later, he started to produce for the home programmes services and he came to edit and present as well as produce a weekly arts features programme called *New Comment*. This was not a poetry programme, but it did give MacBeth the scope to include poetry within its brief. This series ran for six years and gave MacBeth the niche or slot he sought from which to extend his artistic interests. It was not long before he was editing and bringing to the air waves a poetry programme entitled *The Poet's Voice*. This was to become the best known of all poetry programmes, *Poetry Now*. It was through this that MacBeth was to aid the oral development of poetry more than any one other single figure. *Poetry Now* remained MacBeth's own programme until his resignation from the BBC in 1976. Additionally, he also introduced, edited, presented and produced literary features programmes, most of them related in one way or another to poetic arts, and poetry specials, such as the complete presentation of Ted Hughes's *Crow*, read by Hughes himself with some assistance from actors where this was deemed useful to the interpretation of the poems.

It is worth knowing something of the manner in which George MacBeth operated his programmes. Firstly, though, it is important to understand that he was fully conscious not only of his responsibility to his programme series but also to his performers and the poetry that they represented. Whatever MacBeth did include in his half-hour programmes, the only criterion applied to the material was that it was of a sufficiently high standard to be worthy of inclusion. Whether or not the poet could read his work was immaterial: his position in the poetic hierarchy was similarly of no consequence. This meant that a poet with no first collection published could easily find himself sharing a programme slot with the greatest living poets in the land.

Each poet always read his own work on the programme and, under MacBeth's tutelage, was never a failure. Tremendously aware of the power and abilities of the spoken word, MacBeth taught many poets how to read for radio and, therefore, for an audience. Large numbers of young poets passed through his expertise and the result was that, indirectly, MacBeth stabled and nurtured much of the roots of the new oral developments. What was as important, if not more so, was the manner in which, through his programme, MacBeth encouraged poets and gave many of them a confidence and identity. His policy being as wide as it was, demanding only good standards as a criterion, meant that many struggling newcomers found themselves placed alongside their superiors and mentors thereby giving poetry a unity that it rarely had in the outside world. In the studio, with MacBeth as ringmaster, all the performers were equal.

With skill and no little panache, MacBeth gave his programmes, especially *Poetry Now*, a personal touch. All the programmes began in very much the same way and followed the same presentation pattern. Quite often, the programme would consist of an interview or review slot with new poems added or included as a beginning. A typical programme, an issue of *Poetry Now* broadcast on 18 July 1969, began:

> 'Later on in this evening's programme, you can hear new poems by D. M. Thomas, Alan Brownjohn, Rosemary Joseph, Jean Overton Fuller, John Daniel and George Wightman, and Peter Porter will be reviewing a new anthology of school songs, but we are beginning with a new poem by Ted Walker.'

The poem would then follow and MacBeth would customarily make a terse but critically very astute comment on it, linking into his next contributor. (It is also interesting to see who was in this particular programme – only two of the poets, D. M. Thomas and Ted Walker, were not members of The Poets' Workshop or had not been members of The Group. This was not MacBeth's usual way of operating for he was not a clique-monger. A more accurate assessment of his catholicity might be judged from other programmes, for example that broadcast on 8 June 1970, which consisted of new poems by Alan Brownjohn, Patrick Galvin, Paul Mills, Edwin Morgan and John Smith with Roy Fisher reading and talking about his recent prose poems.)

Listening to tapes of those old programmes now, one can hear that they have not dated and one can understand at the same time just how important they were. A platform was established for poetry *as a whole* upon which anyone with capability could stand and perform: it set up a central shop, as it were, a booth from which the wares could be called.

After MacBeth left BBC, poetry broadcasting underwent a slightly rocky period when little of import was aired. *Poetry Now* continues to be produced under another producer, but with different presenters and a lack of editorial cohesion, something MacBeth gave it and which was one of its strengths. What is more, under the post-MacBeth production, the programme is inefficiently run: in former days, MacBeth accepted or rejected submissions within forty days whereas now rejection can take up to fourteen months, manuscripts submitted being lost in a morass of in-trays, one assumes. It also seems that the producer now favours a certain branch of modern verse and the wide approach has gone. The result of this is that many of those connected to the poetry scene no longer listen, certainly not as avidly as in the earlier years when the programme was seen as a central focus. As the programme does not have mass appeal any longer, even within the poetry *cognoscenti*, the value is greatly diminished. Another part of the old days has gone.

It must be added, though, that other editors in the BBC such as Alec Reid, Brian Miller and Brian Patten (not to be confused with the poet) have taken up the poetry banner, bringing out new programmes of merit and interest that reach well beyond the limited audience of the poetically keen. However, the fact remains that there is no longer a viable successor to MacBeth's *Poetry Now* productions.

It is somewhat of interest to hear that the BBC have received, in the latter years, an increasing correspondence from the public demanding more poetry programmes of both a traditional and contemporary nature, so much so in fact that this correspondence was commented upon on Radio Four in early February 1983. This suggests that the demand for an overall increase in poetry presentations is required and that there could lie in this a renaissance of such – the narrowing of *Poetry Now* in recent years has obviously been felt. It is not impossible that the public have also become bored with the mundane poetry often included in this programme series. Certainly, new producers are coming up through the BBC, often rising or moving over from drama production, who have a considerable and considered desire to meet the poetic demands.

Whilst still on the subject of broadcasting poetry, it is lamentable that television has hardly bothered with it. Occasional snippets appear in *The South Bank Show* as a result of a national poetry competition, or when a major poet is being featured: *Omnibus* (on BBC1) has featured poetry, but not very much. It is more or less accurate to say that poetry has not been featured on more than two dozen separate occasions in the last fourteen years. True, there was for a time (on BBC2) a series of *Closedown* programmes where an actor read a poem, but these came at the end of the evening's viewing, often after midnight, and can hardly claim to have captured the mass audiences associated with television. The nearest that television did come to a major poetry production was at some time in the early 1970s when there was a poetry documentary made around the poems of Seamus Heaney. The programme was distinctly successful. It has never had its format repeated. Poetry, which can expand its boundaries of appeal through television, has never had the chance. The scope of visual imagery linked to word, of rhythm linked to video-film techniques, and of poetic beauty linked to language, has never been explored. The poetic use of the video, it seems, remains in the hands of the pop musicians and their film-makers or promoters.

Quite why poetry has never made it to the square screen is a mystery. Television has made huge leaps and bounds in the last decade, computer graphics are common, split-screen techniques (not to mention wavy fades and the like) simple and production highly skilled and polished. But poetry remains lost.

Is there the mass media audience for verse? The answer has to be an emphatic yes. The public are always keen to see experimentation or the lifting or stretching of boundaries – a look at television humour since the early 1970s shows how much that, for example, has changed, broadened and become popularist. At the height of MacBeth's power at the BBC, *Poetry Now* had an estimated audience of 50,000 plus: that figure is much lower now that the programme is run by another. It should be noted that this figure did not take into account audiences directly related to education. *The Poet's Voice* began in 1957, long before the poetry explosion, under the hand of Donald Carne-Ross; MacBeth took it on in 1959. Both must be particularly saddened to see into what all their efforts have dissolved.

MacBeth sought to show how powerful a good text could be in a good studio performance. This was not a process restricted to the bowels of Broadcasting House, though. It might have received a positive stimulus from that direction, but it was to manifest itself in a thousand other places. Poetry readings began to take form and a network erected upon which they could be hung.

The Dylan Thomas-type reading has been mentioned and so has the critical reading. The other thing that came about was, perhaps, the biggest phenomenon of them all.

Poetry readings grew in popularity. They were not attended by the well-educated and the toffs. They were attended by ordinary people, their children, dogs and friends. They became forms of entertainment, amusement and artistic participation.

A potted history of the reading system and its foundation is hard to plot. Already many of the primary sources have vanished from sight, stopped organising or withdrawn from the reading circuits, such as they now are, to other things. Many have ceased to operate in the face of reduced grant aid, the reduction in audiences and the lack of support, the latter two factors brought about partly by the mundanity of the present poetry.

Quite why poetry readings became popular is equally hard to assess. In an age of mass entertainment in the home, one would least expect live poetry readings to be successful, but many were and a few still are. Attended by 'real' people, they attracted interest and excitement and – the key – involvement. The audiences were real because they cared, because they gave and took with poetry. From these there developed two different audiences aimed at two different types of reading, although the persons attending often overlapped.

Firstly, there were the big top readings. These were heavily subsidised events that took place at major literary festivals or at major, national venues. The Cheltenham Festival, the Stroud Festival, to some extent the Edinburgh Festival, the Royal Festival Hall and the Queen Elizabeth Hall have all seen mammoth poetic events in their time, although it has to be said that Edinburgh often ignores the literary arts unless they are directly related to the theatre. In order to bring these jamborees about, several large patrons came together and between them spent large sums of money – inordinately large sums, bearing in mind the money could have been spent more fairly and productively by spreading it around a bit – and attracted large audiences, at least by British standards. Thousands attended the readings at the Royal Festival Hall, hundreds still go to the Cheltenham Festival and the Ilkley Literature Festival. However, these should be set against greater figures that are achieved in other countries and were already in the late 1960s. The Russians, ironically, had vast audiences for some poetry readings and, in the USA, poets have been known to read to audiences of five figures. No one in Britain has quite made that yet.

Of the venues for the big readings, several stand out as worthy of note. Two are festivals, one mentioned already which is held at Ilkley in Yorkshire, which has to be one of the most unlikely sites for the worship of poetry that can be imagined. Ilkley is a small town far from anywhere, in the north of England and considered by the London poetry crowd to be distinctly out in the sticks. It is a difficult place to get to – by any form of transport other than car, and it has a population that one suspects would find it hard to muster a football team, never mind a major poetry reading audience. But it does, for Ilkley has become a mecca in the north, its festival anticipated and nationally famous, that fame partly spurred on by the fact that some years of the festival have produced remarkably fine publications, one by Ted Hughes and another in celebration of, or as a tribute to, W. H. Auden. Readings, talks, lectures and similar side events make up the festival. In recent years, it has become somewhat bent towards the ear of the new 'poets', but it is nevertheless a major festival of literature and one that now ranks with such standard events as Cheltenham.

The other festival, that runs in Cambridge, needs a little putting into context for it appears to draw for part of its design upon some of the big, international readings that were staged in London in the late 1960s and early 1970s.

These massive showpieces were most memorable. In 1969, the Poetry Society booked the Royal Festival Hall for the 'Poetry Gala'. This consisted of a three-week-long exhibition of poster poems, mobile poems, machine poems, poetry journals, manuscripts, record sleeves, book covers and the rest of the literary ephemeral art sidelines, culminating in a recital (as it was rather archaically termed) on 3 February. The line-up was never-to-be-forgotten: Basil Bunting, Spike Hawkins, Ted Hughes, Christopher Logue, Hugh MacDiarmid, Brian Patten, Tom Pickard, William Plomer, Stevie Smith and (health permitting, the press hand-outs read) Ezra Pound. Music was provided by Larry Adler and the evening's producer was George Melly. The domain of the symphony orchestra, the opera or visiting dance troupes from Outer Mongolia was for one night taken over by the muses. The audience was huge and the evening a rocketing success. It was the peak of public poetry and the height that readings seldom aspired to, never mind reached, at least in Great Britain. For the Poetry Society, it was a gamble that paid off for it set a tone going that was to overlap into that second festival. But first, one must say, there was another remarkable gig at the Royal Festival Hall, this time in May 1972. This was staged by the Poetry Consortium, an unlikely alliance between the Poetry Society, the Greater London Council, the Institute of Contemporary Arts (where poetry seldom ventures except as a product of elitist thinking or snob-audience appeal), the Greater London Arts Association, the London Poetry Secretariat and the National Book League – unlikely in that several of these bodies were arch-opponents in the literary field.

The event that they staged was called 'A Festival of Poetry with Music'. The poetry was provided by Pablo Neruda, Stephen Spender, Brian Patten, Adrian Mitchell and Neruda's translator who read the poems in English. The music was provided by the then-bestselling group, Lindisfarne. The action was provided by several people in the audience who heckled and rankled Neruda, shouting abuse of a political nature at him and generally getting a series of shushes and shut-ups from the audience. After all, this was poetry, not politics! You don't mix them. Not in England. The excitement was silenced when, with apology for some error but not much, the heckler, in mid-voice, was as equally loudly clunked with a shoe on the top of his head by those seated behind him. His vociferous complaints reduced to mumbles and his demise was cheered. The readings progressed interupted only by the band and applause. The line-up was not as impressive as the Poetry Gala's had been, but it was another unforgettable event.

One man's dream, however, caused there to come into being an event that outstripped all the rest and continues so to do into the 1980s, somewhat diminished but still larger than its peers. Richard Burns was a poet who worked as a lecturer in a college of technology in Cambridge and published a number of sound if slight volumes and, for these, he became a little known. A man with considerable drive and ambition, he conceived the idea of having a Cambridge poetry festival that would be a biennial event drawing to itself poets from all over the world and forming into one of the most important international events of its kind. As ever, money was to be a considerable problem, but that aside, Burns saw it was a distinct possibility and he set about trying to get it together.

This was to be no mere festival of readings such as the Poetry Gala had been, nor was it to be limited to academic poets that association with such a university city might imply. Big as his ideas were, Burns saw his festival as being the biggest poetry bash ever, something that was unrivalled and unequalled in Britain or a good many other places. In the early 1970s, he set about planning, aiming to stage the first event in 1975. And so was born the 'Cambridge Poetry Festival'. It is of interest to see how it came about for there is nothing on a par.

Burns at first contacted everyone he could obtain addresses for and sought their advice, condemnation or indifference. He then built around himself a committee of dedicated members who, with various expertise, could assist in making this happen. The Cambridge Poetry Festival Society, as it was called, became registered as a charity and then sought patrons to support it, and the list of these became extensive and considerable, including patrons of the arts, Cambridge colleges, publishers, booksellers, Cambridge City Council, big businesses, sherry importers, newspapers, arts councils, the Poet Laureate and foreign embassies. The last was a shrewd move, for they assisted in obtaining their nationals as participants.

Once finance seemed settled, if not totally assured, Burns and his committee began planning readings, exhibitions, lectures, films, competitions and related events that included music and dance, symposia, poetry forum sessions and book and magazine stalls. Venues were arranged around Cambridge but centred on the university's Cambridge Union Society building in Bridge Street. Day tickets were issued, event tickets followed and an overall 'season' ticket was introduced. A programme was designed and printed and carried considerable advertisement from around the poetry world, most of it based upon British publishers, associations and magazines. In the meantime, the cast for the extravaganza was being assembled. When arranged, it looked like a who's who of modern verse and included in its not inconsiderable list Roberto Sanesi (Italy), Ted Hughes, Miroslav Holub (Czechoslovakia), Jon Silkin, Charles Tomlinson, Nathaniel Tarn, Chinua Achebe (Nigeria), a group of German poets including Rolf Dieter Brinkman who was tragically killed just after the festival, Duncan Glen, John Ashbery, Lee Harwood, Roy Fisher, David Gascoyne, Takis Sinopoulos (Greece), Elaine Feinstein, William Cookson, Peter Dale, Sorley Maclean and others. American and British poets rubbed shoulders with many, many others and the selection of events made the festival exciting, to say the least. Films of Wilbur and Lowell reading, on Hugh MacDiarmid and Ginsberg, films by poets, song-cycles and poetry about music, lectures ('Imagination and Invention in Contemporary British Poetry' and Kermode on Wallace Stevens and other talks) and discussions, matinee events and a children's poetry competition added to make an almost fair-like atmosphere.

The festival took place over six days in the spring of 1975. It was an outstanding success from start to finish. It did not cover its costs, but it made the television news, and radio broadcast special features on it. The programme became a collectors' item and the festival's own issue of poster poems became much-sought-after sheets. Burns was worn out to a frazzle but he saw his dream become reality.

There had been nothing like this before. A week encompassed all aspects of the art as internationally as was possible with only oriental poets being obviously absent as a group or genre. Concrete poetry rung its bells next to the most rabidly traditional verse and a small press publications exhibition stood equal ground with a showing of sixteenth- and seventeenth-century manuscripts and early editions. A unity was forged across what was beoming a divided artistic country.

What was more, a precedent was set that other committees, with or without Burns, who eventually retired from the scene, built upon: the 1977 festival was highlighted by Robert Creeley, Robert Duncan, Fielding Dawson, Seamus Heaney and Geoffrey Hill; in 1979 appeared Allen Ginsberg, Hans Magnus Enzensberger, Kenneth Koch, Peter Orlovsky and a suitable supporting galaxy of names; 1981 fielded Vasko Popa, Anthony Hecht, Yehuda Amichai, Stanley Kunitz, Joseph Brodsky, Ed Dorn, George Barker, W. S. Graham and Edward Brathwaite and many others; the 1983 festival continued the tradition but with a little less flamboyance. The 1981 festival was notable for being funded, along with the National Poetry Secretariat, the Eastern Arts Association and the British Council, by Clive Sinclair, the owner of the massive micro-computer company and the 'inventor of the British pocket calculator', and his involvement shows a keen interest by some entrepreneurs outside the immediate confines of the poetry world to support such a festival. Indeed, the party Sinclair and his wife threw for the poets and festival staff just before the opening night has already gone down in literary history for its superlatives: a good deal of gratitude is due to people like Sinclair who patronise such events not only with cash but with kindness as well.

Burns's Cambridge bash occurs every two years and it is the exception. There is nothing else like it, although there could be. The Edinburgh Festival could take poetry a bit more to its heart than it does. There could perhaps be another festival in the in-between years of the Cambridge one, but that might flood the market and cheapen the goods, so to speak. What is important is that the festival in Cambridge is established – indeed, it is so much so that, from 1983, it appears to have gathered its own fringe festival, a sign of acceptance and the big time if ever there was one.

Such huge events as those mentioned were, at best, annual. What went on in the interim months was just as thrilling, if not on such a scale of magnificence. Certainly, they did not take place in such auspicious surroundings. Church halls, school buildings after hours, tiny arts centres, public houses, private houses and Boy Scout huts have all seen their parades of the muses. The venues stretched all over the country, from Falmouth College of Art to the wilder reaches of the shadow of Hadrian's Wall and beyond, although primarily readings occurred in England and Wales, the Scots being not so keen upon them, it seems.

Audiences consisted of poets, poetasters, school teachers with or without pupils, poetry lovers, poetry readers, the curious, the uncurious and the drinking man and his wife. Organisers were invariably local poets or those who felt that poetry was important. (The decline in readings since 1975–6 – it can be dated as accurately as that winter – can be attributed to the dwindling of numbers of those who believed in poetry's importance. They must have come to lose interest because poetry now has lost some of its importance. Read the present-day 'martian' mush and appreciate one of the reasons: for an interpretation of the adjective 'martian', read on.)

Just as it was best to outline the small press activity by naming a few of the firms, so it seems best to illustrate the types of reading organisations by listing some of them, beginning with the better-known:

The Poetry Society/National Poetry Centre is situated in a building in Earl's Court Square, in west London, sandwiched between small London hotels and facing what more than one poet has titled 'a shagged-out London square of trees'. The Poetry Society holds a wide variety of events under its roof, in the better days including a good and intimate bar, a bookstall and a loan library. Readings used to take place in a recital room equipped with spotlights and a disconcertingly large mirror, a piano and a movable dais. In recent years, the whole place has become a little shabby, but between 1969 and 1975, it was a delight to enter. Audiences sat on reasonably comfortable chairs, poets were given a glass of wine (and a microphone, if they needed it) in the library by the general secretary, in those days Michael Mackenzie, and the number varied from thirty-five to several hundreds, spilling over on to the balcony, into the library and up to the stairs. The acoustics were terrible but surmountable. The fee paid for the reading was always in accordance with the laid down rates.

The Old Fire Station, Oxford housed poetry readings (and other events) for some years after the fire engines moved out and the arts moved in. The building is next to the central bus station and stands between it and George Street. As an arts centre, it was somewhat run-down, but lively. It drew in some of the university undergraduate population, but not much: most of the audiences came from local non-university students and would-be poets. The best readings were organised by the poet Anne Stevenson, in a freezingly cold room (in winter), who managed to rustle up good audiences. Needless to say, there was competition from the next named.

Oxford University Poetry Society. Readings for this society or its associated organisations could take place in a college (Hertford College in 1979 when the organiser was a member of that college) or the bar of a pub. Readings for the Oxford University poetry festivals occur in hired halls or – on one occasion at least during the 1970s – the debating hall of the Oxford Union, a distinctly awe-inspiring place in which to read.

At this point, it is worth mentioning that a good many readings did – and do – occur in university or college premises. Students, fired by their freedom and artistic licence to do as they will inside and outside their courses, are avid poetry swallowers and just as well, for it is from their midst that the next generation will more than likely come into the poetry game: the trouble is that, often, they bring not only new enthusiasms and ideas but also the narrowing of their education. And when they are entertained by boring poets or those who thrive on gimmickry and hollow shells of art, then what hope for the future? Readings to students can be positive and constructive for all concerned and poetry at large. They can equally be just as destructive and distinctly harmful. On the side of fortune, however, is the fact that students are young and therefore resilient and critical. They do see through the shammers. Yet, if they see and hear only shammers, then what are they to do? It is here that readings as a whole carry a considerable responsibility.

Words Etcetera was the name of a bookshop run by the poet Julian Nangle and his wife at 89 Theberton Street, Islington, in London. Readings ran for about a year at the end of the reading boom around 1976, taking place in the bookshop's cellar, a book-lined, red-brick cavern that was cosy, intimate and good to read in. Audiences were limited by the size of the room but a glass of wine in the price and the seriousness of the audience made it all worthwhile. There were times when, as Nangle hoped, the atmosphere ventured towards being like that of readings at Harold Munro's Poetry Bookshop in the 1920s.

Nottingham Poetry Society has been going for a good many years and it conducts readings, members' (and open) competitions and has, from time to time, published its own slim booklets. The central organiser changed from time to time, but one of the leading background figures was (and is at the time of writing) Betty Parvin. She keenly supported the local society and one of the near-rituals of reading for the group was a meal at Betty Parvin's house. Meetings often took place at the New Mechanics' Institute building in Nottingham and the list of poets to have read there must cover most of the important poets of the period.

Local poetry associations flourished in the late 1960s and continued for a decade, the hardiest going on beyond that time and re-appearing each year rather like the fairy rings in a lawn, always in the same place but under a new stimulus, chairman or secretary. These societies – for example, Ripley Poetry Association in Kent, Ruislip Literary Society (Middlesex), Portsmouth

Poetry Society, Surrey Poetry Centre, which operated under other similar names in Guildford, and many others – formed a major part of the live poetry reading network. They were essential to the development of oral verse and the widening of the audience to which poetry could appeal. Those attending meetings were seldom fewer than forty and were sometimes considerably more, especially if the poet was nationally famous or on a schools examination syllabus. They were also a major poetry market place. Some poets, carrying a stock of their latest books with them, often sold out at such meetings and books that were a little older, sometimes purchased by the poet from his publisher as remaindered stock, went too. I personally cannot recall a single event of this sort to which any publisher arrived to sell books, or arranged to have books sold on sale or return terms by the organiser or a helper. A market was lost, once again, due to the ineptitude or narrow attitudes of the publishers. Small presses, needless to say, made hay in this sunshine. Even in London, publishers ignored readings of this sort. It was only in the late 1970s that publishers occasionally took to having a reading by their latest poet, usually at the National Poetry Centre. By then, it was too late.

St John's, Smith Square was a church in Westminster that was changed into an arts centre. They have made a superb concert hall and the crypt was a bar-cum-restaurant in which lunchtime poetry readings were held. Few churches ever took in poetry, even of the religious kind – and it can be argued in the light of today's ecumenical attitudes that much poetry is religious – so to read in a crypt was a strange experience. Audiences came from lunchtime eaters or those who wanted a bit of art in their break.

Berkhampstead Library in Hertfordshire has seen a good few readings organised by John Cotton, the poet, under the auspices of his Priapus Press. Audiences for these readings were of average size for the poet concerned, but were distinctly literary and keenly critical and inquisitive. Readings were lively and pleasant to give.

Libraries might seem the ideal place for a poetry reading but most librarians seem to shy away from contact with live poets. There are a few enlightened spots that do let the writer in to mingle with the shelves and give a show of some sort, but they are thin on the ground. Some local literary societies meet in their local library – *Friends of Essex Poets* used to meet in Saffron Walden Library, for example – but on the whole such an idea is foreign. There seems no historical reason for this disregard. It seems ridiculous that writers are excluded from libraries – it's rather like refusing to sell alcohol in a pub, or preventing doctors from visiting surgeries.

Readings in public houses have long taken place, either under a distinct organisation or spontaneously. One of the most success-ful was *Toddington Poetry*. This was set up by Alan Harris, a lecturer at the Open University in nearby Bletchley. Toddington is a large village just north of Luton and conveniently just off the M1 motorway. It is a sprawling dormitory village, with a remarkable number of pubs, set upon a hill. Its situation was part of its appeal to the poetry reading network; not too far from London where many poets live, in the centre of a part of the Home Counties that can be adequately described as a cultural desert, surrounded by people for whom poetry (and drinking) had a purpose and within (just) the boundaries of Eastern Arts Association funding limits, a regional arts association which for some years has been the most avid literature supporter under a succession of highly competent literature officers. Harris's read-ings took place in the Sow & Pigs public house, a homely and unpretentious hostel with an open coal fire, an amenable landlord and locals who were not quite sure how to view the onslaught of long-haired men with satchels, briefcases and women in long dresses and matching hair. Readings inevitably began late and involved one or two imported poets, a musician or two, some local poets reading their work (including Alan Harris) and an exhibition of some local artist's handiwork – carved bowls, bread sculptures or paintings. The audiences were usually in excess of sixty and packed out the upstairs room of the pub where the readings took place. Beer and other beverages flowed and the evenings warmed and were a joy to attend and perform at . . . in the summer, Harris arranged a poetry picnic that lasted all day and included readings, a band, a barbecue, a mural painting session, a visit from William Shakespeare (an actor being his double and spouting apt sonnets here and there) and an assortment of latterday hippy activities. Toddington Poetry was the last of the big-time, local venues. At present they seem dead but poised for a revival. In the West Country, a local group have established an arts centre in a disused chapel which promises to turn out well, and others are hidden in the countryside.

Other pub meetings that have a niche in history are those held under the aegis of Norman Hidden and his *New Poetry* set-up, *Pentameters* (again in London), and readings that took place in Surbiton, under the guidance of Valerie Sinason, where the landlord was distinctly antagonistic towards 'bloody poets' despite the fact that they drank over the per capita norm.

Plan B was for organised poetry readings in a private arts centre. Established by Monica Darlington and her husband in a barn behind their home in Stone (Staffordshire), it was the epitome of what local enterprise and enthusiasm can do. The barn was tastefully redecorated, cosy and warm and strewn with cushions. Poets who read there were treated to considerable hospitality and a good audience that seemed to flock in from the darkness of the West Midlands. (I read there on the night of 2 January 1976 and was, I believe, the last performer: it was a night of tremendously high winds and, during a guitar-player's set, I was leaning on the wall of the upstairs performance room when I felt it move – imperceptibly, but definitely. Poplars in the garden blew down that night: slates from the roof cut the wing mirror off my small car and I was blown – car and all – on to the soft grass of the M6 going home at midnight. Shortly after the reading ended, the barn wall fell out, injuring no one. It seems poetry reading venues cease by acts of God as well as mere apathy.)

Matchlight ran a series of readings in London throughout the period this book covers. Eileen Warren, now sadly deceased, made this small circle a one-woman crusade for poetry and it was held in high esteem. Readings followed a different pattern from most and were held in the Orangery in Holland Park, West London. A poet was invited to read and a guest reader also came along, to read whatever they liked. The latter included well-known public figures, actors and actresses of renown and poets other than those who produced their own work. Books were on sale: Eileen Warren was one of those people who demanded books from publishers to sell and got them. Coffee and biscuits were served. Poets whose work was read by others received a royalty – a small one of but a few pounds, but cash nevertheless which gave the whole process a certain dignity and more than pecuniary value. When Eileen Warren died, so did *Matchlight*. The extinguishing of both have been sadly missed in poetry rounds.

There were many more of these types of venue, some of them allied to local arts festivals, some to nothing at all save the organiser's enthusiasm. And it is to this latter that much can be attributed. Without such drive and determination, the poetry appearance would be restricted to the university lecture room and the school classroom, the 'famous' poets and the equally 'famous' venues. The lamentable fact is that the purveyors of poetry books never bothered to join the ride save on the off-chance when they put on a reading from a new book of theirs at the Poetry Society. It was enthusiasm that caused Richard Burns to make his Cambridge Festival and Eileen Warren to start her much smaller comings-together.

One of the rare exceptions to the rule was something that the National Book League and the Poetry Society put on with the actual (rather than covert) blessing of the London publishers. It was called, rather euphemistically, the Bedford Square Book Bang and it ran from 28 May to 11 June 1971. This consisted of a kind of publishing fair to which most of the publishers contributed both cash and authors (and, remarkably, books), and events were staged where authors could meet the public, discuss, read, perform, lecture and generally do their turns. Poetry being, by 1971, a major performance art in highlight in the literary whirl, it followed that poets would take a fair slice of the action, and they did. A book was published of the poems that were commissioned of various poets, the only requisite being that the poems should be 'committed poems' that would invoke a 'fresh representation of a phrase that is rapidly becoming a cliché'. The cliché was to be given added strength just two years later with the appearance of Jon Silkin's anthology, *Poetry of the Committed Individual*, published by Penguin and based upon Silkin's *Stand* magazine. Quite what the poems were committed to in the case of the Book Bang book, entitled *Responses*, is somewhat vague. Perhaps they were simply committed to being good poems which most of them were and which, surely, must be the best commitment of them all. But the sad thing is that it is the only major occasion on which the big publishers have bothered to come together to push their product so well and so massively, and poetry with it.

There is one sort-of event that has become popular in recent years, that is a hybrid of the public reading and the broadcasting of verse; indeed, it is hard to know exactly where to mention it. It is the proliferation of poetry competitions run in association with either big newspaper concerns or television. The first of these giants was the 1980 Arvon Foundation/Observer newspaper/London Weekend Television competition which earned money for the former of the three organisations and set the trend. A total of 35,000 poems was submitted, each with a slim entry fee (not over £2 per poem), competing for a first prize of £5,000 *for one poem*, with other poems earning £1,000, £500, £250 or £100. It is quite ludicrous that one poem should win such a sum – more than many an author might earn for a full-length novel in hardback – but it did once again bring poetry to the public eye, and on television, for the winners had their poems read out on the South Bank Show, an artistic weekly magazine programme of the general arts. (Significantly, the poets did not read their own poems themselves, which was a shame; if that had been allowed, then the real value of the prizewinning poems might have been assessed.) Since then, other competitions have formed in relation to magazines and other poetic bodies. In 1983, Arvon Foundation in association with Sotheby Ltd, the fine art auctioneers, brought about another of these massive lotteries. The first one produced a book that was certainly of as much value as the prize. There are those that argue that such contests of poetic gladiators bring the art into disrepute and there is something to this, but on the other hand, it does get controversy going. Not quite a public event in the sense of those already mentioned, it is nevertheless a fact that these big sprees are just that – a publicising of poetry, albeit with a pecuniary motive. How moral they are is left to the moralists.

It was Horovitz's enthusiasm that set up *New Departures*. As time passed, one senses, he began to grow frustrated that his magazine was just that – a magazine. He has for years, indeed since the 1950s, been performing poetry with jazz, music, actors, other poets and the whole gamut of potential performers, but as the reading circuits closed down in the second half of the 1970s, one feels that Horovitz more than any other has felt this decline most obviously. Quite probably, the narrowing of the reading field hit his own income hard, for he has earned a good slice of his financial backing from performance, but this is not to imply a mercenary character hidden behind his shoulder-bag of poems that he carried like a British, latterday Ginsberg. Horovitz's enthusiasm, allied to his powerful acumen in publicity and self-publicity, brought about a new move in poetry performance, a hybrid that appears now to be sired by the non-establishment muse and the Festival Hall readings. In 1979 Horovitz began to pull together the strings that made the first Poetry Olympics come to life in September 1980; there has been another event since. As Ted Hughes wrote to Horovitz, in a letter which the latter reproduced in facsimile in the special edition of *New Departures* that came out with the Poetry Olympics' opening reading, 'It's so long now since those international poetry frolics passed away, this is probably a good time to start something fresh.' Horovitz could have received no greater approbation.

It began appropriately at Poets' Corner, Westminster Abbey with the 'voices of Dylan Thomas and Wordsworth on Westminster Bridge', followed by readings by, amongst others, Stephen Spender, Anne Stevenson, John Cooper Clarke and Linton Kwesi Johnson. Also listed were Dennis Lee, Edward Limonov, Gregory Corso, Derek Walcott and Janine Pommy Vega. Quite who some of the latter were left the audience in some quandary. Horovitz was doing his usual in bringing in his friends and acquaintances and ignoring others, sometimes those the public might have wanted. Nevertheless, he did bring poetry to life again and he hit the headlines. The national papers covered the event and it was universally justifiably applauded. The impact was, sadly, short-lived. As with anything that appears in the press, the public saw it and then ignored it as it passed by.

But the value of the event lies not in what it did on the night, but what it did to poets, revitalising them to some extent. The sad thing is that not all the poets could share in the afterglow which has been reserved for the Horovitz round. (One can hardly call them a clique, for there's so many of them.) If Horovitz had done a Burns, the overall outcome would have been stupendous. There is still time, though. Horovitz has only just been born to this; his aim was to 'encourage a rebirth of the spirit of poetry and of the public's interest in it' and, to some extent, he has gone a way along this road, but he has yet to travel such a distance as to make poetry a force again which has lorry drivers talking of it and BBC producers producing it in likely and exciting quantities. One can only hope and wish more strength to Horovitz's elbow.

Poetry in performance is as old as the hills: the Greeks did it at Delphi, the Anglo-Saxons did it in their longhouses, Shakespeare stuck in with it and it had a renaissance in the 1960s. Now its popularity is going through apathy and poor writing, not to mention poor reading by readers. The old adage that a poet is the last person most qualified to read his own work, so massively disproved in the 1960s and 1970s, now seems to be gaining relevance again. A major direction in poetry is being lost and it will take years to overcome the loss. The few hiding in the bush and keeping the flames alight, the Burns and Horovitz mentality, are fighting a strong wind of non-interest. Opportunities are disappearing that poetry could snap on to. Soon it will be considered, once more, words on a page. If poetry is to move with the times and enter the video world, the sound world of cassette tapes and radio, the electronic media, it must rapidly get with it, as they say.

13

It is apparent that what is badly needed is a healthy poetry scene, a poetic culture that is progressive yet traditionally aware, responsible yet willing to take risks. Yet how does one define such a state of affairs?

It is not complicated. What we need to have developing and quickly developed is a poetic culture that seeks to promote the art in all aspects, to be artistically non-partisan and consciously against the formation of a sense of being set apart from people.

Poetry is a form of art that is one of the most accessible if only it will let itself be so. It is within the reach of all, educated or otherwise, not only as an art to be appreciated but also one in which to join in and create. It is not something elitist and singular but a common denominator that is wonderful and should be shared by everyone.

Poets need to be conscious of this, that they write for people and not themselves or their in-crowd associates. They must accept that they have a responsibility to the truth and to the core of all art – to enrich and enlighten others and lift their minds up to greater or deeper or meaningful heights.

A drive must be made to interest people in poetry and to give them the opportunity of getting to the art, to encourage readings that are interesting, promote books, establish magazines, increase broadcasting. In short, try to reach the levels that existed in the decade from 1964 to 1974. Poetry must start once again to mean something more than the pretty or skilful engineering of words and images. It must be relevant to society.

To do this, of course, the poetry must match the aims. It has to start to be something people first want and then need. Like music, it must be something without which people feel the poorer. It has to seek to fill the void that exists in many souls in an age that is increasingly filled with loss and despair and apprehension. Poetry must speak for and to more than poets.

It has a role to play. It has to be controversial, outspoken, aware of the internal drives that work within men – politics, religion, the basic emotions. An example of what it can do and should do in Britain is given on page 183 in Robert Bly's poem, 'Kennedy's Inauguration'. Never before in modern Britain has the stage been so ripe for poetry's influence to burgeon. Poetry must come out of the closest of cosiness and start to grapple with the matters of concern in our world – search for beauty, criticism of things that worry or amuse or are generally a part of life.

There are poets who are striving to set up such a culture, conscious that it will benefit them but equally knowledgeable in the fact that it is somehow their duty to set the poetry machine in operation once more. They are struggling against heavy odds, as this book points out, but they must eventually reach their aim.

Given this, one will then have a poetry scene or culture that will mean something and will give the art the credibility it has either lost or is fast losing.

PART TWO

The lunatics, the lovers and the poets

1 THE GROUPS

Having now looked at the poetry world, it is time to look at the poets.

Poets are a strange breed: it was Shakespeare who put into Theseus' mouth the words

> The lunatic, the lover, and the poet,
> Are of imagination all compact

in *A Midsummer Night's Dream*, and he knew what he was talking about. All are made of imagination and make much of it, too. In the period from roughly 1964, there was certainly a fair smattering of lunatics and lovers in the poetry scene.

It has not been unknown for poets to come to blows over their art, an occurrence not uncommon in the Poetry Society in the second half of the 1960s, to form everlasting enemies and to hate, despise and harangue their fellow craftsmen at every opportunity. However, poets as readily form solid friendships with co-defenders of their poetic faith. Not surprisingly, therefore, poetry is riddled with groups, cliques, schools, sects and cults and there are few in-betweeners who ride across these artificial boundaries.

Accepting that this is the case, it might perhaps be useful to look at these divisions before studying the members of each one. Needless to say, the boundaries aren't totally inflexible and there are some poets who have crossed boundaries in mid-career.

Furthermore, it is important before embarking upon the remainder of this book to realise that what is being presented is not a text for examination candidates, a sort of study-aid notes. As has been stated, the trouble with poetry today and its relationship with the world outside is that it has become too much a property of the academic and the teacher whose interests lie only in interpretation and not enlightenment. What is intended is a scenario, a presentation of who of value was writing, what they were writing and how they fitted into their part of the landscape. In some respects, that they are related to others far away or near at hand is by the way. Essentially, poets and poetry are solitary beings and they thrive best when they are not overtly under the influence of each other; in poetry more than in any other art, incest is rife and destructive. Where links and relationships do occur they will be noted and brought up, but the end result is not really intended to be that the reader looks at Poet 1 and says that that character belongs in Group A: and not all the poets writing today will be included. Some must be dropped because of the dictates of space and, more importantly, because they have contributed little or nothing to the art.

Ultimately, I hope that what follows will provide active proof of what British poetry and its makers can achieve when the atmosphere is conducive and the stage is set. With fortune blowing, it might give directions again that the craft might turn with the wind and sail rather than struggle against it or tack aimlessly to and fro making no headway. I would also hope that the comments that are not favourable to those at whom they are directed will indicate something of what is wrong in the present trends in British verse. Additionally, I trust that, in the true spirit of Poets' Workshop meetings – not to mention those of the Group – adverse comment is not taken as being destructive and personal but simply a means of showing what I think is at fault in poetry today in Britain. Personal animosity is not intended. It is contrary to the spirit of poetry that should and must be engendered if the art is to thrive. There is already enough animus about, tinted with self-interest, and it is working its evil as it is.

The divisions: what are they? How was the scene set prior to 1964? Poetry prior to, say, 1958, existed in three main streams. There was the poetry of the Movement, the poetry of those who had made their reputations before 1955 and there was, for want of a better term, the new poetic underground.

The Movement consisted of poets whose primary concern was to revalue poetry by reacting against the romanticism and traditionalism of the post-war period that was so dominated by poets of those two leanings – Dylan Thomas, for example, who was the last of the great romantic poets. The new reactionaries were spearheaded by Philip Larkin, Thom Gunn, John Wain and Elizabeth Jennings. They looked at the everyday world through their poetry and there was a sense that they were seeking to deal with the ordinary rather than the flights of poetics that their predecessors found so absorbing. However, they did write in a style and with a form that was still really too poetic for the average reader. They wrote for the poetically educated, not the man in the street. Their values, however, were important in establishing the atmosphere which was to nurture the poetic revolution of the 1960s. Of course, a number of them wrote well into the 1960s, too, continuing to publish verse that altered to suit the times: a few of their number did not evolve with the times – D. J. Enright, John Wain, Donald Davie – and they faded. One, Kingsley Amis, made himself more felt as a novelist than a poet and here it is interesting and important to consider how his novels took the creed of the Movement and used it to such effect in prose writing. His poetry did not develop as his fiction did.

Those with solid reputations clung to them. They were the greats of their day, the sage-like figures that were respected and read but again only by the poets; few outside were concerned with their output at all. Auden, MacNeice, Day-Lewis, Edwin Muir, Graves, Blunden . . . they were there, but had passed their day. Only Betjeman stayed on in the public's mind, partly because his poetry has always traded upon the two staples of British popular poetic success – nationalism and nostalgia in tandem.

And then there was the underground. They were not known as that at all. They were entitled, by themselves, The Group, and they were to have an impact of considerable strength and to form the next generation. The background of The Group has been mentioned already. What follows is a look at the members and their influence and importance.

By 1963, The Group poets were beginning to make themselves felt in no uncertain terms. Their books were being published or had appeared in the preceding two years to consolidate reputations that were now building rapidly. In this period of growth and popularity in poetry, other factions set up shop and may be classed as follows, always being borne in mind that they were, throughout the 1960s and early 1970s, secondary to The Group. They are not given here in any specific order. They cannot be classed chronologically for they developed so organically. Similarly, they cannot be placed in rank order for they each worked in their own fields. And there were many poets who belonged to no one clique, or belonged to more than one in the course of time.

For want of a better term, there were (and still are, to some extent) the Mainliners. These were poets outside the framework who, through expertise and earned influence, were the leading figures. They are Ted Hughes, Sylvia Plath, Philip Larkin (a Movement poet, but one who carried through the doctrines and found a voice that fitted the period), Geoffrey Hill and, included in a listing of another group, Seamus Heaney. These five became known to the world, were public people so far as their art went although it is a point of shame to the British that these poets would hardly have been known in a street of passers-by: the British have honoured and admired poets, but seldom recognised them in their lifetime.

The Liverpool Poets appeared in the heyday of 1967, the name coined or conjured up by Edward Lucie-Smith who made it current with his anthology of the poets in question which was called *The Liverpool Scene*. The main characters were Brian Patten, Adrian Henri and Roger McGough but there were others who rode along on the wagon. There was a hard core of poets who were influenced by, or were subsequently to influence, rock music who might be put under the same classification, for they were similarly held under the charms of what rock music poetry could do – and it could do much, as the summer's release of The Beatles' *Sergeant Pepper* album was to prove. The best of these poets was Pete Brown who was to write many of the Cream's major hits. Certainly Eric Clapton, the world's most important rock guitarist, rode to considerable fame on the lyrics that Pete Brown wrote.

The Group gradually evolved into The Poets' Workshop, as has been mentioned. The poets who made up the workshop were also to become influential and important although it is fair to add that they did so because they had the backing, both materially and intellectually, of The Group. George MacBeth in particular was very important in this direction through the use he made of poets from the workshop in his BBC programmes.

Few publishers have, in recent times, made an impact with their lists. One that has, and which has almost set a genre in publishing the poets that it does, is Carcanet New Press. The publisher has been listed earlier in the book, but it is important to state here that the company has established its own clique which has, as a firm centre, a body of poets who are young – under the age of 40 in 1980 – and who, though they are joined by older figures, form a kernel to one poetic nut.

Less of a clique or school and more of a fluid movement in itself is The Performance Poets. The explosion of poetry into a performing art that the 1960s saw produced a wide number of poets who wrote primarily for the reading circuit or to be heard and seen rather than simply read on the page. They are not a coherent bunch. Many poets from the other sections of the art have joined in from time to time – even the most academic and middle-of-the-road poets have, from a desire to join the trend, written quirky performance work that has, in a few cases, been amongst their best work. Performance has also been an integral part of poetry emanating from The Group/The Poets' Workshop. The very nature of meetings, where poetry was read out loud, militated towards performance of some level or another.

Another less solid group, but one that nevertheless existed and still does to some extent, was The Metropolitan Poets, who wrote for Londoners, the environs of London and the city life in general. Their work was and remains topical and of little, or reduced, meaning to those who inhabit the non-urban areas. Again, poets from other fields have ventured into this arena only to quit it at a later date. And, once more, poets from The Group/The Poets' Workshop tended also to be in this bunch as the meetings, from the early 1960s onwards, took place in London.

The Irish Poets came into being with the arrival on the poetry shelves of Seamus Heaney's first book in 1966. It had been a long time since a band of poets was based upon one man's literary output, but with Heaney, this became the case. To be more accurate, they might be named the Northern Irish clique, for most of these poets came from Ulster rather than the Republic and they were yet another indication of the Ulster identity asserting itself and using Seamus Heaney as its starting handle and lynch-pin.

As is so often the case, what is outside the structure of the scene becomes a part of it and the vacuum left by one movement becoming respectable is filled by one that isn't, as yet. This was never more true than in the case of the Concrete Poets. Poetry and form have long fascinated the avant-garde, whom some would prefer to label the way-outers, the oddities and the cranks. The freedom of expression and the release that the 1960s brought to all aspects of life, the permissiveness that was all-pervading, manifested itself in poetry with work that was not necessarily poetic in the traditional sense. Art and visual form, sound and physical texture and original means of producing these brought about a wave of visual and sound poems which caused many to tears of laughter and others to weepings of rage. The poetry did not catch on and remains to this day very much a minority side of the art, but it does exist and it came into new strength in the 1960s with the desire of all to push out the boundaries of the possibilities of poetry. The new performance helped. So did the new methods of printing that allowed concrete poems to be expressed in print with ease and comparative cheapness. The availability of tape recording equipment that appeared in the early 1960s, within the reach of most people's pockets, also meant that the new forms could become more widely produced and distributed.

Not so much a school as a phenomenon in poetry is the category of poets who wrote directly for music or were influenced by it to a far greater extent than the Liverpool Poets who were still concerned with books and the state of the art rather than the actual aim of hitting the hit parade. They might be called the Rock Poets. Few people consider them as poets. They are musicians. But the fact cannot be lost that they are still poets in the basic sense – troubadour-like figures who use words set to music to say something in which they believe. It is more easily seen when one thinks of the copyright notice on many records of the mid-1960s: music by Joe Dough, lyrics by Phil Stim. Lyrics are poetry.

In the second half of the 1970s a new group of poets reared its head. They were called the Martian Poets after a poem by their leader which formed the title of his second collection, *A Martian Sends A Postcard Home*, by Craig Raine. Not a large band of poets, but a most influential one, the Martians have impinged themselves upon British poetry and to its disadvantage. The main creed of the poets seems to be to write of everything from life in such a way as to plumb its most basic ideas, as if studying it through the eyes of a total newcomer from another planet. This attractive but facile viewpoint does not seem to be catching on in either literary or wider circles, largely because Martian poetry has to have, it seems, lengthy explanations to justify itself. (Attendance at Martian poets' readings confirms this comment.)

Then there are the Outsiders. These are the poets who do not fit a category as such. They may meander into one but they leave it and write individualistically. They do not pander to 'market forces' in poetry, they do not bother with cliques and new attitudes. They merely write and others take them or leave them. Some of them are major figures – like Ted Hughes – and others are not.

Other groupings may exist but I think that the above are the main ones, the ones that built up the spine of British poetry from about 1964 onwards.

It is difficult, if not impossible, to set a rigid chronological framework to the various divisions of poetry but, as a summary guide, it might be said that the Movement ceased with the end of the 1950s. The Group came to prominence in 1962-3 (Brownjohn's first book appeared in 1961 and *A Group Anthology* came out in 1963) and was no longer a unified clique by 1972, after having gone through its metamorphosis into The Poets' Workshop which ran from 1966 to 1972 in any worthwhile form: it continued until the late 1970s, but with no real promise in its ranks. The main poets have carried on through the whole era. The Liverpool Poets appeared in 1967 and, although they are all still writing, they ceased to be a unit by 1976 when Brian Patten's collection, *Vanishing Trick*, more or less ended that style of poetry that so typified the school from the Mersey. The Carcanet Poets started to appear in 1970, with the publication of booklets of verse by such poets as Roger Garfitt (ex-Poets' Workshop), Marcus Cumberlege (subsequently published in book form by Anvil Press), Sally Purcell, Michael Schmidt (founder of Carcanet),

Grevel Lindop and Anthony Rudolf (also ex-Poets' Workshop); the grouping, much enlargened, continues through to the 1980s. The Performance Poets have no set dates but poetry in performance in a major way can be said to have started in the 1950s with the arrival in Britain of what was called the Poetry-and-Jazz Revival, exported here from the USA. There is not, nor has there been, a collection of poets who only perform and, for this reason, the term Performance Poets is but a grouping of convenience. By the early 1960s poetry was being performed in connection with jazz concerts. As jazz faded under the onslaught of rock music, the poetry stayed on its own. Poetry is still performed but not anything like as widely as it was. The best years were 1964 to 1974. The Metropolitan Poets are just as amorphous a grouping as the last and there have been poets who have drifted in and out of it. They are those who write of, for and by the city life. They do not look at the countryside, or hardly – and if they do, they see it from the townie's viewpoint. An example of this sort of poetry might be the earlier work of George MacBeth who writes a kind of poetry divorced from contact with the soil: compare this to his later books – say *Poems from Oby* (1982) – and one can see the change. The Irish Poets commenced with Seamus Heaney, as has been stated, and still go on strongly well into the 1980s. Concrete Poetry is old, perhaps older than any other traceable grouping, but because of its esotericism it has never become a major force: suffice to say that it began around 1924 but it started to be rediscovered or reborn in 1964 and was to become, for a short while, something to watch. It ceased again to be popular by the end of the decade and it has, once again, gone underground. Rock Poets came into being with The Beatles, The Rolling Stones and the birth of British R & B music in 1963. As a genre and as a poetic animal, the rock poet survives. The Martians landed in a book called *The Onion, Memory*, written by Craig Raine in 1978. They have not yet taken off and, indeed, seem not likely to for they have occupied, even colonised, British poetry and look to be set for a long occupation now that two of the three leading Martians have acquired editorships of established London publishers' lists.

The Outsiders as a category are those who have not sought to be members of schools or cliques. They have carried on regardless. They always have. They are timeless and they work for the art without bothering themselves with side-taking and faction-making. Perhaps it is in them – and those who belonged to cliques but have had the sense or courage to quit them – that the future hope lies.

In the final count, though, what is important is not the various pigeon-holes into which British poets can be slotted. To try to categorise them too closely is to give a false picture. The best poets do not keep to the sides of the poetic fences, nor do they sit on them. They leave the field for pastures new and start a fresh harvest going in newer, more fertile soil.

The groupings are only useful in the long run for two purposes. The first is that they tidy up a complex world so that the students and the academics have a board upon which to pin their thoughts. The second, more positive, purpose is to give poets a starting point in their careers and a shared experience with others from which they might learn or understand to discriminate. This book therefore acknowledges that these units exist, or existed, but that poetry seen through just this corridor of facts is misrepresented. What counts is the poets themselves.

2 THE POETS

Where to begin presents a quandary for there are so many criteria by which the poets may be placed upon the field of action. Degree of talent, fame or influence all offer themselves but, in order to try not to show that one poet is better than another, and to indicate that every poet has, either positively or negatively, contributed something towards the whole canvas of the art, I am going to start with one small collection of poets and work out from them, building up the grapevine in much the same way that the poets themselves did in the exciting years. Those mentioned first do not suggest a heightened position but simply a convenient point of entry.

As has already been mentioned, The Group came to its strength in the early 1960s and, by 1964, had produced a large number of the poets who were to set the scene in their own, individual ways. What was at first a random assemblage of young poets, joined only by their intelligence and ambition or fire, became an influential core, a kernel from which grew a number of major oaks. Alan Brownjohn, George MacBeth, Peter Porter, Edward Lucie Smith, Philip Hobsbaum, Martin Bell, Adrian Mitchell, Peter Redgrove and David Wevill all came from this stock. In later years came a new bunch – Frederick Grubb, Roger Garfitt, Jeremy Cartland, Anthony Howell, Fleur Adcock, John Carder Bush, Christopher Hampton and lesser lights – who continued the tradition of starting in a small school and working out to the big world at large. The masters, having learnt the lessons, taught them to others.

Alan Brownjohn seems an appropriate poet to commence with for he was fairly typical of the new breed: born of an ordinary background in south London, he was educated in state schools, rose to Oxford from where he moved upon graduating into school teaching, then lecturing to would-be school teachers and finally, having been made redundant by the closing of his college, into full-time writing. He is a methodical poet who works his muse well, is careful with the making of his poems and produces quiet, witty, human poems that caused poetry to take off for his subject matter is always accessible to the general public, or was in his earlier books. He writes of common experiences and places in poetic but down-to-earth terms. This was a trait learned at The Group, and when it later altered, The Poets' Workshop. Criticism was aimed towards poetry being still involved with the 'mystical arts of writing', but in a manner that did not promote esotericism. Poems were to be understood and enjoyed for their meanings and not their hidden, academic nuances. The Group was, in many ways, reacting against this trait that spawned the story of Robert Graves asking an Oxford student, purportedly in the mid-1950s, if she had enjoyed a poem and she replied that poetry wasn't for enjoyment but interpretation. As The Group began in 1955, in Cambridge, one can see that it was ripe to overcome such restrictive attitudes. With Brownjohn, the teachings of the group discussions had good effect. He wrote well and achieved a large public following with poems that touched a nerve of the times – a poem about going to see the last rabbit in England, travelling through a wilderness of concrete to get there; 'A202' about the road that sprawls out through his London birthplace; childhood poems about the war . . . the ease of understanding made these great themes and successful ones. Even when he was, in his quiet way, innovative, as with a poem that was a macabre, child's skipping-rhyme, Brownjohn was never beyond reach. Love, disappointment and a loss of the past recur in his poems, sometimes heightened by being placed into the mouths of fictitious characters whose lives became, in later books, a Brownjohn trademark: in his fifth book, *A Song of Good Life*, which was his first with Secker & Warburg after he was dumped by the closure of the Macmillan list, he goes so far as to include a verse play with these characters utilised to the full. Yet despite the seemingly simplistic line of his work where he seeks to present understandable poems, Brownjohn is a true poet who seeks to plumb human souls. The grand ideas of poetry that previous generations had given to readers in rhetoric and complex forms were now laid out in a manner that gave them a far greater impact. In this respect, Brownjohn was one of those who made the new poetry because he spurned the elitist ideas of cleverness and artiness and wrote in lines of truth, often self-mockingly and modestly, though always with passion. An example of his better work, 'William Empson at Aldermaston', from his first book, *The Railings*, shows a common theme written in poetic terms that highlighted the emotion, but didn't hide it in skilfully oblique waffle:

> This is our dead sea, once a guidebook heath.
> Left and right hands worked busily together
> A parliament of two,
> And there she stands:
>
> Twelve miles of cooling pipes; concrete and secret
> Warrens underground; clean little towers
> Clamped with strong ladders: red, brisk vans
> Which hurry round. . . .

This was poetry readers knew and it was the sort of thing they came to want and expect over the period from 1964. Ironically, Brownjohn tells of showing this poem, with its clever political puns on left and right and its horror of images of nuclear death at the carnival of the march to Aldermaston, to William Empson on a subsequent event, asking if he'd read it. Empson replied that he had and that he couldn't see it was very much about him and he went on marching. Obviously, the reference later on in the poem to the man with the 'Chinese beard' – for Empson had a distinctive beard that hung below his chin and grew on his neck (or seemed to) – was not one he liked or wanted to acknowledge. On the other hand, Empson might have been applying the wrong criteria to the poem: what his generation had wanted was convoluted literary-isms and Brownjohn avoided them. His later work did not achieve such efficient avoidance.

It was with the likes of Brownjohn that a trend was set towards writing poetry for the masses, not patronising them but seeking to emotionally and intellectually inform them, widen their lives or enrich their beings. It worked and it was for this reason that verse became so alive.

Another of The Group poets, as they came to be termed, was Martin Bell, now sadly dead. Bell produced only one major book, his *Collected Poems 1937–1966* (also Macmillan's production – that firm became almost The Group's exclusive publisher for a while) but it was to have its impact. He was the old man of his peers, born in 1918 when most of the others in his little circle were born around 1930. He worked as a teacher and university lecturer and became Gregory Fellow in Poetry at the University of Leeds in 1967. (He also wrote under the pen-name Titus Oates.) His verse was not so easily absorbed, but once it was, the reader was astounded by its wit and range. He wrote skittish poems about his fellow poets (in particular one to George MacBeth, that 'Harlequin glinter and Frisker!/What a gay air of "I'm Colonel Death!"/Sets twitching each end of his whisker'), carried out a dialogue with Corbière who was a strong influence on Bell, celebrated Eddie Cantor and took the micky out of The Group's meetings in a poem entitled 'Mr. Hobsbaum's Monday Evening Meeting', which ends

> Poems condemned must lose their bowels:
> Knit brows acclaim the execution –
> Expressive consonants, rich vowels
> By ladies trained in elocution.
>
> A slow breeze stirs a beard Lear-sized
> (Edward not King) to stringent rage:
> 'Not in the poem! It's not realized!
> 'An abstract statement on the page!'

It was Bell's poem, *Headmaster: Modern Style*, that made him famous, though, despite the fact that it was omitted from his selection in the third of the Penguin Modern Poets series. This is a deliciously bitter attack upon a pompous headmaster and, so rumour goes, it killed its subject who found a duplicated copy upon a staff-room table, went into a rage and suffered a consequential coronary. Everyone knows a headmaster and Bell's 'Conk' is typical. The poem contains some allusions that might be lost to the ignorant general reader, but most of the poem strikes home and the imagery at the end is common to all:

> Give him a surplice of toffee-paper and hymn-book leaves.
> Let bottle-tops stinking of yesterday's milk be gathered for
>   his medals.

To what extent should poetry follow this direction, this deliberate bending of the public's eye and ear towards something it knows of? One poet who was in The Group and who has written in both manners indicates firstly how well The Group lessons could be turned into effective mass-appreciated poetry and, secondly, what the result is if the readers are discounted. The poet in question is Peter Porter.

Porter was born in Brisbane, Australia and held a number of jobs before turning to live from his pen – he was variously a journalist, clerk, bookshop assistant, advertising copywriter and warehouseman. His first book was *Once Bitten, Twice Bitten*, published after he came to live in Britain, and it shows a skilful talent. These early poems were powerful and struck a cord in many readers, establishing Porter as a poet who tackled the harsher themes of modern life – 'Annotations of Auschwitz', 'Soliloquy at Potsdam' and 'Your Attention Please' have become standards. In the former, he writes of the concentration camp and draws the parallels between it and modern life in a London not quiet yet swinging:

> On Piccadilly underground I fall asleep –
> I shuffle with the naked to the steel door,
> Now I am only ten from the front – I wake up –
> We are past Gloucester Rd, I am not a Jew,
> But scratches web the ceiling of the train.

Whilst in the latter poem, Porter writes as the broadcaster giving the last broadcast to the nation after a nuclear attack has been launched upon it: to a nation aware of nuclear threat and conscious of the CND movement growing (interesting how Brownjohn was concerned with this, too: it was as if, at last, poets were the conscience of the people and were trying to show the truths in the magnificence of words, giving the ideas a terrible and new potency), this poem was rapidly popularised and spread. The irony and futility of the poem are just as valid today as in 1961 when it first appeared. Through his next two books, Porter retained this immediacy but, gradually, it slipped. His verse began to be heavily influenced by the classical writers and their ideas, Porter's love of Italy and obscurity. His poetry moved away from being about immediate ideas and concerns to a kind of poetic reverie wherein little was of direct application to most readers. Porter had become the academic poet, satisfied with pleasing himself and his poetry – and a few other poets – rather than his readers. Lines like

> Novelist by day,
> chucker-out in a brothel by night,
> the stoicism of prose
> and the garrulity,

paradigms
of the making of money

became more his stock-in-trade. He translated Martial to great effect, but the randiness of the Roman poet doesn't come through as readily as it might for Porter's language is too remote. (Martial's language, of course, wasn't remote in his day.) Ideas that could turn into fine poems that could go out to all concerned with reading get lost; Porter was, in the 1960s, a fine performing reader of his own work, but later that work must defy him. He loses the ability to make the language speak and mean. Porter has become a poet's poet, fallen into the trap of limiting his not inconsiderable vision to that which he exclusively shares with his contemporaries and equals. He has let his work and his skills down and now only writes for those with an education in poetics, not poetry.

On the other hand, George MacBeth, to whom Porter dedicates his third collection, has never let his poetry turn to the arty. He has been continually aware that poetry must meet the people on their terms, not on its own, although a clever manipulation does turn the people on to the poetry and so saves the latter from becoming a sop to poorer things. It is no surprise that MacBeth is so conscious of the need of people for poetry – he was so long in control of poetry broadcasting that he must have known the demands of the relationship; but they were demands he learned early on.

To list MacBeth's output is hard for he is one of the most prolific poets of the century and his work ranges over such a wide poetic countryside that it is, in retrospect, astonishing. He has written serious, emotional poetry about his dead parents, verse narratives, experimental sound and concrete poetry, flippant poems aimed at a mass entertainment audience, erotic poems, long poems with convoluted ideas relating to the war, rural poems of peace and quietude, poems of violence and poems of love and poems of autobiographical fragments. A look at the following lines, from assorted poems, shows the poet's incredible virtuosity:

> So this dead, middle-aged, middle-class man
> Killed by a mis-fired shell, and his wife
> Dead of cirrhosis, have left one son
> Aged nine, aged nineteen, aged twenty-six,
> Who has buried them both in a cardboard box.
>
> (of his parents' belongings in 'The Drawer')

One night we ate, and then lay down
   Under a slab of stone.
The Green was dark, and dog-shit stank
   Against my ankle-bone.
               ('Lovers')

       Gemmed with a dew
of morning tears,
       the weeping armadillo
has brought his shears:
       the droop-ear dog
and the lion came,
       dipping their long waists
to meet the drum.
            ('To a Slow Drum')

AN – AN CHI – CHI
AN – AN CHI – CHI

CHI – CHI AN – AN
CHI – CHI AN – AN

CHI – AN

CHI – AN CHI – AN CHI – AN CHI – AN CHI
AN – CHI AN – CHI AN – CHI AN
           ('Pavan for an Unborn Infanta')

The first day of this month I saw
Their active spearheads. Dry and raw

They rose from grass, beside my pond,
In a white stockade. And now, beyond

Far evergreens, more gather, and
Advance on dead ground. Dour they stand. . . .
           ('Snowdrops')

And consider this for a list of some of the subjects of some of
MacBeth's poems or sequences: a mother giant ant tells its baby of
the last man alive; a man who'd like to be a broad bean; the death
of a pet cat; Yuletide in the Norfolk broads; an escalation towards
nuclear warfare seen through the metaphor of two arguing
neighbours; gonorrhoea; a pastiche on 'true love' romance

stories; a parody of John Betjeman's work; being at his dying mother's bedside; the thoughts of a U-boat commander, a Spitfire pilot, a German soldier and a British tank officer in North Africa, all told as a book-length sequence of war stories in verse; vegetables and their characters; various animals including owls, dogs, cats and bats; a childhood memory of having the family house blitzed; saving sheep buried in snow drifts; an elegy to a Ferrari, now sold and then scrapped, and many, many more.

All this made MacBeth exceptionally well-known and popular: he has since the mid-1960s been much in demand for poetry performances and readings. His considerable skills with rhyme and metre made him easy to grip, fun to read and satisfying to understand. His complex poems came alongside simplistic ones. One entire book, *The Orlando Poems*, was a surreal, poetic romp, though disguised as the 'first disposable epic', and it brought down houses with laughter and can be seen now as a forerunner of the punk poets mentioned later, a link between the nonsense poetry of Edward Lear and the modernesque, bitter humour of post-Monty Python ideas. And this is the key because, for all his jokery and seriousness, for all his evident writing for a large audience, MacBeth is part of a growing tradition in British poetry which is a direct continuation of what poetry has been in all of its golden ages – that is, a means of public entertainment in the senses.

At its best verse provides an entertainment; but if it did only this, then perhaps it would be of less import. Fortunately it doesn't, and MacBeth's verse proves the point: poetry can be light or slight yet simultaneously it can instruct and explain the deeper coils of the human existence. It is rare that this is achieved all in one poem, but with poets like George MacBeth one has an artist who is seeking alliance of entertainment, immediate thrill and understanding but at the same time a deeper consideration of the underlying actions of human living. 'Poem for Breathing' is an example of MacBeth trying to marry entertainment with intellectual and deeper thought. This is not to say that he achieves the end of writing the Perfect, Far-Reaching Poem, but he goes a long way towards this with a piece that is simple yet deals with greater themes:

Trudging through drifts along the hedge, we
Probe at the flecked, white essence with sticks. Across
The hill field, mushroom-brown in
The sun, the mass of sheep trundle
As though on small wheels. With a jerk, the farmer

Speaks, quietly pleased. *Here's one.* And we
Hunch round while he digs. Dry snow flies like castor
    Sugar from the jabbing edge
Of the spade. The head rubs clear first, a
Yellow cone with eyes. The farmer leans, panting

    On the haft. *Will you grab him from the*
Front? I reach down, grope for greasy fur, rough, neat
    Ears. I grip at shoulders, while
He heaves at the coarse, hairy
Backside. With a clumsy lug, it's up, scrambling

    For a hold on the white, soft grass. It
Stares round, astonished to be alive. Then it
    Runs, like a rug on legs, to
Join the shy others. Ten dark little
Pellets of dung steam in the hole, where it lay

    Dumped, and sank in. *You have to probe with*
The pole along the line of the rest of the
    Hedge. They tend to be close. We
Probe, floundering in Wellingtons, breath
Rasping hard in the cold. The released one is

    All right. He has found his pen in the
Sun. I dig in the spade's thin haft, close to barbed
    Wire. Someone else speaks. *Here's*
Another. And it starts again. The
Rush to see, the leaning sense of hush, and the

    Snow-flutter as we grasp for the quick
Life buried in the ivory ground. *There were*
    Ninety eight, and I counted
Ninety five. That means one more. And I
Kneel to my spade, feeling the chill seep through my

    Boots. The sun burns dark. I imagine
The cold-worn ears, the legs bunched in the foetus
    Position for warmth. I smell
The feathery, stale white duvet, the
Hot air from the nostrils, burning upwards. And

    I crouch above the sheep, hunched in its
Briar bunk below the hedge. From the field, it
    Hears the bleat of its friends, their

Far joy. It feels only the cushions
Of frost on its frozen back. I breathe, slowly,

Trying to melt that hard-packed snow. I
Breathe, melting a little snow with my breath. If
Everyone in the whole
World would breathe here, it might help. Breathe
Here a little, as you read, it might still help.

Others associated with The Group achieved this wide vision to
other extents. Adrian Mitchell, whom one does not think of as a
'Group poet' to the same degree that one thinks of MacBeth,
Brownjohn or Porter as such, appeared in The Group anthology
before his first book of verse was published. His verse is
characterised, perhaps more than that of any of his contemporaries', by biting social comment and what seems at first somewhat
flippant but is soon seen to be an actual and very serious humour
that meets all the requirements of universal poetry. Mitchell
writes politically incisive material, outlines social wrongs and
evils, hits at the establishment values that he judges to be two-
sided and two-faced, writes to shock, awaken, alert and instruct.
His poetry is not always as trenchant as it might be; he can write
slightly and sloppily with a strong reliance upon rock music lyrics
and the techniques found in them.

Well North Riding girls taste of cedarwood
South Riding girls cook the wildest pud
East Riding girls melt your soul like lard
West Riding girls well they try bloody hard
North East West South side by side
What do you care so long as they ride
So ride your lover
Get on your little lover and ride

The above, from 'Hello Adrian', addressed to Adrian Henri, is a
lift-off from the rock standard, 'Ride Your Pony', which made the
hit parade sung by Lee Dorsey in 1961. But he can equally write
with a force few others can match.

Now, nobody likes manufacturing madness
But if we didn't make madness in bottles
We wouldn't know how to be sane.

He covers topics that might be *verboten* to many: the above comes
from a powerful attack upon chemical warfare factories. Mitchell

125

is a peacemaker and much of his work advocates peace, radical harmony and an end to other injustices and horrors. He writes critically but he writes also in the tongue of the people. He seeks to be understood but he uses poetry's bag of tricks to reach this criterion. Rhyme, imagery, obvious metaphor, alliteration, metrical forms – they all come into play. His muse is simple, direct and effective. No one can miss the point of lines such as

> The rich are rich because they fuck people about.
> They call it the Quality of Leadership
> And they have special school-machines producing
> Leaders to fuck people about

or those from the poem 'Fifteen Million Plastic Bags',

> I was walking in a government warehouse
> Where the daylight never goes.
> I saw fifteen million plastic bags
> Hanging in a thousand rows.
>
> Five million bags were six feet long
> Five million were five foot five
> Five million were stamped with Mickey Mouse
> And they came in a smaller size.
>
> . . . .
>
> So I've taken my bag from the hanger
> And I've pulled it over my head
> And I'll wait for the priest to zip it
> So the radiation won't spread

Many of the critics of this kind of poetry, with its relevance especially to events of the day – the above came out at a time when it was discovered that the government were indeed storing plastic sacks for just such a use – say that it cannot last, that it will date rapidly and therefore is sub-standard. This is piffle. Mitchell's collected poems appeared in 1982 and not a line of the book had lost its effect. (Has Milton dated? Hardly. Yet we live in a world where many of the values of *Paradise Lost* are long since lost.) It is not with a little humour that one considers one of Mitchell's 'literary' poems, *The Oxford Hysteria of English Poetry*. Long ago, he foresaw just what was happening in British verse, and had happened. The poem ends with the poet safe in his literary cocoon, having been

> . . . given the Chair of Comparative Ambiguity
> At Armpit University, Java.
> It didn't keep me busy,
> But it kept me quiet.
> It seemed like poetry had been safely tucked up for the
>   night.

Mitchell has never let complacency run away with his poetry. Poets are not special people who deserve to be cossetted and preserved but living people with a job to do for other living people. He reacts against the preciousness of verse and he wins.

Naturally, The Group has a large number of members who were not to become such important poets; some became well-known through small press or magazine publication, some published but one or two books and then faded from view, others became writers in other spheres of literature and some left poetry altogether for a non-literary world. Of this greater body of membership are such names as Paul Clarke, who was the chairman for some years of The Poets' Workshop and who contributed to its organisation but did no public verse at all; George Wightman who was a member for most of the entire span of Group/Workshop years but who published comparatively little verse, although he did co-edit a Penguin book of eighth- to tenth-century Arabic poetry: Tom Marshall, the Canadian poet; Taner Baybars who did write some very good poetry but who published only a few volumes and then seems to have ceased operating . . . the list is long.

However, some are worthy of more than a mention either for their poetry or for their contributions towards the activities of The Group and its subsequent sibling and, for ease of mention, The Group and The Poets' Workshop are here considered together.

One member who is remembered by all is Frederick Grubb who was a member (sometimes dissident) throughout at least a decade. He contributed a good deal to poetry. As a member of the reading sessions he was an adroit and sharp-minded critic with sound and clearly-defined objectives. He wanted to see verse that was intricate yet straightforward, unpretentious yet conscious of itself as both art and expression to others less endowed with poetic acumen. He was forcefully vociferous but never unthinking. He disliked the rule that no alcohol would be permitted at readings and he was known to bring – and ostentatiously consume – either sherry or a bottle of wine. He occasionally damned The Poets' Workshop by dubbing it the 'shirkshop' for he considered (rightly as it happens) that in the later years, it did start to dodge the issue of poetry and slip towards becoming an ego-board for those in attendance. His own poetry was thin on the published ground. He wrote but one book of verse that appeared in 1961 from Longmans. It was entitled *Title Deeds*, put into practice all Grubb's teachings and philosophies and it was a typical book for a participant in the coterie for it was one of poetry that sought to dispel the bunk of poetry but keep to its ideals of beauty and emotional expression. Grubb also wrote a critical book on liberalism in modern verse which was to anticipate critical attitudes to come. He was, for example, the first book critic to seriously consider Ted Hughes's animal poetry as well as the poetry of the then-developing Peter Porter.

Three poets who were members in the later years formed their own poetry unit, Sallaticum Poets. The three were Tony Buzan, Jeremy Cartland and John Carder Bush. They did not pass on to a world of poetry publishing as such. Buzan became famous as a teacher of study-aid learning systems whereas Jeremy Cartland, on the brink of what would surely have been a well-founded and talented poetic career, had his health and his future destroyed by an horrific episode in which his father was brutally murdered whilst on a camping holiday with his son in southern France, resulting in an inept and atrocious situation in which the French police accused Jeremy (who was himself seriously wounded by the unknown attackers) of the crime. John Carder Bush, like his friends, appeared in small press publications but he was the only one to publish a book of his poetry and that did not appear until 1980 and was a particularly interesting publication in which poetry was transposed with photographs. Entitled *Blink*, it had a foreword by Hugh Casson and, with the poems being experimentally printed upon onion skin, it looked very much like a book that might well have appeared twelve years previously. It was typical of the boundary-pushing, state-of-the-art book that might have come out in the swinging poetic 1960s. Bush has had another impact upon the world of poetry in that he is the elder brother of the rock singer, Kate Bush, and he was to influence her way of thinking in poetic terms that has culminated in a new direction of rock music writing, as is mentioned later on.

A young poet and undergraduate at Oxford, Roger Garfitt joined The Poets' Workshop in 1968. He was not to come under its considerable spell but he indeed did learn much from it and, when he subsequently moved towards being published by Carcanet, firstly in 1970 with a booklet entitled *Caught on Blue* and later with a full-length collection, *West of Elm* (1974), he was to prove to be an odd fish in their tank for his poetry does not follow

the dense poeticisings of that school of poets but is light, free and
beautiful as well as being accessible:

> Under the hissing trees
> the lank cattle,
> their coats greased with wet,
> roll the night's hay
> in cud through their molars,
> chewing over a week of thunder in June.

Garfitt has published little since his last volume and his
silence – to a small extent – bankrupts modern verse for his
style and type of poetic directness is much in demand these days.

Another poet who has vanished or faded from view is Anthony
Howell. Born in 1945, he attended meetings sporadically. He was
a figure always galvanised into action, a former ballet dancer with
the Royal Ballet and someone of strong opinions. His poetry was
attacked by other more staid figures as being complex, hard to
understand, thickly heavy reading. Looked at now, from the
perspective of fifteen years, it is itself quite staid and very typical
of its time with its untraditional structures that are really quite in
keeping with the past and its images that at the time rang new but
now are just another aspect of the age:

> Tonight, it may be night, a gale snores
> through the gargoyle's nostril on the outer wall;
> for all we know this morning, it is quite likely
> morning, I glance at my watch, prefer this hour
> to be dark – though it might well be morning. . . .

Howell's two books, *Inside the Castle* (1969) and *Imruil* (1970)
received wide critical notice and seemed to indicate that he was
going places. The talent, however, never materialised into
permanency.

Another Workshop poet, but one who has built up a considerable reputation, is Fleur Adcock. A New Zealander who came to
England much as Peter Porter did, she joined the circle in the
mid-1960s and published her first book in 1967. Called *Tigers*, it
was proof that a newcomer to The Poets' Workshop could
produce the goods when required. She had not been a member
through The Group years and this book was, in part, a vindication
of the possibilities of listening to the activities of what went on in
meetings. In truth, *Tigers* was her second book – another had
appeared in New Zealand in 1964 – but it was her first as a result
of the kind of 'poetic tutelage' one received through being with

the Brownjohns/MacBeths/Porters and those of that ilk. Since *Tigers*, she has published three other collections, a book of selected poems and a book of translations from the medieval Latin. Fleur Adcock's poetry is quiet, sometimes distinctly feminine, and often looks at common experience through fresh eyes, always using a language that all can enter. That her poetry is unremarkable partly marks it as coming from The Poets' Workshop, but that is not to be seen as condemnatory. She follows the adage that what can be clearly understood can be best appreciated which was one of the unwritten codes of the poets of that group. She writes typically in a poem called 'In the Dingle Peninsular' from her fifth book, *The Inner Harbour*, published in 1979:

> We give ten pence to the old woman
> and climb through nettles to the beehive hut.
> You've been before. You're showing me prehistory,
> ushering me into a stone cocoon.
> I finger the corbelled wall and squat against it
> bowing my back in submission to its curve.

Selected Poems was published in 1983 and contains poems that are taken from all the books plus a section of newer, unpublished ones. All of them show that Fleur Adcock has kept her talents at a standstill, writing similarly throughout her career. Her work is very much the product of The Poets' Workshop and its teachings and her poetry can fit easily into the 1960s. But it is not dated when read now and indicates that the best point to come from those lessons was the one that prevents the poetry from ageing. The same thing applies to the poetry of Christopher Hampton who did not publish a book of verse until 1980. Like Fleur Adcock, he writes in keeping with the tenets of his learning and his work too still stands up to scrutiny when seen even so long after The Poets' Workshop ceased to be influential.

Other poets in the slot are Roy Bennett, David Tribe, Margaret Owen, Rosemary Joseph and Shirley Toulson. All showed considerable promise. Roy Bennett, who was secretary of The Poets' Workshop for some years, wrote widely for small magazines but only produced one booklet and a book. Without knowing he was a member one can see the influence at work in his poetry – the stance of his work has not been able to escape the dictates of emotional responsibility, plain speaking, access of ideas and the demand of using the poem to raise the levels of experience and thought. Bennett, like Fleur Adcock, has visited the prehistoric Dingle buildings and he writes as follows, quite in a similar vein to her outlook:

> . . . Soon, wild rain
> and bleak Atlantic winds
> Knifed at their legs like nettles.
> Boulder on boulder, the hills
> Climbed into mist. And so
> They raised these hoops of stone.

Repetition of subject matter is not unknown in poets from The Poets' Workshop and this might be said to be one of their weaknesses, that the close meetings bred an incestuousness into their verse. But this is not really the truth. They simply saw things a similar way and yet were able to give everything that they did see a freshness and new light. Margaret Owen was present in *A Group Anthology*, but she did not continue to publish verse and is now a painter. David Tribe was a member of The Poets' Workshop, a man with a quirky sense of humour and a keen sense of critical awareness who was a major contributor to discussion. He was also a contributor of poetry that was high up in the standards ratings of his peers. He has disappeared without publishing save a few small press broadsides and a couple of magazine appearances. Rosemary Joseph was in the 1963 anthology too. She has published no book. Shirley Toulson was also in the book and was, in The Group days, Alan Brownjohn's wife. Her poetic talent was positive and she, like her contemporaries, had a well-defined sense of artistic direction. Her first publication was a booklet, *Shadows in an Orchard*, and she was fortunate enough to have been in the Scorpion Press list with that title, a publisher which has already been shown to have had a considerably important role in the furthering of poetry in the early 1960s. Yet, even with this much of a start, Shirley Toulson has gone on only to publish two more booklets of verse, both from the Keepsake Press. Her poetry deserves a wider audience but she has not been able to achieve it. She now lives as a writer of archaeological, countryside interest and travel books.

There were others who came and went, gave and took, learnt and argued and then disappeared. Even the first two leading lights have trod the path of poetic withdrawal.

It is a sad fact that the two founders of The Group have, in recent years, quit poetry, or at least quit publishing poetry. Philip Hobsbaum published a number of books in the period 1964–72. He was the first chairman of The Group and started the ball rolling in 1952. It is true to say that he was the father – or at least the midwife – of the rise of British poetry, helped by his co-writer and the next chairman, Edward Lucie-Smith. Hobsbaum's poetry never achieved the heights of that of his fellows. He was at best an adequate poet who wrote directly and didn't turn his work into clever trickeries, but on the other hand, he never let it liven up. Nevertheless, he wrote poetry within reach:

> That Sunday I was at classes, I remember,
> But we didn't do much work. The teachers all
> Were clustered in another room listening
> – We clustered round the door, listening –
> To tones which trembled as a life's work fell:
> 'That Note has not been received. . . . War is declared.'

Edward Lucie-Smith has become a revered art critic, but in the 1960s he was a live wire in poetry. His first book, *A Tropical Childhood*, preceded only by a Fantasy Press pamphlet in 1954, was published in 1961 and became a Poetry Book Society recommendation as well as winning the John Llewelyn Rhys Memorial Prize. Lucie-Smith was born in Jamaica in 1933; the title poem of this book was a powerful evocation of childhood memories seen from the distance of adulthood. This was a theme that quite a number of Group poets used. Once again, the poetry was direct and easy to understand:

> In the hot noons I heard the fusillade
> As soldiers on the range learnt how to kill,
> Used my toy microscope, whose lens arrayed
> The twenty rainbows in a parrot's quill.

Later books of his stood away from the everyday reader but still, at times, sparkled through and whilst they seldom turned to obscurity, they often became set pieces as opposed to actual poems springing from the core of the soul. They took on the sterility of exercises. And they did, when weakest, strike poor metal. Few can say that this is what modern verse should be and the lines come from a poem in Lucie-Smith's collection of 1974, *The Well-Wishers*:

> *The night is long, Lord, and sleep is yours.*

> Et venit iterum; et invenit eos dormientes; erant
> enim oculi eorum gravati.

> So let me sleep, Lord, Ah heavy word!

Where Lucie-Smith did contribute heavily and valuably to the scene was not, sadly, in his own poetry, but in his editing jobs. He produced a number of anthologies from a variety of publishers, all of which are books of immense interest and importance for, being in the swing of things, Lucie-Smith had his finger on a number of pulses and he knew poetry very well indeed. In 1970, he edited an anthology of science fiction verse for Rapp & Whiting called *Holding Your Eight Hands*. No one had attempted such a book before and although it did not become a bestseller, it did become a classic and included some major writers seen either in a new light or in a new form – poetry – as, for example, John Brunner was included along with Thomas M. Disch and Brian W. Aldiss, in the contents lists. Some new, 'young' poets were there too: D. M. Thomas and Brian Patten are published. He also edited a number of Penguin anthologies, of which the most important was *British Poetry since 1945*. Although it had gaps in its listing, it was by and large a book that did much for the spreading of knowledge into the development and growth of poetry in the period. What is more, it set up in the later pages some of the poets who were to become major influences and poets in the years to come, but who would never see the inside of a big London publisher's. Lucie-Smith gave a considerable boost to poetry in that he published some of the outsiders in a 'respectable' slot.

He had done this boosting to a far greater extent, however, in another direction three years previously, with the publishing of the anthology, *The Liverpool Scene*, also published by Rapp & Whiting. In this, Lucie-Smith collected together the poems of the Liverpool poets and a few others who lived and wrote on the periphery of the poetry world, where it met the rock music world. The book preceded the first of Brian Patten's collections – and Roger McGough's and Adrian Henri's. It was to be the first important anthology of its kind which contained and looked at the new direction that poetry was moving in. The last movement in verse was, through Lucie-Smith, setting up the next whilst at the same time not destroying itself. This was the natural progression of poets building into new poets, assisting and encouraging and promoting the next generation. This is what poetry should do, through its creators, and it is what it does not do nowadays, in the years after the big boom.

The Liverpool poets were a group of poets who came out of the cultural explosion in that city that had spawned and been spawned by The Beatles. They wrote for young people in simplistic forms but, like the best of their forerunners, they had something to say as well.

The core were a trio – some might say triumvirate – made up of Patten, McGough and Henri. Others that came into the arena included Pete Brown, Spike Hawkins and Henry Graham. The general characteristics of the poetry were slickness, witty humour and pungent comment. The background was working-class, the humour was obvious and the message was not so much the medium as the end punch in the gut. Puns and plagiarisms abounded:

> a three-piece suite for my sweet
> a frigidaire to keep frozen my despair
> a fitted carpet for the inside of my head
>> (Henry Graham; the first line puns a
>> Searchers tune, 'Sweets for my
>> sweet, Sugar for my honey. . . .')

> Take me back to Gotham city
>> Batman
> Take me where the girls are pretty
>> Batman

> All those damsels in distress
> Half un-dressed or even less
> The Batpill makes 'em all say Yes
>> Batman
>> (Adrian Henri, 'Batpoem')

> They've had a hard day
> helping clean up the town,
> Now they hang from the mantelpiece
> both upside down.

> A glass of warm blood
> and then straight up the stairs,
> Batman and Robin
> are saying their prayers.
>> (Roger McGough, 'Goodbat Nightman')

For several years, McGough, Henri and Patten held court and travelled the country either together or separately like a thriving poetry circus. McGough teamed up with others, amongst them Paul McCartney's brother, to form a quirky pop group called Scaffold that made it to the Top Ten three times and had a number 1 hit with a song entitled 'Lily the Pink', the words of which were a Liverpool poem. He has continued to write verse through to the 1980s, but much of his work is similar to his earlier material and, though that was good, one can have too much of it: McGough has also turned his talents to other writing. Adrian Henri has fallen into the same groove. His early work was exciting and original but he has continued through the years to produce a like style and content with no departures or progressions.

The person who has most benefited and developed of all the poets is Brian Patten. From the start, his poetry was different, both from his peers' work and that of anyone else being published. He wrote with a naive sophistication, a simple complexity, an innocent experience. He was enigmatic and wrote poems that were so odd as to be acceptable.

Along with the others, Patten wrote for a very young audience, just as the pop musicians aimed to please a similar following. Whether by design or accident, the Liverpool poets started to produce what young, intelligent teenagers wanted to read and hear. Riding on the wave of affluent youth, the poets pleased with a kind of verse that had not been seen before. It was directed at the young, but it reached all ears. What was more, it was strongly oral. The tradition of hearing poetry returned with a wham. (Patten produced several albums of himself reading his poetry and these sold, for poetry and against the rock music sales, surprisingly well.) The thing was this – the poetry did not try to be what it wasn't. It was truthful, plain-speaking and blunt. It was not without deeper meanings or emotions or intentions. But it did not try to get these across in some rhetorical manner, some holier-than-thou, I'm-a-poet way. It said and that was that. Thousands, tens of thousands listened. Poetry was at last something to take in, something that was out of the bounds of the lecture hall and classroom. (In fact, some poets felt so strongly about keeping poetry pure from the adulterations of education that they said as much – Adrian Mitchell's book, *For Beauty Douglas: Collected Poems 1953–79*, states clearly in the preface, 'None of the work in this book is to be used in connection with any examination whatsoever.' This is a huge pity, for this is the kind of poetry school pupils should be studying alongside others, in order to see what poetry really is. Luckily, Mitchell is now set for public examination.)

Brian Patten used the best words for a mass audience. He did not prostitute his art though and he did not patronise his listeners-cum-readers, nor did he lose his artistic integrity. What he did was what the best poets have always done, from Roman times onwards. He wanted to say something he believed in and he said it in a way his audience could take. It is important to note that Patten and his fellows admit a considerable debt of influence to Adrian Mitchell who, from his own poetic training, realised the value and importance of speaking to an audience in its own terminology and on its own terms.

Of the Liverpool poets, it was Brian Patten who became the leader and it is he who has maintained his artistic hold and development, leading his ideas and muse on from earlier work to later progressions. If the intention of art is always to be under change and flux then Patten's poetry is just that, for it is not a fixed point but always in motion.

The first book, *Little Johnny's Confession*, was hailed as a masterpiece when it appeared in 1967 from George Allen & Unwin, who did not (and do not) have a poetry list but did have an eye to the main chance. The poems became rapidly popular and were soon common currency in the poetic repertoire of many a poetry-lover, poet and youngster. The title poem had a blend of dream, violence and pathos in it: little Johnny gets a wartime, souvenir machine-gun belonging to his father and kills a number of his small enemies. He runs away, but the police are after him, asking

> 'Have you seen him?
> He is seven years old,
> likes Pluto, Mighty Mouse
> and Biffo the Bear,
> have you seen him, anywhere?'

In the end, the boy is trapped for the tracker dogs have his lollipops. The amalgam of innocence, bizarre situation, childhood daydreaming, pathos and tenderness were characteristic of Patten's work. And this was what the young audience wanted at a time when the world was violent, mazed with conflicting moralities and turning towards the hippy peace era. Patten was to the period 1967–74 what Ginsberg and the Beats had been to the previous generations – a poet who saw and exorcised inner feelings by saying it how it was. 'Little Johnny's Final Letter' to his mother, telling her he's grown up, is moving and sad but strangely optimistic and it reflected the growing independence of young people in the years of increasing wealth and freedom. 'Schoolboy' did likewise:

> Before playtime let us consider the possibilities
> of getting stoned on milk.
>
> . . . .

>   Poet dying of
> too much education, schoolgirls, examinations,
> canes that walk the nurseries of his wet dreams;
> satchels full of chewing gum: bad jokes, pencils;
> crude drawings performed in the name of art. Soon will
> come the Joyful Realisation in Mary's back kitchen
>   while mother's out.
> All this during chemistry.

This was the kind of poetry that broke down all barriers, that spoke with a common voice but with considerable artistic skill and control. Patten was a mouthpiece for a vast section of society. Not all of his poems were so straight and laid back, though. 'Somewhere Between Heaven and Woolworth's', which was to be superbly set to music on an album of Patten's poetry, was a sad song for loss of innocence and the void that filled many young hearts in the years of the 1960s. It was a poem with simple, relevant metaphors ('A girl dressed in denim/With boys dressed in lies') and a tone of the sub-culture that was the teenagers' world and which was to be the dominant culture soon afterwards. Patten's second volume, *Notes to The Hurrying Man*, outsold the first which, incidentally, was still in print in its umpteenth edition in 1980. Now more famous, he was aware of writing for an audience that would also hear him. The poems were punchy, direct and suggestive of peace: a bird finds its way into a cinema and smashes on to the screen where a love scene in a garden is taking place – it is killed; a small dragon is found in the woodshed, nesting and fading away in the coal . . . these were the kinds of ideas that Patten developed and made his own for it is true that no one could write as he did. He was a phenomenon and he was original and unique. More books followed, always with the theme of innocence and discovery as their centres yet, as he grew older, so did his poems. They were aimed now at an adult audience, one who could sense his feelings as they had when younger. Patten, if anything, was taking his audience into age with him. The girl at the teenage party became the civil servant who resigned his job to love and follow a concert violinist, and the dragon has metamorphosed into adaptations of Aesop's fabulous animals or a scientist's regeneration of the dodo. At all times, Patten's verse was a re-affirmation of faith in life, its coils and turns, its fates and its abundance of goodness, possibly tinged here and there with the beauty of melancholy. Yet this was what the mood of the times dictated and Patten caught it, either deliberately or by chance. He wrote what people understood about themselves and wanted to have explained. Not many have followed his example of marrying fine poetry with common experience, much to his good fortune. He had no rivals when he appeared upon the scene and now, in the 1980s, he is starting to affect a new generation of young poets who are not reliant for effect or expertise upon a university education or the slick practice taught by academic study in schools. The most important thing about Patten's work, which few thought possible on the publication of his first book, is that it has not dated in the least: the innocence of the 'flower power' years has not been lost in the subsequent years of social violence.

It was perhaps because of the fact that experience of life and living counted for so much in the work of these poets that Patten survived for so long and the others did not. True, they wrote from experience, but not so much of it. There was a flippancy to the work of the other two major Liverpudlians that made for a lack of depth. In their time, they were tremendously popular but this has not kept up although, even in the 1980s, there is a feeling that they still write relevantly. Penguin Books, who made such a splash (and income) from the Mersey Sound edition of the Penguin Modern Poets series, reissued this in 1983 along with a companion volume.

Roger McGough and Adrian Henri, so far as their poetry is concerned, cannot be far divided. They write in similar moulds of similar subject matter and it is sometimes hard to tell who wrote which poem when the authors' names are removed. What is more, it cannot be said that one is better than the other. It is not so. They are very much on a par and can be seen as twins in artistic terms.

Their poetry is typified by copious wordplayings, a somewhat stylised sense of wit and a certain sadness at times which manifests itself in the form of lost youth, sorry loves and the downs of life in cities, the latter especially concerning a loss of what can best be described as with-it-ness.

Frink, A Day in the Life of & Summer with Monika was McGough's first published work in book form, the Frink section being a short novel and the remainder poems. It was published in 1967 and was well received, setting McGough on to a literary career. He was born in 1937, the son of a Liverpool docker, and was educated in Liverpool and at the University of Hull from which he obtained a degree. He taught for some years at school level and then formed a group which – as has been mentioned – reached the hit parade. As well as being a singer and poet, he has also become a successful playwright.

The influence of lyric writing for music and the need that this dictates to be immediate in impact is evident in McGough's work:

monkia your soups getting cold
its cream of chicken too
why are you looking at me like that
why have your lips turned blue?

and

Do people who wave at trains
Wave at the driver, or at the train itself?
Or, do people who wave at trains
Wave at the passengers? Those hurtling strangers.
The unidentifiable flying faces?

There is little depth to the poetry, little literary subterfuge or
hidden innuendo, clever stuff for the students to get their teeth
into in essays. This is its charm. It has no pretensions and can be
likened to somewhat skilful word (and reader) manipulation,
stripping the thoughts to basics. Young people, in an age that
fought against academicism, took to this kind of poetry and, to
some extent, still do. But the poetry, because it dodges the main
issues of life explanation and only scratches the human surfaces,
is not of very great value. It does not expand consciousness so
much as embellish it or polish it up to a former gloss.
Throughout the 1970s McGough has continued to write like this.

And so has Adrian Henri. His work is wittier and less sad but it
is nevertheless the same pudding served on a different plate. The
oldest of the Liverpool poets (and not strictly a Liverpudlian as he
was born in Birkenhead, across the Mersey from Liverpool itself),
Henri was born in 1932, was university educated in fine arts and
subsequently took to teaching in a number of art colleges: he is
still a painter and an award-winning one at that. He came to
poetry partly through pop music, having formed a poetry-'n'-
music group in 1967, but he was not to achieve the acclaim of
McGough in the charts. His first book appeared in 1968, entitled
Tonight at Noon. Its quirky title and the style of his poetry caught
on and, as he was such a performer of his work in common with
Patten and McGough, he grew to heights of popularity in
university student literary circles as well as at club level. The
musical background of his life was a major influence, as was the
beat generation of American poets. One of his early poems,
'Adrian Henri's Talking After Christmas Blues', owes more to the
poetry of Ginsberg and the music of the British R & B movement
than it does to traditional, British verse. It begins:

Well I woke up this mornin' it was Christmas Day

And the birds were singing the night away
I saw my stocking lying on the chair
Looked right to the bottom but you weren't there
there was
>   apples
>   oranges
>   chocolates
>   . . . aftershave
– but no you.

Like McGough, Henri has gone on to playwriting and with
success but his verse, right through to the 1980s, is still of the old
sort. There has not been the change that occurred in Patten's
work: perhaps being the youngest, Patten was more amenable to
change than his peers.

Although not Liverpool poets, there are a few others who fit
the mould, poets whose work was influenced by rock music, the
general laxity of 'rules' in poetry that came about in the 1960s and
a desire to be free.

Pete Brown, who is mentioned later in this book because of his
rock music writing – he wrote a Top Twenty song called 'I Feel
Free' which expressed only too well the emotions of many –
came to temporary poetic prominence in the mid-1960s. He was
one of the first to earn his living from poetry readings, he co-
founded 'jazz poetry' with Mike Horovitz and he preceded The
Beatles in Liverpool with his beat-like poetry: indeed, it is highly
likely that John Lennon, the art student, came into much contact
with Brown and one might well cast a thought into how much
Brown might have reached through to the early Lennon for the
latter's weirder song lyrics from Beatles days are not dissimilar to
some of Brown's poetry. By the late 1970s, Brown was no longer
writing poetry but he was still working in the rock music world
with Jack Bruce and his own band. Pete Brown's first book was
published by Migrant Press in 1966, but his major collection
came out from Fulcrum Press in 1969, *Let 'Em Roll Kafka*. It was
not unlike the poetry of Henri and McGough in content, but
Brown is sharper and more penetrating in his views of humanity.
Poems like 'My Friend Made Love To Her Before Me', 'Sad is the
Man' (in memoriam for a prison suicide in 1965) and 'The
Confidence' show that Brown has a worthy talent. His poetry
does play with 'popular' image and metaphor, the kind one sees
in the simplistic end of the pop music spectrum, but this does not
lessen its impact:

When some unsteady hand

has emptied the last
champagne of night
from sky's flat windows
so high above streets
where we might walk. . . .

And, certainly, Brown's experimental sound poems were not only good, but funny and effective when printed as well. 'Swaqk/ Liverpool Soundpoem' shows this. It begins:

Forswaqk sqaukn torqt?
Adswaqktion rapt swaqts the bare
sswaqkts-round-the-face/cataswaqkt pulted gheists
and gehwinzsquakst vorpt im yovvel!

There is not a little e.e. cummings or James Joyce here.

Sadly, Brown was not to produce another trade collection and his slight but important contribution to the poetry of the times was like that of two others of his sphere, Spike Hawkins and Henry Graham.

Spike Hawkins's first and only major book was *The Lost Fire Brigade*, published by Fulcrum Press in 1968. He was well-known throughout the hippy/flower power in-set of the underground arts revolution. His poetry appeared in small magazines that came and went like mist in the mountains but they had readerships and he was also published in such big slots as *Encounter*, the *International Times* and the *Guardian*. His poetry was mainly made up of very short poems, epigrams or haiku-like fragments that were sometimes effective but often not. Like those mentioned above, he looked at the society in which he lived and saw its strengths and pits of despair and he wrote about them. The poems were very full of the kind of emotions that worried teenagers – lost love, ruined worlds, the state of things in a post-A-bomb culture. Drug imagery was not absent from the work of many of these poets, too. This was a phenomenon of the times: whether or not one smoked hashish or imbibed of other things, grass and dope images could not be missed. They impinged themselves upon everyone (especially after the release of The Beatles' *Sergeant Pepper's Lonely Hearts Club Band* album in 1967), and Spike Hawkins's work was not left out. One poem of his, 'grass out of voice', is a good example:

My machine sits in front of me. I am alone on a beach. Soon she will come to me in a standing door. Oh why do her hands and arms lie helpless at her sides. It is the

trembling earth and the flying stones that lie about us. If I
say to her, she stares as I kick in the waters of her
eyes. . . .

Henry Graham shares a background with Adrian Henri. He is
an artist who also wrote poetry in the late 1960s and early 1970s
but, unlike Henri, he has not broached the poetry scene since.
His first book, *Good Luck To You Kafka/You'll Need It Boss*, was well
reviewed and his second, *Passport to Earth*, published in 1971,
drew such comments as his earlier book had done, including one
from Edwin Brock, the poet of wit and sensibility, which stated
that Henry Graham's poetry 'differs from the others by coming
out of his head and being a good deal more subtle than Ee-Aye-
Adio'. Being an artist, Graham wrote in visual imagery but he
also used this to comment upon the world we all saw in the
second half of the 1960s, a world of good living, mass media, an
expanding economy, permissiveness, personal freedom and the
Vietnam War. In one poem, *Poems of Love and Hate*, from his
second book, Graham shows just what he could do when the idea
struck.

A man and wife, newly wed, pose
for a photograph with the decapitated
body of an Asiatic terrorist, newly dead.
He has a massive erection, from which
they avert their eyes trying to smile,
in spite of the inconvenience of the blood
on his spats and the train of her dress.

Although his poems were not short and succinct like many of
Brown's and Hawkins's, Henry Graham's work fits in with theirs
and that of the Liverpool Poets proper because he does as they do
in linking intense feelings of how life is (or was then) with almost
dispassionate attention and a throwaway tone. Interestingly,
both Henri and Graham taught at Liverpool College of Art at the
turn of the 1960s and into the 1970s. Art colleges at that time were
famous for their avant garde approach to all things and they
spurned, as art colleges usually have throughout the ages, the
limitations and limitings of a strict, academic education. They
looked for expression of originality more than expression of ideas
within an excepted framework and, with the age being one of flux
and violence and the all-powerful validity of personal experience,
it is hardly surprising that they produced, at least so far as poetry
goes, the work that they did and the environment that could
nurture it.

Having mentioned experience, violence and the ills of an introspective academic training, one comes almost automatically to the poet who has had the most influence upon large sectors of British verse since the appearance of his first book.

Ted Hughes has had a good number of critical tomes appear on his work in the second half of the 1970s. Some are excellent and some very sketchy and dubious indeed. All do him a disservice for they drag his work into the eye of the course student rather than the life student. Of all the poets of the period, Hughes is the one who most appears to work against the demands of a considerable academic training. He received his at Pembroke College, Cambridge where, it is important to note, he avoided reading for a degree in English.

Born in West Yorkshire in August 1930, in the village of Mytholmroyd, Ted Hughes was brought up in the rugged surroundings of the Pennines and its deep, forbidding valleys. The area was rugged not just for its geography but also for its ways of life, rooted firmly in the industrial heartland of the north where the mills and factories cringed in the valleys and the harsh rock mountains and moors, with their scrubby moorland farms, towering over them, indicated that the alternative life was little less difficult. The omnipresent power of nature and man in conflict was something that shaped Hughes's work and continues to do so to this day. Through him, it also affects much of modern British poetry and especially that which was written between, roughly, 1968 and 1974.

Those who require a deeper look at Hughes's work need to move on from this book where he is introduced merely as a figure in an entire scene of the art, seeking greater insights in the specialist books dedicated to Hughes's poetry. The reason he is looked at here is to understand how he has done so much towards the livening up of British verse and the helping of it along a path that took it towards the considerable popularity that it held. Noticeably in recent years, where Hughes's influence has tended to dwindle a bit, British poetry has slumped into complacent states of moribundity.

From the very start, Ted Hughes was writing poetry that was well within the reach of all readers, educated or otherwise, if only they were prepared to share in the poem. There was no clever magic to the work, just a skilful observance of realities and a writing of these with a sense of diction that was fresh and untapped to date. As the post-war years developed into a time of considerable social change and innovation, as violence crept increasingly upon society and the awareness of nature became more positive, so Hughes became more appreciated, writing as he was from his roots with reference to the violent aspects of the world and those who lived upon it. His first book, *The Hawk in the Rain*, came as a bombshell upon the poetry world. Published in 1957, it was to set a norm – or, rather, a pinnacle – towards which many others strove, often in vain. His ear for sound and his sense of diction amazed many. Of a parrot, a macaw, he wrote:

> In a cage of wire-ribs
> The size of a man's head, the macaw bristles in a staring
> Combustion, suffers the stoking devils of his eyes.

This type of writing was to set the way. It was powerful and taut, it looked at ordinary objects in a mystical way, it used the rhythm of spoken words for its force, it was controlled and yet it was wide as a field and it was understood. In the same book, Hughes published 'The Thought-Fox', a poem in which a fox is a poem writing itself across the page in a night room. This relationship of art and life was the key to the best of British poetry to come. The opening two verses of the poem were to become almost a mini-manifesto for those poets who were to rise to prominence during the 1960s and early 1970s:

> I imagine this midnight moment's forest:
> Something else is alive
> Beside the clock's loneliness
> And this blank page where my fingers move.
>
> Through the window I see no star:
> Something more near
> Though deeper within darkness
> Is entering the loneliness. . . .

The close personal relationship that exists between the poet, his poetry and the reader is central to this poem of Hughes's and it was to be as important to all those poets who sought to write in the years that followed not so much this first book of Hughes's verse but his second and third collections, *Lupercal* (1960) and *Wodwo* (1967). In the interim gap of seven years, much happened in British poetry but Hughes was not to publish a book in that time. His influence and reputation were already substantial and he more or less sat back from what was in evolution, appearing only in magazines and with other books that were either on the writing of poetry or were aimed specifically at children rather than a wider audience.

Lupercal set a mood and a stance that was already begun in the first book. It consolidated this and it enhanced the target area that others were now aiming at. 'Hawk Roosting', 'View of a Pig', 'Pike' and 'Relic' all come from this book and have become so well known now through umpteen anthologisings that they are almost entire poem-clichés. They are, however, still more than worthy of partial quotation at least not simply because they are so astoundingly good but also for what they do: they take reality and, if anything, make it all the more real by extending and applying the experiencing of this reality to the full through the abilities of language.

> The pig lay on a barrow dead.
> It weighed, they said, as much as three men.
> Its eyes closed, pink white eyelashes.
> Its trotters stuck straight out.
>
> . . . .
>
> They chop a half-moon clean out.
> They eat cinders, dead cats.
>
> Distinctions and admirations such
> As this one was long finished with.
> I stared at it a long time. They were going to scald it,
> Scald it and scour it like a doorstep.
> > ('View of a Pig')
>
> I found this jawbone at the sea's edge:
> There, crabs, dogfish, broken by the breakers or tossed
> To flap for half an hour and turn to a crust
> Continue the beginning.
> > ('Relic')
>
> I sit in the top of the wood, my eyes closed.
> Inaction, no falsifying dream
> Between my hooked head and hooked feet:
> Or in sleep rehearse perfect kills and eat.
> > ('Hawk Roosting')

This is the best of modern poetry and few British poets can equal it. It has masters and equals only in Eastern Europe and the USA where the restrictions of stolid learning upon language have been reduced to a mere whim. In such places, poets deal in such similar realities rather than self-conscious and introspective meanderings as will appear later in this book. Hughes's poems show a mind at work that is a true bridge between the intellect, the normalities of reality and the inner souls of men.

Wodwo carried this further. The poems in this book showed an increasing craftsmanship over earlier volumes and, if anything, indicated a new awareness of the boundaries to which language could be pushed. What is more, the poems show an awareness of the poem as an oral performance rather than just a cold print on the page. Hughes was, by the mid-1960s and with his solid reputation, much sought after for readings and he toured Britain and overseas reading his work and talking about it, something that he ceased to do in the mid-1970s on anything like the same scale – it is interesting to note that from that time onwards, his verse was becoming denser and less attuned to the ear, more the inner mind.

Poems such as 'Wino', 'Gnat-Psalm' and the title poem show this conscious commanding held by the voice:

> Grape is my mulatto mother
> In this frozen whited country. Her veined interior
> Hangs hot open for me to re-enter

and

> When the gnats dance at evening
> Scribbling on the air, sparring sparely,
> Scrambling their crazy lexicon,
> Shuffling their dumb Cabala,
> Under leaf shadow.

Wodwo itself was to become one of Hughes's most powerful early poems for the voice, he reading it with an awesome violence and mystical prowess that haunts anyone today who ever heard it:

> What am I doing here in mid-air? Why do I find
> this frog so interesting as I inspect its most secret
> interior and make it my own? Do these weeds
> know me and name me to each other have they
> seen me before, do I fit in their world?

This book also contains a number of short stories, rich with violence and poetic concept, including the now-famous 'Sunday', 'The Rain Horse' and 'The Harvesting' which are less prose pieces than extended prose poems.

By the time *Wodwo* appeared, Hughes was a central figure in the whole of British poetry. He had obtained this position not only through the excellence of his books but also through his considerable performance reputation, and it was to performance that Hughes's next work turned, being as it was for that as much as if not more so than for the page.

Ted Hughes's voice is rich, deep, very powerful and has a presence that one would normally associate with an international actor. He has a strong but not overpowering West Yorkshire accent which is both musical and lyrical without being somehow earthy and basic. It was this that made him so very popular with a wider than average poetry audience. Many who would not know poetry normally knew of him; in the true sense of the poet and in the best tradition of the times, he spread his work outside the confines of poetry in the normal context – that is the classroom, lecture room and tiny poetry society. Through his public appearance and poetic personality, Hughes did a huge service for poetry for he showed that it was possible to write intelligently and intellectually without the trappings of elitism and artistic thought in the narrowing sense; because he was such an important poet to the poets as well as the public, he influenced the movement towards the wider popularising of poetry, albeit unintentionally or subconsciously. The spreading of poetry was due not only to his writings but also to his presentation in the person. The public saw that poetry was alive, vital and, more importantly, that it had something to do with them. This is not to say that he made it as popular as football or as easily understood as cricket, but he did give it a fillip that none other had done. To be fair, though, others were riding the bandwagon with him and gave ballast to the cart.

When Hughes's seminal book, *Crow*, was published in 1970 (and subsequently republished and lengthened two years later – it has reprinted many times since) it took both the poetry and the ordinary world by storm. It sold as many copies as a successful novel. It was poetry for performance. It relied for its power not only on its subject matter but also on the way in which it was to be presented. Interestingly – and this can happen with the best poets and in many ways is a mark of their superbness – it was a 'deep' book concerned with basic and primeval emotions and concepts and yet it sold and was understood by a big public. To know it truly, one has to hear it and, luckily, there is an album record of the book available read by Hughes himself. However, just seeing the poems or fragments of them on the page gives more than an indication of their possibilities and astonishing force:

There was a boy was Oedipus
   Stuck in his Mummy's belly
His Daddy'd walled the exit up
   He was a horrible fella
             Mama   Mama

You stay in there his daddy cried
   Because a Dickybird
Has told the world when you get born
   You'll treat me like a turd
            Mama   Mama

The violence was appropriate to the world. The primitivity of the poems was suitable to the times. Hughes was writing for performance, for everyman, for the historical context of his life in the early 1970s. Crow, the archetypal black angel, creator of chaos and order, adversary of God yet God himself, was a figment of the way things were. In the poem 'Examination at the Womb-door', one has lines that were deeply significant yet accessible to poetically untrained readers.

Who is stronger than hope? *Death.*
Who is stronger than the will? *Death.*
Stronger than love? *Death.*
Stronger than life? *Death.*

But who is stronger than death?
                   Me, evidently.

Pass, Crow.

In a world torn by the Vietnam War, increasing nuclear arms build-ups and the beginning of the New Decade after those exciting 1960s, a decade that was very soon to see oil prices rocket and recession commence, these poems meant something and did not require a learned mind to unravel their message.

Poetry should never need a trained mind in order to be understood. It must have a free mind, an open mind that is ready to accept outside stimulation without having to muddle through obscure constructions to get at its core. This does not exclude skill and metaphor, allusion and hidden directions. What it demands though is a key to the door to these, that the meaning beyond is enriched by the skills of the poetic craft and not camouflaged or hidden by them.

Since *Crow* was first published, Ted Hughes has written other verse books. Two were distinctly poets' volumes that were not within the easy reach of the average reader – *Gaudete* was a poem that started life as a film scenario but somehow translated itself on to the page. It is rich in visual images and has a complex plot, being not so much a set of poems as a long, narrative poem about a priest who is kidnapped by the dark powers, replicated and returned to the earth to minister as he sees fit. The climax is when the changeling is faced by the original and the powers of the occult are balanced. The narrative is well told, but the concepts behind the poem are not so readily seen. And the whole is not a performance sequence as is not the other volume, which came out the following year (1978), *Cave Birds*, sub-titled 'an alchemical cave drama', and which had superb and malevolent line drawings by Leonard Baskin with whom Hughes was increasingly working in artistic partnership. This is a strange and darkly mysterious sequence which is even more complex than *Gaudete* in its origins. The poetry is strong stuff indeed, but the book was not a popular seller. It went over the heads of most of Hughes's followers:

> Big terror descends.
>
> A drumming glare, a flickering face of flames.
>
> Something separates into a signal,
> Plaintive, a filament of incandescence,
>
> As it were a hair.
>
> In the maelstrom's eye,
> In the core of the brimming heaven-blossom,
> Under the tightening whorl of plumes, a mote
> Scalds in dew.

It is exceptional poetry but it is narrowed to the few who understand its implications.

However, Hughes has not lost his ability to create deeply moving and sensed poems that all could enter and replenish the inner man from for, after *Crow* and before *Gaudete*, Hughes published *Season Songs*. This, too, was a Baskin collaboration and consisted of twenty-eight nature poems arranged according to the seasons and based upon the poet's farming experiences in Devon. The poems set a new light burning in modern British verse, one that tended towards simplicity of expression but not at the expense of considerable emotive force:

> The crocuses are too naked. Space shakes them.
> They remind you the North Sky is one vast hole

> With black space blowing out of it
> And that you too are being worn thin
> By the blowing atoms of decomposed stars.

Where *Cave Birds* and *Gaudete* extended the directions of the *Crow* poems, the other poems took further the aims of the earlier poetry, to explain life and the world in poetic terms. Hughes's move into a rurality that was always in his mind was what people wanted to read and did. *Remains of Elmet* (with photographs by Fay Godwin) and *Moortown* show this development and, in 1981, *Under The North Star* furthered it, although Hughes claims that the latter is more a book for children for it had its conception as a collection for a young girl.

Remains of Elmet deals with the West Yorkshire landscape of his childhood – Elmet was the ancient kingdom of the area and one of the last to fall to Roman occupation. Liberally spliced with outstanding photographs, the book has been a success for it brings verse and the English starkness of landscape together and in a way all can understand. *Moortown* is, more than any other of Hughes's books, the one that appeals to all tastes. It holds rurally inspired poems like *Tractor* and *Dehorning*; it contains *Crow*-like poems in the sequence earlier published as a limited edition only, *Prometheus On His Crag*; it has a series of poems under the title *Earth-numb* that are for the general reader and includes another sequence previously hard to come across, *Orts*; finally it has the mystical sequence of poems, *Adam and The Sacred Nine*. The subject matter of the poems is a pot-pourri in many ways. The rural poems go with the complex which in turn sit next to such poems as 'A Motorbike', based upon a machine that Hughes's elder brother had had through the war years, an old BSA. It was bought by a young man returned from the war and bored by the slowness of peace, who

> A week later, astride it, before dawn,
> A frosty, misty morning,
> He escaped
>
> Into a telegraph pole
> On the long straight west of Swinton.

This is a poetry that people understand. It does not shirk its responsibility to enlighten and enrich, to evaluate experience, but it does not at the same time try to set itself up as grandiose. It is matter of fact.

In 1983, Hughes published what is most likely his finest book of work associated directly with nature and natural forces and magic, *River*. Like *Remains of Elmet*, it was a sequence of poems that appeared accompanied by full colour plate photographs by Peter Keen, but in this new volume the marriage of photographer and poet is complete: in the former alliance of this sort, one sensed that Hughes's work was not completely in artistic sympathy with the camera.

As the title suggests, the poems are about rivers – the life around them, the act of fishing (Hughes is an expert trout and salmon fly-fisherman), the animals and the atmosphere. They are mostly about English rivers, with a few exceptions, and they are all exceptional. Hughes's ability to join the commonplace with the beautiful comes to a climax in the book, which is not a book for fishermen or water-lovers but for anyone who seeks re-affirmation of the power of natural forces in an age of technological 'marvels' and believes in the positivity of existence and the optimism that nature promises for the future. Consider the opening lines of 'That Morning':

> We came where the salmon were so many,
> So steady, so spaced, so far-aimed
> On their inner map, England could add
>
> Only the sooty twilight of South Yorkshire
> Hung with the drumming drift of Lancasters
> Till the world had seemed capsizing slowly.

Or the following, of an 80-year-old fisherman:

> He holds
> The loom of many rivers.
> An old rowan now, arthritic, mossed,
> Indifferent to man, roots for grave.
>
> He's watching the Blackwater
> Through Hotel glass. Estuary nets
> Empty. The river fishless. He's a trophy
> Of the Great Days – his wrinkles, his tweeds,
>
> And that armchair. And the Tussaud stillness.
> Probably he's being tossed
> Across a Loch on Harris.

This is remarkable poetry, lines that speak of wonder and yet speak of it to anyone and everyone. It does what good poetry should do and that is reincarnate experience and emotion on a grand scale so that others, unconnected with the original impulse or stimulus, might share in the feelings and their implications.

Ted Hughes is such a good poet not because he writes poetically but because he writes with artistic integrity for the universe of people, widening reality in their terms but on his poetic ground. He raises consciousness, excites life and, by doing so, he achieves what all poets should seek. He goes beyond the work of others because he plumbs souls through life study, the anthropologist in him playing off.

Perhaps partly because of his accessibility and wide scope of vision and partly because of his justified fame, Hughes is now starting, like many others before him, to suffer from the onslaught of the academics. Recent years have seen a spate of 'studies' appear on the market, catering for every level from school examination candidates' needs to the upper end of the PhD students fumbling for esotericism.

Complexity of academic 'research' into poetry can only do it harm. Much of what is extolled as masterful imagination and the activity of genius on the part of the poet is really just a skilfully contrived interpretation of what was never intended by the artist in the first place. Once this kind of cleverness is applied to the poet, it begins to drive interest away from his work for a series of barriers are then set up between the verse and the reader who, for his part, has his mind turned away from the poem as a poem into seeing the poem as an extension of the educational system that seeks to insert a wedge between the creation of art and the understanding and appreciation of it.

Most poets to whom this fate occurs are able either to ignore it or accept it with a pinch of salt. However, they are often affected by it at the artistic level, finding themselves driven into the depths of the textbook and away from the readers who really want to see poetry. A comparison may be drawn with those who visit national art galleries who don't go there to criticise the paintings, but to enjoy them or at least react to them. They are spared the infiltration of 'art criticism' and its phoney language. With the poetry book, it is different: quite why is hard to understand. There is something, possibly instilled by the ways in which literature is taught, that has people 'studying' poetry where they would not do so to music, visual arts and even prose writings.

Once critical books that are overloaded with esotericisms and convoluted interpretations (often presented as deliberations and finite ideas emanating from the poet concerned) are accepted and read, then the public who fall into their reaches start to see that the poetry is really a con-game, a means of disguising thoughts, hiding truths, a covering up of simplicities with wordy gimmicks, and they react by leaving well alone. Who wants to read Shakespeare only to be thinking all the way through just what King Lear's motivation really was in seeking to demand allegiances of love from his daughters? Enough that he did and we should sit back and let the literature happen, not try to discover why it does what it does. When one thinks of it at its most basic, why did Shakespeare write plays? To appear on the examination syllabus four hundred years later? No: in truth, he wrote plays because he enjoyed it, he liked the theatre, he found he was able to create and the money he earned paid for his board and lodging. He had the integrity not to write garbage, with a few exceptions of course, but he did not set out to confound his audience or provide a living for generations of critical interpreters.

Hughes is like this, as are many of his peers. He does not set out to write verse that will puzzle, but poetry that will explain – quite the opposite – and he also tries to make a living at it. It is the academic leech, riding on his skin, that has to build up the aura of arabesques in order to live, as well, feeding on the poetic blood.

The question now is to wonder if Ted Hughes, or his poetry, will be affected by the critical meanderings that are being published and no doubt will increase to greater proportions as the years pass. Will essays that deal with oriental mythology in *Wodwo*, or speculate upon the need for another essay to be written on the relationship between *Crow* and children's literature, affect matters? Or will they be ignored as the rantings of professors who don't create but live in the scientific-mind end of the literary world, an irony when one considers that Hughes has condemned the scientific analysis approach to life and, at second hand therefore, to his life-giving poetry?

Of course, there are studies of Hughes's work that are beneficial in that they explain without seeking to embellish upon the original. *The Art of Ted Hughes* is one such book, written by Keith Sagar and published, updated, in 1978. This tries not to go over the top, though in places it does. A more recent book (strangely edited by Sagar), *The Achievement of Ted Hughes* (1983), really does a major disservice to the poet. It contains the most obscure stuff.

Most likely, Hughes will be unaffected by this university-inspired seeking to reduce his work to the level of the lecture room. He looks at it all with a humorous, mild detachment. Yet it remains that poets in general, as they become better-known, face this ridiculous side of their art. But Ted Hughes shows, and will continue to show, all of life in his work, or as much of it as he wants to see and illustrate. Many other poets half achieve this.

One such is the poet, editor and critic Jon Silkin. He has been around since the mid-1950s when his first collection, *The Peaceable Kingdom*, was published. In this collection and his subsequent ones – his next appeared in 1958 and 1961 – there are poems that founded his reputation. They are moving poems that often speak of death and one, 'Death of a Son', is probably the most sad and moving elegiac poem of this century. Throughout his poetic career, Silkin has written poems that uplift the mind but he has also written some very heavy material indeed. Again, it is skilful and controlled, but it is narrow and does not either do his talent justice or further the reaches of poetry. In short, it is his more openly made poems by which he will be remembered.

> I am a form disgorged; magma's forms pelt
> their splintered minerology. The souls
> of angels suck the rubied tracts of blood.
> Crystals turn ichor in the divine mouth.
>
> But gentle rains discharge their benefacts.

These are not memorable lines. They are obtuse and obscure, even when seen in context in a poem called 'The Deformation', a poem that is religious but unsatisfactory because of its obscurity.

What is it that makes poets go to these extremes of statement, these astoundingly narrow confines of art? It seems foolish when one considers that these people have already learned the lesson to be gained from writing with accessibility. Silkin knows that he is famous. He knows also that he is famous for his poetry that is read by many for whom he has opened the many doors of the mind. Yet he writes poetry of recent years that even his peers have to pore over. This seems like madness.

At this point, one has to wonder what it is that has brought about this tendency in recent years towards the obscure and the complex, what it is that has forced so many excellent poets to feel that it is necessary for them to involve themselves and their poetry in such a mire and give added credibility to the statement that the best way to disperse an English mob is to mention the word poetry.

The cause has several roots.

Firstly, the blame must lie with the education system and the teaching of literature at all levels which demands an analytical approach to the writers' arts rather than an intuitive or emotional one. A glance at the manner with which poets were presented with poetry in school and university shows that the prime concern of the teacher was not the act of artistic creation but the evolution of that, at second hand, which might be interpreted from the original. Poetry becomes not a life art but a sort of parlour game in which the idea is to guess at what might be meant rather than what was.

Thus it is that the student does not try to see why a poet wrote of a certain subject, only what it was that he produced and what this might imply in terms of academic interest. In other words, the implication of a poem is more important than its reason. With this being the basis of literature teaching, one can hardly be surprised that poets write with this partly (or totally) in mind. They are, therefore, writing for the system, not the human. (Interestingly, in the USA, where the teaching system as regards literature is very different, the poets who have gone through the mill do not become academical, but continue to write outside the traditions of the classroom which are limiting.)

Secondly, poets are basically selfish, more so than artists are generally. They believe that their art is precious and that it is up to the reader to rise to the poet's level, rather than that the poet should climb down or seek to raise up the reader himself.

Quite why this should be is a puzzle and one can only suggest an answer or two: that it is traditional, that the poet was always someone special; that it is related to the fact that poetry is by definition a very personal art form; that poetry is itself a narrow art form, which some poets regard as being so though they have to be misguided, and has a certain exclusivity about it; that poetry is simply snobbish.

Thirdly, poets enjoy playing games. After all, there is a game quality to poetry making, with its concerns for tight structure, image and diction. Additionally, poetry having its roots in prayers, spells and incantations, it seems only natural that it should retain some degree of obscurity. Of course, this is to the detriment of the root, too: prayers were meant to be understood by all the supplicants.

Fourthly, many poets have a vision. Poetry is visionary. When the receiver of the vision has had his mind stultified by academic disciplines though, he is unable to interpret the visions adequately and must revert to the only means of interpretation at his command, that of the lecture hall and tutorial room. The poet whose vision is grand and universal is therefore hog-tied by his 'training' before he begins. He is left with only the resources of his education as a means with which to explain what he sees.

This suggests that the better poet is the one who refuses to accept the restraints of education. A look through modern poetry shows this to be the case for many of the more popular poets, those who reach their audiences, have either shunned their schooling or not had it in the first place.

Despite this, though, I believe that some poets become academic through a perversity of nature only linked to the education that they have received. I cannot believe that poets do not realise what they are doing when they write in such a way as to know others will have a hard time unscrambling what it is they are penning. Others are academic because they want to be: they are not interested in expanding awareness but simply with plying the trade they know best – introspection. These people, in my mind, are not poets but mere continuers of the academic tradition.

Poets believe themselves immune to common criticism and they see themselves as 'special'. With this frame of mind, what else can they do but be self-indulgent and if this involves complicated writing which requires a code to break it down, then so be it.

In the long run, however, they will suffer for it. Their art will become even more obscure, even more suited for the eyes of specialist students. They may well have started off writing so that all might learn from their visions but this has gradually dispersed into material for dissection and not revelation.

The poets that follow in the next few pages have done this; they have begun by building firm reputations as poets and subsequently shot themselves down in flames of verbosity, self-indulgence or simply poor writing. It is not a series of cases where the muses have fled their masters for whatever reasons but just ones in which the masters have corrupted the magic of poetry in their souls and, to some extent, they have prostituted their talents.

Hugo Williams is one such. In 1965, at the age of 23, he was one of the new poets of the 1960s who was driving towards the new directions. His first book was well received and justly so. The first volume, *Symptoms of Loss*, was followed in 1970 by a second collection, *Sugar Daddy*. This was a highly accomplished book with poems that were moving, intense but not complicated. Some were short, astringent pieces that somehow summed up the mood of the times for which they were written: all were of the type that the public could take up and enjoy, both on the page and in the ear as well as in the inner ear of the mind.

'I am in a little saloon
Drinking lemon water

And thinking of many things
And I am sorry. . . .'

But what's the good of that my love,
If we are strung out like runners,
Losing ground?

This is typical of this book. It might be said that Williams was writing for those in their late twenties and early thirties while Patten was writing for those in their teens and early twenties. An age was encompassed between these two who, with other poets, were semi-chroniclers of their times, at least of the emotional core of their times.

It was not to last in Hugo Williams's case: his next two books, *Some Sweet Day* (1975) and *Love-Life* (1979) show him abusing his abilities. The language he uses slackens, the poems have lost their beauty and Williams seems to have fallen into the general rot of the mid-1970s.

'A little inaccuracy,' said O'Sullivan
'Runs deep.' And used to hold on
Like a dildo-fancier to make it last.
He knew the object of his mirth
Was mounted on a railway, like a hare,
And used to speak of it as if no skill
Were so suspicious were it danced upon the moon.
'We'll bury Mary later, in a rush or gradually.'

What a simile in line three! What appalling diction and construction in lines six and seven! What could he have been thinking of? And the fourth book is no better. True, there are glimpses of the earlier prowess with words showing through here and there, but it is generally very much a case of a few shafts of light through a very overcast sky. Compared to the sad first six lines of 'The Sailing Wind' in the second collection below, one sees the collapse:

All day we fooled around the port,
Spending the money like reprieved lifers,
We are as happy as lovers, talking

As if your going ended here
In this blue Ocean Dining Room the last day
Of a month gone on ahead of us.

Perhaps the decline in Williams's work was also seen by his publishers for his fourth book was not placed with Oxford University Press (as had been the others) but with a marriage of Deutsch and Whizzard Press.

As it was with Williams so it has been with Peter Reading, a poet almost entirely created by the centre of the establishment, which he has seldom ventured outside. He rarely places work with magazines, save for *Encounter* and *Ambit*, has not had to go through the small press mill of publication before hitting the big time with a major publisher – his is Secker & Warburg, a fact of some interest as will be shown – and he has a low profile in that he does not widely travel the reading circuit. His books have been fêted by all the literary critics of the major (but poetically minor) journals and he has a sound poetic but not popular following.

Born in 1946 and educated as an artist, he is now a lecturer in art history; he has had a Poetry Book Society recommendation and in 1978 he won the Cholmondeley Award which is quite an astounding achievement when you consider that, unlike most poets, he hasn't had to run that apprenticeship but gone in straight at the top. And he did so with a very good first collection. *For the Municipality's Elderly* appeared on 4 November 1974. It was a new book in a number of senses. The poems most definitely shaped up a lot of the time to the type of material that would appeal to all readers of real verse; *Removals* begins,

> (Not actually) written in dust on the rear of the van:
>
> Living here has had its advantages I suppose
> but we're tired of the place and the time has come to
>   depart.
> The Coal Board will make us redundant and pension us
>   off.
> You can stuff Conservation Year – let's get it over with
>   quickly.

There was hope that here was a poet who might develop into a new popular poet in the mould of Logue or Mitchell or Patten.

Here comes the catch, though. Peter Reading is published by a company the poetry editor of which, Anthony Thwaite the poet, is not only the editor of the magazine *Encounter* but also someone who, because of his position, can dictate tastes, and his own tastes do not follow along the lines of the popularist poet. He is someone who does not necessarily see that verse has to widen its horizons. Indeed, a look at the work that appears in *Encounter* and in many of the poetry books published by Secker & Warburg shows this; he is a poet who is caged by his academic training and not his considerable intellectual skills. Consequently, he tends to nourish poets who are not only his sort (for want of a better phrase) but also those that he has somehow shaped himself. In Reading's case, he is practically a Thwaite discovery via *Encounter*'s columns.

This is distinctly incestuous and cannot do the art good. Of course, one cannot escape influence, but here one sees these going to extremes and Reading, sadly, has suffered from it. Mind you he has also benefited – he has had more books of verse published by Secker & Warburg than any other poet on their list. He has produced six to date, since 1974.

How has Reading's verse stood up to the test and the limitations? His second collection, *The Prison Cell and Barrel Mystery* (1976), showed no decline in promise of being a book for all and was certainly not a book for poets. In fact, his poetry stood the test of time, as it turns out, for it is still good when looked back at from the present and it seemed as if there was a revival going on in Reading's mind. He was writing with a style not unlike the mid-1960s one, but updated somehow. In fact, there was a time when I wondered if Reading wasn't a semi-pseudonym for several poets in their late forties. There seems to be so much in his work that rings of others without being imitative or derivative. At his best, he's good:

> Mr Bottomley taught us French and Eng. Lit.
> We called him Otto Van Bumph, I don't know why now.
> When we were in 4D he was absent
> nearly a whole term. When he returned
> he got tired climbing the stairs and short of breath.
> We took the piss with a rare tenderness.

The rot was creeping in, though. Either because Reading had fallen for the trap of having discovered a formula that works and was therefore sticking to it, or was unable to widen his work and develop it, or was aware that his editor would require such-and-such for a new book and that he was to write to ensure an acceptance, one cannot say. But his poetry has remained ever since much of a muchness except that it has lost much of its get-up-and-go that the first two books contained. The fifth volume indicates this only too well: *Tom O'Bedlam's Beauties* appeared in 1981 and although it was well reviewed in a few establishment places, the book received little note elsewhere. This was because it was not a new book but a reissue of earlier work. Certainly, the poems were all new, but the poetry was not. And it lacked spark.

It had fallen into the mire of self-indulgence and narrow-minded artistry:

> Susurration of rushes,
> deck-chair poised at the weir edge,
> strepitumque Avon avari.
> Valetudinarian gent,
> knitted as for a safari
> in pith helmet and white ducks,
> has sat unmoving for four hours.
> A cleg enters him by the nose.

This might be clever but is it good poetry? It can't be, for half of it is lost on the reader who lacks Latin for a start – and these days, that is everyone, more or less, under the age of 35. (In that poem, 'A Departure', one assumes that the old boy's dead but it isn't that clear even at the end when the St. John's men raise him from the river's edge.)

Once again, a poet who starts the race well flags after the third lap of the track. In Reading's case, that's sad. In him there is – or was – a sense of the new life coming. And it came, but the important thing is that it didn't stay. This is surprising for Reading's style is highly suited to the public reading; but he is not a performance poet, it seems.

To a lesser extent, Peter Reading's editor fits into this category, too. Anthony Thwaite has been a poet for a long while. He is a contemporary of Brownjohn, MacBeth, Hobsbaum and the others of that period, but he was not a Group poet. He has been a university teacher in Tokyo and Libya, a BBC talks producer, a literary journalist and newspaper editor, and a publisher's editor amongst many other things. He was first published – like MacBeth and Larkin – by Fantasy Press in 1953 and since then he has produced a large number of verse collections as well as other titles. He, too, wrote early poetry of force and excellence and his book out in 1968, *The Stones of Emptiness*, which contained poems written in or about Libya, justifiably won the Richard Hillary Memorial Award. Since then, his work has deteriorated into something less than extraordinary and certainly below his original ability. His 1980 collection, *Victorian Voices*, shows his decline. Compare this (from the late 1960s):

> At Asqefar the German helmet
> Rests like a scarecrow's bonnet
> On a bare branch.
> The shreds of coarse grey duffel

Hang round the gap a rifle
Left in a shallow trench.

'Much blood,' said the shepherd,
Gesturing with his head
Towards the bald hillside . . .

with this (from 1980):

If Lord Somers
Should be inclined to pay this coast a visit,
I would delight to be his *cicerone*. Did I mention
At Apollonia the numerous columns
Of cipollino, relics of Christian churches,
To which the Turks attach no value, but
Which I am sure would be much prized in England. . . .

One shows feeling and life and skill with image and diction: the other shows arty playing.

It is inevitable that when one person edits a poetry list that person shapes it, especially where this involves the taking on of new poets. In the case of Secker & Warburg, this has certainly become true, for the list divides roughly into three – the poets who had built hefty reputations before coming to the list (MacBeth, Brownjohn), American poets (Hall, Sissman) and foreigners in translation (Holub, Rokeah) and new writers. With the first category, no mistakes could be made for these were poets of proven skill and importance with a following. In the case of the second, the publisher was running a risk, but not much of one when one looks at the poets involved: Donald Hall is a very fine poet with a reputation of stature in the USA, L. E. Sissman's poetry is suitable for English audiences, and two others, Anne Sexton and Erica Jong, both had international literary reputations. In the case of the third group, Secker & Warburg have become a little unstuck. Perhaps it would be better to say stuck, for they have become bogged down in the unexciting end of modern poetry with writers who are distinctly ordinary.

A few have over-ridden this statement and come in to this study at a later stage for they cannot be so much identified with the 'Secker School' and are best seen as outsiders or independents. (It should be stated here that the 'Secker School' is not a distinct category of poet but more a term of mild derision for those who write in a manner that has equipped them for a place in the Third Division of that publisher's list.)

Amongst this grouping are poets who are either young or new to poetry in published form in books.

William Peskett is one of them. He might well be classified as one of the Irish poets, for he has more than a tenuous connection with Ulster, but he does not come up to their standard of writing either about the past, the present or Ireland. He was first seen in one of the Faber Introduction books, a series that was aimed at introducing new poets, five or six to a book, to a wider audience without the need to run to the cost of bringing out an entire collection. After that, Secker & Warburg took him on and published his first individual collections, *The Nightowl's Dissection* (1975) and *Survivors* (1980). Both books contain competent but unexciting poetry.

> Snow conceals, everything:
> I tell him it's cold;
> it's white,
> it's like crushed ice from the freezer.
> What else can I say?

Indeed. There is little else to say, even to the Malay boy to whom the poem is addressed. Or consider a domestic poem entitled 'At Home' which is seen to begin:

> Two cats sitting on the mat,
> you're upstairs between the daydream
> and the dark, picking stitches
> from a difficult seam.
> Outside, the wind has dropped.

At the end, the poet turns in bed to 'switch the passion on'. But the passion doesn't come, it isn't there. The poetry is passionless and flat, lacking verve or even a stirring of life. In Peskett's case, it is as if he has experienced life and then deliberately played it down, suppressed it out of his poetry and, therefore, his poetry is poor. It fails life and the experience of life. This is particularly sad in Peskett's case as he has not had his horizons limited by university and typically British provincialism. He is a school-teacher, admittedly not of English but biology, and perhaps this is his fault: he writes as if from the secondhand experience of the teacher rather than the firsthand experience of the doer. It is as if his vision has been restricted by the class- and staffroom. This need not be the case though. He has lived in Northern Ireland and must know of that province's pains, and he has lived and taught in Malaysia. But he was educated at Cambridge and does not seem to have been able to escape the talons of the rigid academical institute that, say, Ted Hughes did.

Freda Downie is another Secker School poet, one who is not young but has come late to poetry publishing. Born in 1929, she has experienced wartime London, rural England and Australia. She has been variously employed and knows life. Her poetry is detailed and neat, particularly accurate in that it seeks to explain with a certain finnicky tidiness. However, she does not write of her life – which is a shame – but of the minutiæ that she sees around her. Her diction is particularly dense and unyielding and the alliteration doesn't work in the following, but one instance of technique that hasn't quite come off:

> Desultory sun reappears
> To lick the sombre grass lazily,
> Pucker the face of the pallid pond
> And play on the soundless floor
> Beneath the oriental gestures
> Of the bandstand's turquoise canopy.

The accusations of mundane writing that are levelled at the last two poets can as easily be applied to the next two. John Whitworth is another poet the publishers took on with a first collection. Born in 1945 in India, educated in Edinburgh and Merton College, Oxford, Whitworth writes as does Peskett – of the narrowings of living. And, like Peskett, he's a teacher. Admittedly, Whitworth writes with more verve than Peskett or Downie, but he still doesn't do much more than cause a titter. His poetry, when it seeks to be humorous, is mildly funny. It might perform well but on the page it's limp and flaccid stuff, a choice of description in keeping with the attempted wit of the poetry. One poem is typical of many, 'Are You Dancing? No, It's Just the Way I'm Standing':

> Oh God, the crawling, appalling party,
> The pimpling dimpling, the hearty arty,
> The humid tumid, they prop the walls,
> Fleery and leary, all beer and balls
> For us, neat meat in flaccid chops, em-
> braced in haste to see if she drops 'em,
> Clutched in the crush of a rush connection,
> (The Belly Clamp on a damp erection),

. . . and so on. Clever stuff, but more words masquerading as poetry than poetry riding on words. George Szirtes isn't as clumsy a writer and he doesn't seek to amuse with what the blurb writer for Secker & Warburg called the writing of 'a latter-day Petronius' on the cover of Whitworth's first book, *Unhistorical Fragments* (1980). However, Szirtes's work is just as lacklustre even if it is technically very good. With a considerable control of metre and rhyme, Szirtes could produce very innovate and thrilling poetry. Indeed, he has everything in his make-up to produce poetry of our age; born in Budapest in 1948, he fled with his family to Britain in 1956. He studied fine arts in Leeds, with Martin Bell the poet as one of his tutors. Had some of that connection rubbed off, one wonders at the outcome. He is an artist and art teacher, is married to a composer and musician, runs a small press and is fast becoming known as an etcher and engraver. He has himself exhibited his work and his first book, *The Slant Door* (1979), won the Geoffrey Faber Award, though quite how one wonders. It might be that Szirtes's quietness works against him for he is a noiseless and gentle man, a charming person in whom one senses much turmoil going on at creation's level. But this does not manifest itself in his poetry which is, to say the least, withdrawn and laid back. From his second collection, *November and May* (1981), one has:

> Your namesake, perversely, is unrelated
> And spends his time underground,
> A warty, tubered thing, and quite unlike.
>
> But fine in soup, served cold in summer,
> Pale and green in lamplight. He dreams of Tasso,
> Nicolo da Tolentino, dark excavations.

That is about an artichoke. Despite the above, Szirtes is an accomplished wordsmith. The trouble is, and it is one he shares with the others in the Secker list who are 'recent discoveries', he works with poor material and should not be looking at vegetables, a door leaning on his garden shed or visiting a shoe shop for a fitting. He should be writing about his childhood, using what he heard from Bell in Leeds. And, with the visual control of an artist, he could really knock poetry sideways. Instead, he is prepared only to shadow-box the muse.

To some extent, these people are given too much publicity, are published too readily. Particularly in the second half of the 1970s, there has been a tendency on the part of many editors to bring out books that are not thrilling to read. And then the directors of the publishing houses wonder why poetry, by and large, doesn't make a profit. The reason is that there are too many Whitworths and Pesketts about and too many editors prepared to let the likes of Szirtes get away with provincially pretty poetry instead of the stuff that lifts souls. When one considers that the editors are, generally speaking, not youngsters themselves (or where they are, they are sadly those who write the boring drivel that has risen to prominence of late) then one might wonder what on earth is going on: the experienced are ignoring their experiences and failing to pay their dues to the art. Promise is overlooked, potential ignored. All that is accepted is the matter of the norm. Publish quietness and keep poetry on a low profile . . . and, where newness is seen to rise to the surface, it is soon either discouraged or swamped. Or the poets see the way the tide is running and they run with it.

This is certainly true of many and one who has not lived up to his promise is Neil Powell, not a Secker poet but a Carcanet one. Powell began his literary career in 1969. At the age of 21 he received a Gregory Award for poetry, one of the greatest encouragements a young poet can have in Britain, and which is worth not only a tidy sum of money but a fortune in fillip and boost. He studied English and American Literature at the University of Warwick, one of the newer educational establishments where new degrees that broke the mould of traditional narrow studies in English university curricula were exciting students, and this resulted in a poet who had already a very extensive knowledge of literatures away from the insularity of the British, an insularity that has long been the bane of British poetry, before he broke upon the scene.

Although Powell was not to place a book until 1977, much of the work included in it was written in the early 1970s when he was still under the influence of the poetry that was current in the country. *At the Edge* contained much of the work upon which Powell had established himself, work that had seen the light of day with such small presses as Sceptre Press, Cellar Press and Mandeville Press as well as in a number of both establishment and underground magazines. The poetry was quiet, subdued and unpretentious and it had skill and life in it. Powell obtained work as a teacher after leaving his studies and this crept into some of his work, initially to its benefit:

> I stop before the door, compose myself,
> Then enter slowly. Certain faces turn
> To contemplate my manner or my tie;
> A few glance quickly, anxious now to learn
> What Wordsworth really meant, and instantly.

I looked around for signs of coming storms,
And swiftly launch into the holy life
Of music and of verse and UCCA forms.

This is a human poem, albeit on a narrow subject, entitled 'Period
Three'. It criticises attitudes towards literature that are fostered by
the educational process and it has a ring akin to some of D. H.
Lawrence's 'teaching' poems. This closeness to reality was but a
fleeting romance for Powell. His poetry soon became what he was
against in the poem above. It clevers up, as the Americans say.
Gone is the seeking for truth and in its place comes a sleight of
hand that seems not what it is. A second collection – Powell is
not prolific – appeared in 1982 and was called *A Season of Calm
Weather*, the poetry of which is certainly in the calms, even the
doldrums. It has no life, either in subject or in self:

I listen to you speak, hear only tone;
I feel the weight of words, not what they mean.
And this seems strange, in words so used and known,
But is (I know not *seems*) not strange at all:
For words are shadows which we move between
From light to light where heavily they fall.
You do not speak thus when we are alone.

Technically quite adroit but emotionally dead. And this is typical
of the entire book. There is an irony to this poem, too for Powell
obviously does feel the weight of words and he sees them in his
poetry as shadows when in truth they are the light by which the
art survives. It is a pun – and one no doubt that many of the
modish new poets will fully appreciate, for most of them are little
better than punsters – to say that Powell has a negative approach to poetry and it is one that he shares with a good number
of his publishers' stable mates.

For Neil Powell is published by Carcanet Press, Ltd, of which
mention has already been made. And this kind of poetry is almost
a universal hallmark of this influential imprint, where youngsters
are concerned. The Carcanet list is considerable, being made up,
so far as poetry is concerned, of a mixture of established poets
and newer ones who are just starting out. Of the former, much
can be said and will be in pages yet to come; they are in many
ways the respectable side of the firm, giving it credibility and
standing. Michael Schmidt, the owner/founder of the company,
has been gallant in his support of those who have been
established but who have lost their publishers due to closed lists,

bankruptcy proceedings or changes of editorship elsewhere and, in his support of these people, he has to be rightly lauded. However, there is another side of the Carcanet plate. It is the side that publishes new poets of little or spurious merit, who are at best dilettantes and at worst mere poetasters and charlatans who are clinging to the art and dragging it down in the eyes of the public and the dreaded literati as well. Of these one can but be dismissive. They write weak verse, they have little poetic spunk in them and they are unworthy of publication especially when set against the far superior work that is ignored because it is not considered heady enough, arty enough, high-flown enough or clever enough. The hallmark of these poets is a kind of poetry that is pretentious and pompous if not downright arrogant. How Schmidt, who is an accomplished editor and has proven it by publishing some excellent poets, can publish these people is a wonder.

The list of these poets is considerable when compared to the lists of other publishers and their new poet intake. Where Secker & Warburg might have four or five, and Faber but one or two, Carcanet has tens of them – Clive Wilmer, Michael Vince, Simon Lowy, Grevel Lindop, Robert Wells, Dennis Keene, Jeremy Hooker, Paul Wilkins, Robert B. Shaw, Ian McMillan, Jeffrey Wainwright, Paul Mills, Michael Cayley, Charles Boyle, Cliff Ashby, Andrew Waterman and more.

All of these have had first collections from Carcanet and some have gone on to subsequent collections; some, like Waterman, have had their books chosen by the Poetry Book Society as runners-up to the Choice position; some have published else-where – Jeremy Hooker, for example, though advertised as having had his first collection published by Carcanet, was actually first seen in covers in a substantial book published by Enitharmon Press – and some haven't and, most likely, never will.

Of course, it is commendable that Carcanet should seek to publish new poets, but this must be done with more than a modicum of editorial and literary expertise and discrimination. Having the most substantial newcomers' list in the country, if not (though it is arguably so) in the English-speaking world, places upon the publisher no small responsibility for the growing future of poetry and this is something that Schmidt appears to have let slip.

It is impossible to quote all of the list above, but let us look at a few examples of shoddy writing that have been lifted up and praised by appearing in full-length collections. Firstly, there is Jeremy Hooker, a poet who has also published essays on poetry (from Carcanet) as well as three collections so far. His poetry is shallow:

> Is the poppy afraid
> Of its redness?
> I am not a dry leaf
> That flares to nothing.
>
> Roots drink at my side.
> Chalk absorbs my warmth.
> And still I am replete,
> Blood-ripe.

The poem is entitled 'Solstice'. Another, 'At Osborne House', begins:

> Under cedar and ilex,
> On lawns to us *verboten*,
> Convalescents watch us,
> From coach and car,
> Mobbing their repose.

What is this but poor verse? Where is its life? It has none. It is a mere observation that leads nowhere: a complete printing of the poem leaves one with little. The result is but an emptiness and an uneasy unfulfilment. It is the kind of poetry that is best suited to school examination papers, for it is hollow and the poetic output of those learning the basics before seeking the real stuff. Hooker hasn't always been a weak poet, as the above imply. He has written, in his earlier times, verse that is accomplished and sound:

> After nightfall in harvest weather,
> Over the lowland clay
> Where the axe has opened hearts of oak,
> A faint wind moves in the rigging of leaves.

But he has not kept it up. He has gained himself a publisher and he has it seems let that go to his head: of all his books to date, one good one could be gleaned. The rest is Carcanetised, distilled poetic wine, indeed.

Charles Boyle is another:

> I lower my eyes

168

To evade the bookseller, as if he were the priest
And I a tourist, a pagan voyeur
Of books that I don't believe in.

Immaculate confections and remedies for gout,
What have these to do with us?
With your painter's instinct for colour and risk?

A weak pun, a cock-eyed image and the poem is not intended to be humorous or, if it is, it fails miserably. Entitled 'Newly Marrieds in the Second-hand Cookery Section', it actually contains the lines:

But here, oh here is our Egyptian dish,
Disguised in print – here are the flies,
The heat, and the carcasses
Strung from the trees like melting wax.

There is little hope for modern British verse if this is considered acceptable for print, and even more astonishingly, Boyle received a Cholmondeley Award in 1981. One wonders what the arbiters were seriously thinking of at the time: possibly, there came into play there some of the old boy network of editor and judge and publisher that so undertows our literary scene?

Thirdly, there is Michael Vince, who has an equally blinkered poetic vision. His is the poetry of the un-tried pen:

A bitter wind flaps at the shades
Of street cafes, their tables taken in:
   Glinting, a torpid winter fly,
October struts its border victory
   With paper flags, the school parades
My son will march in soon. . . .

The craftsmanship is confused in these lines, from 'From the Old Historian', which is to suggest that it's very badly written. Is October really being compared to a torpid winter fly? Why glinting? This might seem pedantic in the extreme, but then poetry must be exacting and this one piece is far from that. It's sloppy and, in keeping with the other poets in the youngsters' list, it has little aim. These are poems for poems' sake. They aren't great art and they are not likely to be so.

Others that fit into the Carcanet net are of even less substance than Hooker, Boyle and Vince. They are poets that typify this publisher's apparent desire for quantity rather than quality, poets with little to commend them to readers and who, in twenty-five years, will be adorning the shelves of secondhand bookshops as unknowns and un-achievers. Such shelves are today full of the poets of this kind who appeared between 1890 and 1925.

Consider the poetry of Ian McMillan, a Yorkshireman whose first book, *The Changing Problem* (1980), claims to be entertaining but in truth is not a little prosaic. Can the following be considered as poetry or truncated prose?

> It really is a shock to find a new place
> a few miles from home, in old country
> near the back windows of Doncaster.
> A block of a few houses and a farmhouse,
> and that home-made sign
> painted Melton Brand
> into the centre of the day's canvas
> where there should only have been a few fields

It has little conscious use of poetry's diction or nuance. And Paul Wilkins, Surrey-born but by now an adopted Ulsterman who teaches (see how often these people are teachers?) in Derry. His work is of a similar variety, lacking poetic awareness:

> I choose the later train.
> Vague as any tourist, discreetly
> I thumb my A-Z, wander
> east from London Bridge;
>
> and find I can remember this:
> Tooley Street's dingy office-windows,
> alleys echoing behind Jamaica Road, narrow
> turnings to the waterfront.

And Keith Chandler (public school, Oxford and another school-teacher) who does what many of these new poets do; that is, being possibly short of actual experience – though how this can be in a modern world, lord only knows! – they have to take secondhand ones and build upon them. Wilkins writes a poem about von Aschenbach that owes a bit more to Dirk Bogarde in the film than to Thomas Mann's original *Death in Venice*, and Chandler writes a poem about Raleigh's last voyage:

> To stand on the bridge of my *Destiny*,

to follow the parabola of the sun
across the tilting table of the ocean
where the charts slide off . . .
feel the boards vibrating, take the strain,
patched sails cracking out in the wind,
spray on my cheeks a fresh rebuff!

Hackneyed similes, worn metaphors and tired imagery seem to be the order of the day with these poets who, in the 1960s, would have had difficulty getting printed in the fierce fire of craftsmanship and artistic integrity. 'The tilting table of the ocean' would have been hacked to pieces in a Poets' Workshop meeting; in a Group gathering, it would not have occurred.

Similarly with David Day's poems in his book, *Brass Rubbings* (1975):

I do not know why I am
here. The letters are like birds
that rise disturbed and wheel
across my page, a little sky.

Or Alison Brackenbury's lines from her book, *Dreams of Power* (1981), which read:

'Strawberries', 'raspberries', whisper the letters.
Until July is a taste, to hide
In reddened mouths, in fields which feet
Can't flatten, tall, soft throbbed with heat.
Where horses shaking gnats aside
Come slow to hand through the darkening grass. . . .

Or, again, Michael Cullup's *Reading Geographies* (1982):

A hand lies over the edge of the bed
Mapped with the dark streets of London.
Eyelids confine visions of light
Breaking over the pavements.

And so on, and so on. Carcanet's list is full of this sort of thing.

Is it any small wonder that people don't buy poetry when they are presented with a plethora of such banal and artless drivel in ranks in the shops that are courageous enough to stock it? Is it any small wonder that the books don't make much profit? As has

171

been said, this is self-indulgent ego-tripping, poems for the sake of poets, not readers.

Why is it that so many of these young poets, now being hailed high on the mountains of Parnassus, as they'd like to think, write such poor verse? The answer may lie in the fact that, according to the blurbs on the back covers of their books, most of them are British university-educated in recent years and not a few of them are Oxford and Cambridge products. The academic creeps in, the intellectual flees. What damage the hallowed halls and spires are doing to our art – for poetry is ours. It has the longest roots bar the Greeks and Romans and it has had more effect and influence upon other literatures than any other. If this is to continue – and it has so far, though the Americans and Canadians are fast catching up in recent decades (thank the gods) – then the future looks bleak.

An interesting final observation: of the Carcanet 'new' poets, several are not all they seem. Dennis Keene writes like this in 'Rimbaud's Childhood':

> Our wartime summer holiday was four
> Weeks in Torquay. A German fighter plane
> Scattered the crowds on the beach but did not fire.
>
> Country of red earth, real farmer's country, so
> One could walk nowhere. No place for a dog,
> So he must stay at home; he must not go.
>
> As well he went when he did, my father said,
> Skin festering, lousy with fleas. He had walked
> In front of a bus, crawled to the gutter dead.
>
> An eight year child makes what he can of death.

This has life, meaning, pathos, emotion, light. And look now at the following lines from Robert B. Shaw's poem 'Gargoyle'. His poetry is humorous and witty, but it has punch and vitality added and the results are effective and – in some ways – he compares with the American poet, George Starbuck and, to a lesser extent, Anthony Hecht.

> An ornamental bung,
> a dragon-dog in little,

a throat without a tongue
to sample its own spittle:

whatever I may be,
harpy or horned toad,
is all the same to me.
I labor to erode.

These two fragments come from first collections, but they are different. Most of the poets in the Carcanet new poets' list are born in the post-war years and quite a number were born in the 1950s. Keene wasn't. He was born in 1934 and was first published from the all-discerning Fantasy Press: his horizons are broadened by the fact that he has lived for twenty years in Japan, not restricted in body and mind to school, university and the English scene. Keene has escaped the narrows. And as for Shaw – he's an American born in 1947 and studied in Harvard under the American poet, Robert Lowell. It shows. He, too, has a vision that is not restricted by the insularity of the British systems of education and thought. It is a terrible thing to suggest, but our poets are dying from lack of freedom of thought and Carcanet New Press, in their drive to produce new poets, are furthering this terrible extreme by fostering the resultant attempts at poetry. What is more, because of the power of publishers and their editors, this poetry is what is being sold, awarded prizes and garlands, hyped and pushed for all it's worth as being the new and good directions – and the only direction, at that. Result? Apathy and artlessness. The cure is to start publishing poetry that is not the result of learning but of living. So much for the Carcanet new poets. Of course, some of them are good, but only a few, and even fewer still are above that. It is true that all poetry lists are like this, but not so massively. Schmidt should trim himself a lot more. His publish-a-lot-and-hope-to-make-a-hit-with-a-few policy doesn't work for it hardens public resolve against poetry when one has to search through a pile of pebbles to find one uncut agate. The expense of publishing these missers should be channelled into the production of more work by the hitters.

The few who are good include Anthony Rudolf (who founded and runs Menard Press and who has escaped the overbearing pressures of an Oxford education), now published in two books (only one from Carcanet) and Roger Garfitt who was educated in Oxford as well, but also escaped it. He was 'brought up' partly through The Poets' Workshop and more considerably through living in the 1960s and letting the years and the life affect him. He was, for several years in the 1970s, the editor of *Poetry Review* and did a good bit towards lifting that magazine from a clique-ridden journal to a publication of repute. His poetry is about the world all see and feel, and in the following section from a poem, 'The Basement', written for the society for the homeless, Shelter, he shows his skills with rhythm and diction and rhyme:

> 'Half past five, look alive!
> It's home to the wife, and the cosy life!'
> – the joke wears thin, when it's cosy
> if there's a drop of warm in the washing pail,
> or an extra candle
> > globs in the dark.
> Whoever ripped the pipes out
> ripped out the time of day: no kettle
> shrills eleven, no taps hum in the wall.

This is what modern poetry is about. Modern life. It is not about the introverted views of a few well-educated young gentlemen and ladies. The youngsters, also, have little to offer. It is the older ones who strike rich.

A look at some of these older poets, apart from those who are listed above as having had first collections out from Carcanet, shows the strengths of British poetry at their best. As has been mentioned, this publisher has rescued many from oblivion. These include, one should add, poets from earlier times – Schmidt has published a selection of the poems of Edmund Blunden and, under the imprint of Fyfield Books, has brought out the work of Chatterton, Smart and (best of all) William Barnes, the nineteenth-century Dorsetshire poet. He has also a substantial list of foreign poets, not the least being John Ashbery and Hans Magnus Enzensberger. So this is not an attack on Schmidt as a whole: he has done much for poetry, but he has also done it irreparable harm with his poor choice of younger poets and his somewhat cliquey ideals. (He published his own first book and then placed his second with Peter Jay's Anvil Press in 1978. Peter Jay's next collection, *Shifting Frontiers*, was published by Carcanet two years later. Both books are good, Jay's the far better, but is this the way to do it? It smacks of friends for friends rather than editors for poets, regardless of amicability. Be it the commodity market, insurance, barrow selling or poetry making, this attitude can do no good in the long run and it is rife in the art.)

Carcanet's older poets are, as has been stated, often those rescued from other publishers' list closures. Some class as outsiders, for they have kept to their own grain and not tried to infiltrate tenaciously into the poetry market place, much to their credit. Some are distinctly insiders and one wonders why any publisher should want to be rid of them: their acquisition was a series of minor coups for Schmidt.

Christopher Middleton is one of Carcanet's rescued and perhaps the one most deserving, for he is one of the poets of the times and a major figure. Born in 1926, he was educated at Merton College, Oxford and, in the 1940s, he published two books but it was not until 1962 that his first important book appeared, *Torse 3*, which won the Faber Memorial Prize and which contained work written since 1949; the first two books were ignored by the poet and are omitted by him these days from any list he compiles. Three years later, *Nonsequences* appeared to considerable acclaim. Until now, Middleton had been published by Longmans but he did not remain theirs and, in 1969, Fulcrum Press published *Our Flowers and Nice Bones* to their credit and his betterment, for the book established him as a poet of power and place. Not long afterwards, as had happened with Longmans, Fulcrum Press ceased publishing poetry and Middleton moved to Carcanet, since when he has brought out three new books of verse and a book of essays.

His poetry cuts across all the boundaries, actual and artificial, as, indeed, does Middleton himself. For some years, he taught in British universities, but since the late 1960s he has worked as a professor at the University of Texas, his discipline being not English but foreign languages – he has translated much from the German in addition to his poetry writing.

He has that uncanny and much-envied knack of being able to write for poets and people simultaneously. A sign of his mastery of verse, Middleton can conjure up the understood and the esoteric in one line, one poem. His writing, from *Torse 3* onwards, captured the minds of his contemporaries but also made him a poet whom the public audiences enjoyed at both his and their own levels. The opening lines from 'The monsters' (from *Nonsequences*) illustrates this. The poem is a surreal, imagist poem with a strange and mythic ending, but at no time does it become obscure:

> They slide from rooms,
> trees, tunnels, and gleam
> in the airy halls, diffusing
> round their bulk the stale
> room-stench, tree-glue, tunnel-twinklings.

The diction is simple but calls up grand feelings of the macabre. The poem ends:

> A time is coming for the monsters.
> They begged their helpings of it,
> the music, and we lent them
> our ears, played into
> their hands our instruments.

Not all of Middleton's poetry was so. He was also one of the first to be published widely outside the narrow confines of the concrete poetry world, yet writing concrete or sound poems. To many who were in the ordinary public who were not in the know of this type of verse, Middleton opened a new world with poems like 'The Joke' from the last section of *Our Flowers and Nice Bones*:

> nun found nude on dunes
> nun found stunned on dunes at noon
> nude nun found stunned at noon
> nude nun on dunes had been stunned & screwed

and 'Armadillo Cello Solo', which begins:

> didl   dodl   dad!
> o   aro   ma
> miomar   miodaar
> a   dio   da

Middleton cannot be set into a category, the sure sign of a top-notch poet: he can write as above yet also one sees in his work such as the following:

> I saw the wire Spring come,
> the first clock beclambering the redbud;
> out of a marble cloud thrush-legs fell
> hitting the grass with a twang.

In later books that came from *Carcanet* one can find also lyrical beauty rare in modern times, except in the work perhaps of Ted Hughes, Seamus Heaney or Francis Warner. The first book from the new publisher was *The Lonely Suppers of W. V. Balloon* and the contents carried on where Fulcrum Press had left off. The poems were sharp and simple and deep. Of a window:

Oddly like a porthole
It contains a thistle

Someone with a hammer fashioning stones
Imagined a deep square hole

And placed it in the wall it was real
Light in the morning returns to root in it

No sea for a hundred miles
Among these unforsaken mountains
The deep square hole is white inside

Middleton's latest volumes are as odd as his overall range of vision. Always one to push poetry to its limits, *Pataxanadu* (1977) is prose-poetry, a long and difficult book (to some), rich with fable, fantasy and convolution. The book is not for the general reader and is, to this extent, not a good one for it restricts its readership to those who can hang into it. Few can grasp a line like

Waxiest cloacas but nullify the culpablest Fascists; the timberman of Bengal cries in spitted grunts of centennial vernacular.

but the book that came next, *Carminalenia* (1980), has Middleton returning to his former poetry but still advancing it to new borders and using poetry as an exploration of emotion and living:

Not crocked exactly, but in a doze,
There I was, before supper time: Elgar,
Stop your meteoric noise, the glory
Leaves me cold; then it was
I woke to the melody –

Back, a place, 1939, and people
Singing, little me among them,
Fresh from a holiday
Summer, beside the Cornish sea, I sang
In chorus with a hundred English people.

This is poetry. It is the realisation of reality. One can hardly say that many of Middleton's co-poets on his publisher's list – especially the younger ones – match anything up to this standard.

Macmillan originally published Elizabeth Jennings's poetry; they shut their list and Schmidt took her on. Elizabeth Jennings is a quiet poet, one who writes very much from the innermost corners of her privacies. She is not a 'great' poet because she shuns publicity: a cruel statement up to a point but one that is valid. Unless poets these days seek out audiences, they reduce their chances of greatness, but what sort of greatness it is is questionable. Our world demands that the great stand in the spotlight otherwise they are lesser. Elizabeth Jennings is nevertheless great as a poet, but she doesn't look it. Few critical books contain much on her, the public at large do not know of her (to their considerable loss) and she keeps clear of the reading circuit and the poetry machine. Her greatness lies in her work, not her abilities to shout about it. (There are those who are great because they shout and yet are poor writers – we come to them.)

Taken as a whole, Elizabeth Jennings's poetry is a corpus of peace and one that many should enter in turbulent times. She lives almost as a recluse in Oxford but from her melancholic and sadly beautiful shell she produces poetry of exceptional lyrical qualities:

> Evader mostly, a glancing cold, a watcher
> Of snow from a warm distance, a clever seeker
> Of the heated corner, the generous lap, the fingers
> Handing tit-bits or filling a shallow saucer –
>> (Cat in Winter)

> Like children now, bed close to bed,
> With flowers set up where toys would be
> In real childhoods, secretly
> We cherish each our own disease,
> And when we talk we talk to please
> Ourselves that still we are not dead.
>> (Sequence in Hospital – IV
>> Patients in a Public Ward)

> I name them now, I think of them always.
> Features stand out whenever children lurk
> Among the crowds. I catch a hostile gaze.
> O children not yet frightened of the dark,
> I fall upon my knees,

> I sweat, am scourged, am crowned with thorns for you,
> Yes, I escaped but Herod took each son.

I'm punished by the screaming mothers too.
Father, where had our endless mercy gone
If there was this to do?

> (Christ Recalls 'The Massacre
> of the Innocents')

Few can match Elizabeth Jennings's musicality. Few try to write religious verse these irreligious days and she is brave to attempt it and highly successful when she does. More than many male poets, she has stayed the course from her first book, *The Mind Has Mountains*, published in 1966. Unlike any other poet of her sex, bar possibly Sylvia Plath, she is a poet of the age, one writing for public consumption. Now she gathers a following, at the end of the mid-century's poetic era, because she writes that others can travel the word journeys with her. Melancholy and quietness seem to go hand-in-hand with turbulent times.

There were also the groovy poets of strangeness, innovation and loud, jolly with-it-ness, such as Edwin Morgan, who followed the Middleton joke-poem direction with things such as

Blea on the baulk the furze kidder rocked
with a bottle of flags and a budget of bent.
Sawning and soodling in a drabbled scrip
he hirpled and jolled hirkling and croodling.

> (The Computer's First Dialect
> Poems: i. The Furze Kidder's
> Bating (Northamptonshire))

A mugger is disgustedly
knifing his victim
who has nothing on him
but a small Raphael
nipped from the Louvre.
Conceptualize.

> (Pictures Floating From The World)

and is well-known for his performance of a large number of witty poems, especially the computer poems that are sound poems with ironic messages. But alongside the groovers went the quieter folk, and one who has lived through the times and writes in a manner not unlike Elizabeth Jennings's, but has a wider horizon, is Michael Hamburger.

His first book appeared in 1950 but it was not until the

publication of his collection *Travelling*, in 1969 (Fulcrum Press), that he became well known and gathered a following about him. A sense of lyricism characterises Hamburger's work which is much influenced by the poetry of Europe, for he is (like Middleton) a noted translator and therefore cannot escape being impinged upon by those whom he makes into English. Often sad and withdrawn in his work, Hamburger is nevertheless a man who writes about subjects many can identify with, as in 'Report on a supermarket':

> First of all, the site:
> Nowhere, I said, put it nowhere,
> Right out of town – some town! –
> Near the motel, if you like, near the filling station,
> But away from houses, all houses.
> You wouldn't listen. And now
> People drive in for a pack or two
> Of cigarettes and – would you believe it? –
> Walk in and buy what they want.

The irony is implicit, the mood of the poem harsh and bitter in its comment upon our world, yet it is also laid back, understressed and unforceful. Yet it still works so well without being forced with loudness or clumsy, clever slicknesses as has become the fashion from about 1978 onwards. Despite the quietness of his work, however, Hamburger does not shirk the responsibilities that all good poets must accept in order to use poetry as it should be used, to look at existence and underline matters of import to all men. In *Real Estate*, published in 1977, he includes a poem entitled 'In South Carolina':

> 'Who's Charles?' she informs the young white couple to
> whom she's lent
> The house her husband put up twenty years ago
> Between two lakes on the newly-bought seventy acres,
> And they don't use now. 'Why, he's the very best
> Nigger anyone ever had.' The next time she comes it's with
> Charles,
> She in her car, he in his, to pick the scuppernong grapes
> She wants for wine.
>   Charles has a farm of his own,
> More of a farm than theirs, larger, worth more, come down
> to him
> From his family's last legal owner.

Seldom has Hamburger been obtuse, verbose or poetically narrow. He always writes with a broad outlook and it is for this reason that he is known and his poetry accepted as important.

Women have not had the impact upon poetry in the period from 1964 that one might have expected when one considers that these years coincide with the rise of what the feminists would want to term the new emancipation. However, those who have come through with force have done it in no mean manner. Elizabeth Jennings is one of these, a poet who has worked right through the decades and, with a small sorority, has made a major contribution.

Ironically, the one poet who fits this category and has influenced the most died before the poetry boom took off. She was Ted Hughes's first wife, Sylvia Plath. As with her husband, much has been written about her and this is not the place to recap upon it all. It is the time, however, to look at her work in the light of those around her and to realise – remember – one important fact. Sylvia Plath was an American by birth and only later became a British poet. Much of her poetic training lies across the Atlantic and it is for this that she is of such importance for she brought it with her and passed it on to Hughes and, from herself and via his work, to British poetry. She was, in the mid-1960s, almost a cult figure not only because of her poetry but also as a result of her novel, *The Bell Jar*. This meant that she was widely read by many, poet and non-poet alike, and she implanted her poetic concepts upon all who took to her work.

Sylvia Plath's poetry was always accessible to any reader. Even when writing about matters that were poetically narrow, she was always able to broaden her scope so that the concepts of the piece took on a wider significance. In this respect, she was like those others already mentioned who are poets' poets yet people's poets too. Inevitably, her reputation is based upon a small number of poems – say two dozen – and it's these that have spread her doctrine of brutal language, exacting imagery and the sense of personal searching within the soul for meanings to apply to the universe. Her work is often confessional in the sense that some of the best American poets of the last twenty years have been; it is easy to say that, in their work, they write about themselves in the light of mankind, highlighting their emotions and weaknesses and strengths in the perspective of others' viewpoints. One thinks particularly of John Berryman and Robert Lowell in this context, as well as Sylvia Plath's friend, Anne Sexton, who was to follow very much in the former's path.

It is perhaps pertinent at this moment to consider what it is that American poets do that sets them up at a higher level than many of their English counterparts and which they have given or brought to British poetry where the latter has been amenable to influence creeping in under its usual insularity.

Apart from those poets who either lived in Britain or were frequent visitors (as Sylvia Plath and Robert Lowell were respectively), most American poets have been ignored in the British Isles since the mid-1960s.

There was a time when the best of American contemporary poetry was published in London as well as in New York or Boston. One publisher, Rapp & Whiting, even went so far as to inaugurate an American poetry series and it was, to say the least, vibrant and exciting, containing as it did books by Galway Kinnell, Robert Bly and James Wright amongst others. These three were poets of considerable stature in their own country who were writing universally aware poetry across national, political and cultural boundaries. Jonathan Cape also published, from time to time, books of American poetry (including another by Robert Bly and the work of Denise Levertov) and they continue so to do at a very spasmodic rate. Secker & Warburg publish some American poetry but only one important living writer, Donald Hall. Faber & Faber also occasionally publish American verse. Other publishers have, by and large, ignored American verse unless the work itself has fitted in with the English pattern of poetic structure and ideals. It is almost as if the British feel that there is a threat from American and Canadian verse, posed by its being so much more direct and clear-thinking, unambiguous and deliberate in its directness. And so the better American poetry, the material that is wide-reaching and universal in appeal and import, is ignored.

What is the 'better American poetry'? It is the poetry of writers from North America who are not intent on being obscurantist and esoteric, but seek always to be expanding consciousness of the human world, the surroundings of the body and the soul. They do this with a plain speech and a sense of the direction in which the man should look in order to understand his world and, by understanding it, to better it or at least prevent its dissolution. This is possibly a very American stance to take: for all its modernity, North America still lives in a pioneering age, a spirit of the need to survive against the odds still exists in the depths of the American mind. British poets, perhaps, no longer feel that they have an outward world to tame or with which to come to grips and so now they seek to self-indulge themselves with 'inner matters' which see no need to relate to the space outside. In short, British poetry is selfish and introverted and American poetry is not.

Modern North American verse – and older writings, come to

that – is the opposite. It looks at the world and relates the man to it, rather than vice versa where the man sits at the centre of his universe and looks out at that which should relate to him. The British poet sees himself as a nucleus of creation whereas the American sees himself as but an electron in the mass of the whole, agitating and playing his part.

Briefly, the best American poets write outwardly. They do not play artistic games, bandy words or try to be clever. They write directly of what they see and feel. There are, of course, those who do not, who try to be very conscious of their poetic skills and use them in intricate, often lost ways but they seem either to be in the minority (in Britain such are the majority) or, wisely, they are muted and seldom seen or picked up by readers or publishers alike.

A few snippets from just a few poets show the force with which Americans can write and to which few British poets can aspire.

KENNEDY'S INAUGURATION

The Sister hands it to me – the seed
of the sweet-gum tree.
New to me, it is the size
of a cow's eyeball.
Dry as a pinecone, round
and brown. Its seeing
is all gone, finished,
exploded out
through the eye-holes.
I turn it in my palm,
it pricks the tender skin.

Dry spikes, beaklike
splinters – hen
beaks widening in fear.
Are the dogs
coming? Where an eye
should be, another
beak is opening, where
an ear should be,
a beak is opening – blindness
and deafness
make the cries more hoarse.

And what did I do today?
I drove on errands

183

twice so as not to pass
the funeral home;
I had three conversations,
all distant.
Well, if I know how to live,
why am I frightened?
I see Lorenzo's head
in my hand, cheek
broken by a cannonball,

one eye dangles out.
The Catholic
strangles the Papal candidate
with a thin cord.
King Leopold's plantation
men cut off
the boy's hands, punishing
the father for missing
work; the boy's hands
lie on the ground
at the father's feet.

In Nineteen Thirty-Eight
Brown Shirts
arrive, smash the contra-
ceptive clinics,
take women away
into breeding hotels.
I look down: Marilyn
Monroe is there.
The arm of the drugged mistress
hangs out a hole
over the side of the bed.

Out of her back comes the Marine's
cry for the medic.
His foot is lying a few
feet away,
his lips are open, the brain
is missing – only
the throat and cry are there.
And the President
in the cold – the old white-
haired poet nearby –
lays one hand on the Bible.

Robert Bly

ON A PHRASE FROM
SOUTHERN OHIO

For Etheridge Knight

A long time's gone.
Now all I recall for sure
Is a long shattering of jackhammers that stripped
Away the whole one side of one foothill of one
Appalachian mountain

Across the river from me where I was born.
It is summer chilblain, it is blowtorch, it is not
Maiden and morning on the way up that cliff.
Not where I come from.

It is a slab of concrete that for all I know
Is beginning to crumble.

James Wright

TRAVELING THROUGH THE DARK

Traveling through the dark I found a deer
dead on the edge of the Wilson River road.
It is usually best to roll them into the canyon:
that road is narrow; to swerve might make more dead.

By glow of the tail-light I stumbled back of the car
and stood by the heap, a doe, a recent killing;
she had stiffened already, almost cold.
I dragged her off; she was large in the belly.

My fingers touching her side brought me the reason –
her side was warm; her fawn lay there waiting,
alive, still, never to be born.
Beside that mountain road I hesitated.

The car aimed ahead its lowered parking lights;
under the hood purred the steady engine.
I stood in the glare of the warm exhaust turning red;
around our group I could hear the wilderness listen.

I thought hard for us all – my only swerving –,
then pushed her over the edge into the river.

William Stafford

185

Certainly, this is the work of famous poets, but the fact remains that this style and direction of poetic thought can be found at all levels of the art, particularly in the USA. The following comes from poets who are not all that well-known – indeed, Krapf has yet to publish a trade collection – yet they are far superior to their equals on the same rung of the poetic ladder in Britain.

HAVANA

The young Cuban at the parking garage,
taking in at a glance, one knowing glance,
questions of authenticity, of style,
the texture of my days, my life's credentials,

says he wishes he had the car I have,
claims it would all be possible with that,
all of it, only not in green, of course,
but in his lucky shade: canary yellow.

I would like to have seen, I say, Havana,
to have stood on the Malecón and watched
the darkness coming down, the first stars rising,
a full tide breaking, wave on Cuban wave.

Herbert Morris

POEM OF A CRAZY MAN

As I pounded a wedge into the heart
of maple logs stacked outside our old
Long Island house on a hot sultry day
in August, my friends said I was crazy.

That day a child was born somewhere in Bogotá.

After one red-streaked beauty split open,
neither my wife nor my daughter, who was
also born somewhere in Bogotá, saw me
kneel on the patio to lick at the sap.

I would not claim to be a visionary.
I did not pause to consider the possibility
that along about then somewhere in Bogotá
a boy was being born. I admit I just
split my log and quietly licked it.

186

But I do know that because I am crazy
enough to split wood on a hot sultry
day in August and am not afraid to lick
maple sap, that boy born somewhere
in Bogotá is going to be my son.

My daughter and I have named him Daniel.
And if he wants to dream of lions instead
of logs somewhere in this old house,
there is no way we will ever stop him.

Norbert Krapf

It is rare for British poets, other than the major ones, to attain
such a height of expression and beauty related to everyday life
and yet it seems that this would not be impossible. All that is
needed is a disregard for being clever and a determination to
speak the truth in language that is careful and succinct, aware of
emotion and impression, well-chosen and sincere to the art and
the subject matter. There is no artiness in the above poetry. It
simply says its piece and is the richer for it.

The confessional Americans did write with a sense of complexity – certainly, Berryman and Lowell did, possibly as a result of
their university education which trained them to look into the
convolutions of which language is capable – but the better ones,
Sexton and Plath, did not try to be so ingenious.

Sylvia Plath's success lies in the fact that her poetry externalises
personal emotions by stating these in the context of the world
around. (It is not easy, for example, for the average reader to
appreciate fully the intricacies of Berryman's alter-ego, Henry.)

Unlike any other female poet, Sylvia Plath wrote in terms of
starkness. The neat emotions and feminine gentleness that one
tended to associate with women's writing were absent. Her work
held blunt truth and, as truth is often violent and harsh, so it was
that the poetry followed suit:

I have done it again.
One year in every ten
I manage it –

A sort of walking miracle, my skin,
Bright as a Nazi lampshade,
My right foot

A paperweight,

My face is featureless, fine
Jew linen.

Suicide was a common theme in Sylvia Plath's verse and this
openness towards death, coming into a society that was accepting
death no longer as a taboo but as a means of final comment,
expression even, gave her an interested audience. Her violence of
idea appealed in a violent world to people for whom the bloody
violence was fast become a sign of the times; certainly, by the late
1960s and the height of the Vietnam War, violence was commonplace and almost gratuitous. For Sylvia Plath, it was but a part of
her world. Anything became game for a poem for her – death,
natural violence and beauty, love, sex, thalidomide crippling,
hatred, fear, longing, desire, places visited seen as emotional
responses . . . all feature in her work and made her a newness in
the poetic firmament. Earlier poems show less the sparseness of
language, but always the emotions are there, raw and unyielding.
Life was, for Sylvia Plath, no compromise. It was to become so for
the retinue who followed her and the rest who followed them.
Sylvia Plath also gave the language of poetry a new direction,
playing at techniques that others either did not try or rejected as
being false. They weren't and one of the important factors
towards her success and subsequent influence was the fact that
her language was that of the everyman, albeit somewhat
Americanised at times, but this was no detraction – English had
long since taken into itself a good deal of American via the movies
and the impact of the mass media. Her most famous poem
perhaps, 'Daddy', shows all of her power as a poet and her
unique use of language that opened up the floodgates on
conservatism in poetry and let things rip:

It stuck in a barb wire snare.
Ich, ich, ich, ich,
I could hardly speak.
I thought every German was you.
And the language obscene

An engine, an engine
Chuffing me off like a Jew.
A Jew to Dachau, Auschwitz, Belsen.
I began to talk like a Jew.
I think I may well be a Jew.

The snows of the Tyrol, the clear beer of Vienna
Are not very pure or true.

188

With my gipsy ancestress and my weird luck
And my Taroc pack and my Taroc pack
I may be a bit of a Jew.

This was poetry people could understand both intellectually and actually. It was still deeply conscious of emotion and the sub-minds, was still poetry in the sense of the traditional meanings, the language of the soul and the world about it, but it hit hard at substance far under the human surface and it made its times. Poets could now write as they pleased for people. Sylvia Plath made it possible for one to speak of the most basic pains and truths without self-consciousness or equivocation. What is more, she wrote as she heard the sounds in her head and, although she missed the main years of poetry performance, she prepared the seedbed of it. Listening to the few recordings that exist of Sylvia Plath reading her own work, one can understand just how important the music of words was to her. It was a facet of her work that did not escape the interest and attention of her followers. 'Mushrooms' stresses the point:

Overnight, very
Whitely, discreetly,
Very quietly

Our toes, our noses
Take hold on the loam,
Acquire the air.

Few accept, from twenty years ahead, that Sylvia Plath had such an influential position, but she had and, although she is not now 'in fashion' with poetry readers, they cannot avoid the fact that her influence is considerable and her lesson one that has become ignored. It is that poetry, no matter how close to the soul and seemingly private it is, is something for the public platform but only if it is presented in a manner such that those listening can grasp it, and if this is done then the subject matter and the art are justified as truth. The truth of poetry is invalid if it is masked or considerably camouflaged by semi-erudite scribbling and esoteric or inappropriate diction, image and structure. As has been shown, this does not reduce the will of experimentation. In many respects, Sylvia Plath's work was experimental to the British and the experiment, backed up with truth and the desire to be truthful, was a success in artistic as well as financial terms. Few poets can have earned as much this century as Sylvia Plath has done, albeit the bulk posthumously. Her death was a major loss to British poetry.

It is unfortunate that few other female poets have matched up to the challenge set by Sylvia Plath. She was taken up by the feminist movement, as well as by women everywhere who could identify with and appreciate her feelings. She wrote from the core of the modern woman's soul and, since so many males also took wholeheartedly to her poetry, she did a vast amount for the female cause. For the first time in a long time, Sylvia Plath showed that a woman could be a prime force in poetry. The drive seems to have died out with not only her death but the now slower purchasing of her books.

Of the female poets who have come to the fore since 1964, few can be listed as great and, although some show promise and hope for the future, they do not shine like the Plath beacon to all and sundry. It is a sorry fact that most modern female poets seem to be writing only for their own sex and the men are ignored; perhaps this is a throwback to the liberation years, but I think not. I think it is another instance of poetry become a narrowing influence and an introverted one.

Who has come to the poetry spotlight? Not many. Yet those who have gained prominence are good and of interest not only to poetry lovers but also to those who would see what the inner minds of women do in verse. Again, unfortunately, the delving isn't as deep as the Plath spade was wont to go.

Some were already on the scene at Sylvia Plath's arrival – Patricia Beer and Stevie Smith spring most to mind, the former still going strong and the latter now dead but as powerful a force as ever and one that is gaining a new readership through a revival in her work and the fact that it has appeared (and survived) listings in public examination papers.

Patricia Beer's work is best described as safe. It takes no risks and is rooted firmly in a security that chauvinists might say is typical of women who are happy and safe in a home, a marriage and a round of life in which they know themselves. 'The Accident' is a poem that roundly supports this view:

Dear Husband, Please come to me.
Yesterday I fell on these stern rocks
And lie in hospital. I was wrong to walk
Here alone. Please come, for both our sakes.

As I fell I noticed the seagulls above me.
Legs dangling, wings pumping, they yelled

Out of white breast feathers and spotted beaks.
Then their cliff drew them back. They wheeled. . . .

Alongside Sylvia Plath's 'Fever 103°', this hasn't a leg to stand on:

Darling, all night
I have been flickering off, on, off, on.
The sheets grow heavy as a lecher's kiss.

Whereas the Plath poem pushes life and experience to an extreme, the Beer one merely states a fact and poetry can and should be made to do more than this. Stevie Smith, in her inimitable manner, did shove poetry into the reaches of the distance. In her case, it was a bizarre, macabre, witty, mystical, strange, wonderful and exotic place where the imagination was Empress and the life she outlined one of melancholic humour. Indeed, Stevie Smith was an enigma. And she was not necessarily a female poet, but just a poet as was Sylvia Plath. Certainly, there are womanly outlooks and ideas at work, but the best poets transcend sexual (as any other) boundaries. (Hence the use of the word poet for both sexes in this book, rather than poet and poetess. The Canadian poet Susan Musgrave always insisted that in her mind was a human, regardless of what might signify its type between her thighs, and that poetry should cut across the sexual lines of distinction. Plath's does. So does Musgrave's, but she's a Canadian and not in the sphere of this book. One of the faults of modern verse is that it draws lines around itself. At least, British verse does.)

In many ways, Stevie Smith was so enigmatic as not to be a product of any time but her own. She came to prominence in the post-1964 period because her kind of humour and wit, allied to considerable feelings of emotion and expression of the human condition, came of age in a society that understood it. What is more, with her strange, musically high-pitched voice and her tiny shape, she was made for the new era of performing poets. To attend one of her readings was to be instantly captivated, instantly charmed and entertained and enriched. Her poetry is child-like, simple and both serious and tongue-in-cheek: it is charged with feeling and pathos. It is the soul bared.

With easy rhyme schemes and common words, Stevie Smith dealt with the core of life as she saw it. To her, it was not a complication to live, but a joy and a sorrow, alternating with each other. She used language simply but with energy and, for this, she was as successful as Sylvia Path, though not as influential simply because she was swamped by the years of the Plath regime in poetry.

A few fragments of Stevie Smith's poetry show just how good her verse was in terms of artistic integrity and achievement as well as public accessibility:

> The City Dog goes to the drinking trough,
> He waves his tail and laughs, and goes when he has had
>   enough.
> His intelligence is on the brink
> Of human intelligence. He knows the Council will give
>   him a drink.
>
> (The Wild Dog)

> All these illegitimate babies. . . .
> Oh girls, girls,
> Silly little cheap things,
> Why do you not put some value on yourselves,
> Learn to say, No?
> Did nobody teach you?
> Nobody teaches anybody to say No nowadays,
> People should teach people to say no.
>
> (Valuable – after
reading two paragraphs
in a newspaper)

And a complete poem entitled 'Bag-Snatching in Dublin':

> Sisley
> Walked so nicely
> With footsteps so discreet
> To see her pass
> You'd never guess
> She walked upon the street.
>
> Down where the Liffey waters' turgid flood
> Churns up to greet the ocean-driven mud,
> A bruiser in a fix
> Murdered her for 6/6.

This was not light verse then nor is it now. It is a comment upon life, a sick joke in the latter poem and one that has innuendo and wit to it that makes it work on more than one level. What is more, this is poetry that all can understand and most poets admire, too. This is the criterion poetry should aim at – to be simple, but deviously artistic, too.

Other female poets of the 'swinging sixties' came part-way towards making verse as universal in appeal. Some of them have vanished now without trace, some have kept going and some have re-appeared. Those who are the best are so because they aren't writing as women but as people, writing for people and not for women alone.

Two who come particularly to mind are Ruth Fainlight and Jenny Joseph. They are alike in that they are both women poets and yet they write for a broad readership. Ruth Fainlight, married to the novelist and poet Alan Sillitoe, was born in 1931 and first published a book (and not a very good one) in 1958, but it was not until *Cages* (1966) that she really hit the market place. Her poetry has since made another six collections, including one that is a limited edition in which she appears alongside her husband and Ted Hughes. This is an interesting volume for one sees in it the power of the argument that poets are at best poets and not men and women. Ruth Fainlight's work stands on a par with her co-authors:

> Lamb of Lucifer
> So suave, so sulphur-white,
> So strong. You hurt me
> When you press into my womb,
> Bite through my lips, obliterate
> All air and light.
> Oh, beautiful.
> I arch beneath your weight
> Become saintly
> As I suffer

and there are distinct similarities in the above between the work of Hughes's *Crow* poems and Sillitoe's *Lucifer* poems of several years afterwards. When in a quieter mood, Ruth Fainlight is a poet to be reckoned with: in 'New Year in England' she shows a positive response to the world around her and she lays it out for all to read and feel, again, the sign of the real poet:

> Red tiles on the huddled village roofs
> fusing into the smoky glow,
> the marshland and hills, the mist which makes
> a floating crimson lake of light
> the sun's last fanning rays illuminate,
> the further arch of winter blue.

The clouds also demand their praise –
those purple banners, and corded nap
of new-ploughed earth. Yet something is lacking.

Jenny Joseph takes this line, too – the one that leads to
directness of vision linked to skilful use of language and the
poetic arts. Her world is different from Ruth Fainlight's, but that
is good, for the more worlds poetry explains the better. One of its
troubles of late is that it is too busy looking at much the same
view all of the time and not seeking to explore away from the
confines of the immediate. A blinkering of vision and experience
has never served poetry well.

Jenny Joseph was born in 1932 and, like many of today's poets
and often to their detriment, read English at Oxford. Her poetry
does not show a slavery to learning, fortunately, and the reason is
that, after leaving university, she went out into life rather than
into a new set of cloisters, be they educational or professional.
(Many poets who have a university education and who have not
been able to kick the habit of it have wound up in narrowing jobs
such as teaching, where they have restricted their own human
growth and therefore their artistic development into the bargain.)
Published first by the famous Scorpion Press, whence have
issued many a good poet, in a booklet entitled *The Unlooked-for
Season* (1960), Jenny Joseph has become over the years a
well respected writer although her reputation is based upon but
three books, there being a gap of fifteen years between her first
and second collections. Taken up in 1975 by Dent, she had one
book out from them (*Rose in the Afternoon*) before transferring to
the Secker & Warburg list where her poetry has gained the
attention it deserves. She writes in the common tongue of life as
she sees it, and it is the life of the human, not the poet. This is
important for poetry tends to be something liking to write about
itself rather than what people want to touch: too much recent
poetry talks of what the poets think we ought to hear rather than
what we actually want to hear. Jenny Joseph reacts against this
miserable trend:

This do here, by the window? The steak's not bad.
– Yes, Elspeth, please, and a carafe of red wine I think.
Brought my friend Jack to see you, so do your best. –
The service is good here – foreign. There used to be
A smashing German. My God, what a bottom!
Mixed grill for you? Well, I'll have steak as usual.
Always do on Friday. It's steak tonight
And what my wife calls steak – well, you couldn't see it.

194

'Treat for you tonight, dear' she's going to say
'You work so hard. Two lovely days at home.'

This striving for reality in verse, at every level from meaning
and diction to intention, is a trait of the people of Jenny Joseph's
poetic generation which includes Alan Brownjohn, Philip Hobsbaum, Adrian Mitchell and Peter Redgrove (of whom more later).
They reacted against the poetry-for-poets world that preceded
them and they might well be taken as an object lesson by those
now seeking to be up-and-comers in the poetry limelight, a light
they go some way towards fugging up.

Few other women poets have done as well as Ruth Fainlight
and Jenny Joseph although they have had ample opportunity and
show in their work more than a degree of talent. Anne
Stevenson, English by birth (1933) but mercifully American by
education, shows her childhood influences in her work and is one
of the more promising of the batch. Her work is interesting in
form and, especially in her earlier books such as *Correspondences*
and *Travelling Behind Glass* (poems from the period 1963–73),
published in 1974, she shows a very solid talent and exceptional
skill, especially in the former which is a poem sequence following
one New England family through 150 years. The promise that this
poet showed has not entirely materialised as yet and one feels there
are considerable strengths to be realised in her future writing.
Elaine Feinstein, best known as an outstanding novelist, comes
into this group. Her work is similarly safely tucked up in its poetic
bed, only on occasion showing the thrill it can give that one
knows from her novels. When she is good (like Anne Stevenson)
she is very good; when she is not, she is quietly like Fleur
Adcock. The following, from a poem called 'Exile', illustrates
what she can do:

> Estonian ghosts of
> riverbirds within the
> temples of his skull, ashes
> of poets, girders of school houses:
> these are the tired politics
> that vein his eyes
>
> scoop a pouch under his lower
> lip. . . .

Since 1975 there has been a clear upsurge in the number of
female poets writing and publishing, but most show little verve.
There are a few who could lead the way into a new consciousness

of providing good poetry that isn't self-aware twaddle, but it is too early to tell. These few possible poetry savers include U. A. Fanthorpe, Frances Horovitz, Nicki Jackowska, Anne Beresford and Penelope Shuttle, a mixed bag as will be shown.

The first, U. A. Fanthorpe, is published by Harry Chambers/ Peterloo Poets and has had two books out to date. She was born in 1929, went up to Oxford (that place again) and then became a schoolteacher for many years until – in her own words – she became a middle-aged drop-out. Her poetry is superb and shows the marks of having lived rather than learnt. From 'Linguist' comes:

> The smashed voice roars inside the ruined throat
> Behind the mangled face. Voice of the wild,
> Voice of a warthog calling to his mates,
>
> Wordless, huge-volumed, sad. We can't make out
> A meaning (though his wife can). Solitary
> He sits, shrouded in his vast noise. How strange
>
> To make so much, none of it any use
> To fragile human ears, except to mis-
> Inform. For we all make the obvious
>
> And wrong deduction: *this poor chap is mad*.

The pathos that develops in the poem is moving and the whole is skilful in its interpretation of human existence. This is a latter-day Plath at work, a poet who does not shirk the unpleasant directions of life, but uses them to explain other workings of being. U. A. Fanthorpe is not one to avoid stretching the barriers of verse again. In 'Carol Concert', she hits a note that is a hybrid of Betjeman's early verse, Larkin's adroit social comment and the best of the experimenters. What is more, her language is that which all know – it is governed by the spoken word:

> Before the ice has time to form
> On the carparked windscreens, before
> A single carol has announced itself,
> The performance happens.
> (sing lullaby virgin noel)
>
> These sculptured hairdos, these fairy-
> Tale dresses, gothic embraces –
> *Sophie, long time no see!* – are they

The approved offering
(sing lullaby virgin noel)

The wit and biting satire of the poem about a public (girls'?) school carol concert is unlike much that can appear from many a pen these days. This is verse at its best. It states. It does not dodge the issues it arouses. It entertains. It explains. It has life in it. It is not restricted to the poet's own world. It is, to use a critic's praise, tender and scathing poetry. That it covers both these shows its excellence.

Frances Horovitz is another poet who writes of realities, but hers are softer and not unlike Anne Beresford's – both are the wives of poets: Frances Horovitz was married to Michael and Anne Beresford is Michael Hamburger's wife. Sadly, Frances Horovitz has been missed by the big publishers: her work has appeared in a *New Departures* booklet and a fine book from *Enitharmon Press*. Her subject matter is quiet and she is not one to draw out a poem to extremes, which is a pity, for her ideas are interesting. For example, in the poem 'Sea-horse', she writes:

> Holiday trophy from Cornwall
> he lies in cotton wool, fingernail long.
> Obsidian eye glitters.
> He is light as a husk, fragile.
> Embryo perfect
> he seems not dead, but waiting.

but the poem ends only with the dried creature forming dust to ride the summer fields. Nevertheless, Frances Horovitz's poetry is accomplished. Why? It uses ordinary speech and she knows only too well the value and possibilities of such.

She was, until her early and untimely death from cancer in October, 1983, an actress by training and she has a considerable reputation as a BBC poetry performer and reader. (It is well to note here that, when Frances Horovitz died, a trust fund set up for her young son was very heavily subscribed from sources throughout the literary establishment and, a month after her death, a major poetry reading was held in Bristol. This was of the magnitude of the big readings of the Sixties and had a line up consisting of Ted Hughes, Seamus Heaney, D. M. Thomas, Patrick Kavanagh, Anne Stevenson, Charles Tomlinson and Libby Houston. Few major poets could, one suspect, draw such a tribute and it goes to indicate the importance of the poetry and the poet over the publication history, for Frances Horovitz was never published by more than a small press.) Frances Horovitz knew the score that diction can demand and it shows in her poetry where she treats words with the sense of sound as well as meaning, much as a musician might regard sounds in a score sheet. Anne Beresford's verse does as much, too. She is well known, with both small press and established company publication behind her, notably a book called *Songs a Thracian Taught Me*, published by Marion Boyars. Typical of her work is a poem called 'Farmer's Fantasy', in which a farmer inherits a talisman.

> It were from a black toad,
> with a star on its back
> found under and owd felled log,
> his grandfather whispering before he died,
> thrusting it into his hand.

The talisman coldly performed farming miracles for him but left him in power but powerless. He decides to rid himself of it, to bury it:

> But he couldn't stop thinking.
>
> 'I must fetch me a spade from the barn,'
> as he left the house,
> the spade coming to meet him
> you could almost say walking.

The better conscious the poet is of the reader and his abilities, the better the poetry. A simple poem about a farmer's wish-fulfilment is just that to some but an allegory for others.

Nicki Jackowska and Penelope Shuttle are very similar and this is not surprising for both have come under the considerable and talented influence of Peter Redgrove, who is the latter's co-author on both verse and prose work as well as being her husband. Jackowska and Shuttle both view life as a magical process and write of it in terms that indicate an acceptance of such fates and motions:

> Across blue fields to find Satan
> White stars above me, roots of fire
> I want to unlock the keys of the piano
>
> On volcanic islands I hear the passage
> of clumsy adults without wings
> I am one of them
>
> *Penelope Shuttle*

And my room is red and warm she said
round and warm of the red earth
berries that fell and bled
the snake whose skin is shed
I wear a mask to capture your head
I am white acid she said, she said.
                              Nicki Jackowska

This is not, however, a contrivance, but a deliberate searching process into the soul's eye and, though many critics damn this poetic stance, the poetry appeals to a large audience because it caters in some strange way to the interest aroused in the public by psychology and the inner mind, an interest that hangs on as a result of the magical-tripping-mystery-tour world of the late 1960s. On the surface, the poetry may be obscure, with metaphors that are weirdly alien or unattached to pre-formed concepts in the mind, but then this is but a stretching of verse and language once more into an area in which the reader can find himself as explorer, not sheep led to the evening fence. (Sadly, Nicki Jackowska's work of the 1980s has become narrowly obtuse and inaccessible.)

For poetry is a business of exploration: the explorer must beat a path through the language of words in order to take his safari forwards. There is no use in building a path – hacking one, perhaps – through a jungle that only closes over as soon as the poet/leader has passed, or is only half a path with stinging, whipping twigs to assail the intrepid follower. Poetry must cut a clear way through the forests of the mind, allowing others to come in and see from its security.

The best poets do this. The better of the new ones attempt or achieve this. They are people who live for their art and do not sully themselves with the mirages of skill, but the actual talents that they have and which are also abundantly present in our language. Going way back to the Anglo-Saxons at the start of the book, one sees that this has been the case all along with good poetry. And good means accessible, understanding and under-standable, interpretative and entertaining.

So far, poets have been classified – the loose 'Secker School', the Carcanet poets, The Group and so on and, whilst some of these are clearly defined categorisations, others are not and there are a good many poets who steer clear of cliques and schools, seeking perhaps to identify themselves with a certain type of poetry but not with a certain band of practitioners. It is time to look at some of these unaffiliated poets who are not allied to a certain ticket. They are presented in no set order of merit or importance but just given one after the other and they are listed for ease of reading. Some have made quite major contributions, others have not. What they have all given is integrity, artistry and a seriousness of purpose that is not restricted to self-indulgence and self-advancement – they are people who live for poetry, not those for whom poetry exists as a tool of self-opinionism.

These are the people who can be called 'Outsiders' for they are in the art, but live on their own. They are variously published by a number of firms (big and small) and we are lucky that they have either slipped through the editorial nets that publishers put up or that their editors have had aberrations and taken their books on in moments of carelessness. This latter might be the case in a few instances for some of them have been dropped in recent years and are now writing without a publisher in mind.

Another point must be borne in mind before embarking on this listing and that is that the classification cuts across others that are not based upon particular cliques but upon techniques or structural aspects of poetry. Therefore one finds in the Outsider grouping a good number of, for example, Performance Poets, who write specifically to be heard as well as read off the page.

It might be a good idea to start with a number of the performers for they were and still are, to some extent, the public face of British poetry who shop-front the art with the likes of established poets such as MacBeth, Hughes, Brownjohn and Heaney who also do a good deal of performing or reading.

1   Gavin Ewart was born in 1916 and first published at the age of 17. He spent many years away from poetry but returned to it with gusto in 1966 with a book entitled *Pleasures of the Flesh*, published by Alan Ross. His poetry is risqué, charming, witty, blunt, rude, serious, touching, flippant and skilful. He is not everyone's choice for there are times (particularly in more recent years when two books appeared from Anvil Press – *All My Little Ones* and *More Little Ones*, containing epigrammatic pieces and limericks – to mixed reviews) when his poems don't quite hit it off, but that is the case with everyone. He realises that he writes for a mass market and therefore it is impossible for him to retain his standards for he writes in bulk, being more prolific than many. He also knows that his work can be rude for he has in one limerick:

> There was an old fellow called Ewart,
> whose verse some despised as a blue art –

In other poems, where Ewart writes with less brevity, he is original, funny and clever in the positive sense of the word. Mostly, he writes for the sophisticate, which might come as a bit of a surprise after the above comments, aiming his work at the city-dwellers for whom his kind of humour, wrapped in the Monty Python mould, is paramount and equates with the sense of with-it-ness that city life holds dear. His poetry is rich with allusion to literature and to the present and, certainly, some of his poetry will date. When he writes of topical events, E. Jarvis-Thribb (17) (of *Private Eye*) and current temporary attitudes, he is witty but just as temporary. Yet Ewart has written poetry that will last and he is the nearest to come to the tradition of Edward Lear. What is more, he is the only writer of his kind today producing such poetry. As a performer, he is superb. With lines like the following, delivered in a rich, deep and humorous voice, one cannot fail to see Ewart's success.

> What bosom tapped me on the shoulder?
>> Sandra.
> What blossoming beauty made me feel much older?
> > Sandra.
> What sweet Italian English made me flinch,
> Then made a man of me, yes every inch?
> > Sandra.

and

> That heavy-featured Turkish face
> reminds me of another place;
> for most of 1873
> we shall be joined in buggeree.

> Your harem trousers filled with grace
> are like balloons in Chevy Chase;
> you are the most delightful she
> I ever filled with buggeree.
> > (from The Noble English Traveller
> > Contemplates Turkish Delight)

2   Peter Morgan has but three books to his name, along with a number of small press pamphlets, but his reputation is large. Born in 1939, he went into the army on leaving school – as an officer – but resigned his commission after six years and, after working variously (including in the old stopgap for poets, advertising, which has held a good few in the last fifty years), took to full-time writing in 1969. He performs his work and his poems look thin on the page but erupt like bombs on the ear. He reads with the panache of a trooper (the pun is one he would appreciate) from the music hall. Such poems as 'The Meat Work

Saga!' and 'Bang, Mister' have given him a large listenership. He has worked the poetry reading circuit of universities, literary societies, clubs, pubs and arts festivals with success: he has written poetically for television and is one of the very few to do this in Britain: he has toured the USA.

It is difficult to show to its full advantage, in print, the poetry of those who lean towards performance for their main artistic target, but the following should give some idea of Morgan's abilities:

> (of Arthur Prance, who was Fred Astaire's stand-in and who committed suicide jumping from a skyscraper)

> The one time only Arthur Prance –
> 'The Man Who Taught The Stars To Dance' –
> possessed an act of wide appeal
> especially his eightsome reel
> danced alone.

> The one time only Arthur Prance –
> 'The Man Who Taught The Stars To Dance' –
> performed his final pirouette
> and heard applause he didn't get.

and

> SECONDS OUT
> ROUND THREE

> (BELL)

> 168 lbs of meat
> can be kosher –
> 168 lbs of meat
> can get crucified –
> 168 lbs of meat
> can also trip –
> 168 lbs of meat
> believes in flags
>   frontiers,
>   and meat –

Where Morgan's work does succeed on the page, it uses at times some interesting techniques. 'The Technicolour Dream' incorporates camera instructions, for example, and the poem quoted above contains a section where the audience are obliged to imitate a nuclear explosion by going 'Whoooosh!' at the end, although this instruction has been omitted from the printed text in Morgan's book, *The Grey Mare Being The Better Steed* (1973), published by Secker & Warburg as was his next, *The Spring Collection* (1979); he is an example of one of that publisher's wiser, wider choices.

3 . . . as was Edwin Brock. Born in 1927, he has worked as an advertising man, a journalist, a policeman and has been in the navy. His poetry reads well on the page but is best in performance and, although he seldom reads in public now, there was a time in the 1960s when he was popular as a reader and his absence from the stage, for whatever reason, is a loss. It was only in 1973 that Secker & Warburg took him on: prior to that year he had an assortment of publishers, but it was his inclusion in the Penguin Modern Poets series that shot him into the limelight. He wrote his most famous poems in the 1960s and those by which he is still most remembered – 'Song of the Battery Hen', 'Five Ways to Kill a Man', 'Symbols of the Sixties', 'Let's Burn Lady Chatterley' and the ironic 'Catastrophe'. Brock's hallmarks are – as is needed in performance-biased poetry – wit, pathos, a commonality of diction, quick-fire punchlines and puns, narrative and, his special trait, a wry and sidelong look at modern society. In some ways, he is like Ewart in this, but Brock has a quality of wistfulness to his better work, a subtle corner that Ewart lacks. Consider the following and think of them being given in a quiet, slightly sardonic manner:

> We can't grumble about accommodation:
> we have a new concrete floor that's
> always dry, four walls that are
> painted white, and a sheet-iron roof
> the rain drums on. A fan blows warm air
> beneath our feet to disperse the smell
> of chickenshit and, on dull days,
> fluorescent lighting sees us.

or

> I destroyed the first cat we had:
> crammed her into a basket one spring-wet
> day and walked angrily to the vet. 'Do away
> with her' I said. 'For a year we've tried
> to train her, and the flat is full of fishbones
> and catshit.' The second cat, a small grey
> one that I loved, pined for the first
> and died a month later.

That poem, 'Catastrophe', ends with a rueful look at how the poet was the Eichmann of cats, hoping that his wives don't go the same way for he might then find that he likes living in this manner. What starts as a poem about a cat winds up as a comment – and a sharply observant one, at that – on the human condition.

This is the sort of poetry that made the art popular. People could understand it and it said something relevant, unlike much of the poetry of, say, the late 1970s. Also, it is interesting to note that the three poets described above do not have a university background.

4   A poet who did not make it to the 'big' publishers, but who was well-known in his day – he seems not to be writing now – was Lee Harwood. His work came out from a gamut of small publishers, including Fulcrum Press and Oasis Books. He was born in Leicester in 1939, but was brought up in Surrey and London. He did attend university in London but seems to have wisely reacted against this training for he obtained very un-graduate-like jobs – librarian, bookshop assistant (at 'Better Books'), stonemason for 'monumental work', bus conductor and Post Office clerk. He took upon himself several writer-in-residencies in the USA and Greece and was widely known as a poetry reader-cum-performer throughout England and the eastern USA in the 1960s. His poetry was accessible but it was not light verse, a term which might be applied to the poetry of Ewart and Brock. His verse is denser and more serious but it was best heard rather than seen on the page for Harwood could bring it alive with his voice. His style is conversational, often using direct speech, and he wrote of matters close to all:

> The children playing on the front step
> the sea is green
> today   the power games
> can't be gentler
>
> The walk along the beach at night
> shingle   back home the animals
> all playing games underlined with violence
> maybe cruelty

The influence of American poetry upon Harwood is great but he does not allow himself to be taken over by it. He uses the freedom of expression and break from tradition that is typical of American verse to good end, to extend his Englishness, for he is, particularly in his earlier work, obviously British in an intangible way.

To move on, but away from poets who aimed at performance, it might be pertinent to state here that most poets read in public given the chance and therefore could all be classed as performers to some extent. The difference is that the performer seeks to write for that end, whereas other poets seek to write poetry the reading of which is incidental to the initial act of putting pen to paper. Those who are to follow give readings but their prime concern is the page.

5   Geoffrey Hill was born in 1932 and was educated at Keble College, Oxford; he has worked since as a university teacher. He has published six main collections and an important pamphlet and it is upon these that his considerable reputation rests. His poetry is the one that proves the exception for it is highly popular yet academic in the extreme. It is thick with allusion and often has an accompanying notes section to explain or annotate the poems: it is best described as learned and it must go over the heads of many of his readers – and yet they are numerous. Possibly part of the audience's preoccupation with Hill's work lies in the fact that he is a mysterious figure who does not seek the publicity that poetry can offer but prefers to remain enigmatic. Another point might be that although his work is very 'literary', it is strangely open at the same time as being complex.

Possibly his most important book, *Mercian Hymns*, published in 1971, is just so seminal because it is so readily accessible. It is a fantasy loosely based upon King Offa, a series of prose poems that look at him living yet dead, a figure worthy of castigation yet praise, celebration of his being yet a lament at his absence. Some of the poems are very tenuous in their link and rely for success mostly upon the fact that they are looking at history (which is also the present) through minutiae. The overriding unity comes from the book's regard for the Celtic homelands of Britain, now and in the past:

> We ran across the meadow scabbed with cow-dung, past
> the crab-apple trees and camouflaged nissen hut.
> It was curfew-time for our war-band.

Whenever Hill writes, even if the meaning is obscure, the poetry is always lyrical and powerful, strangely universal and yet simultaneously very personal indeed. One poem, from his first full-length collection, *For the Unfallen* (1959 but reprinted through-out the 1960s), entitled 'After Cumae', begins:

> The sun again unearthed, colours come up fresh,
> The perennials; and the laurels'
> Washable leaves, that seem never to perish,
> Obscure the mouthy cave, the dumb grottoes.

205

The classics and religion are themes and subjects Hill is fond of and, in many aspects, he seems a natural successor to the religious mystical writers of the last two centuries. Certainly, of all the poets who made up the new revival in the 1960s, Hill is perhaps the most obscure yet still fascinating. His poetry, not written for a market or the times, was caught up by them in the face of the interest in matters magical that were reborn in the period, and he was accepted much as a shaman might be into a crowd of commuters. In later years, his books turned towards a deeper narrowing of vision and esotericism and, with this development, his popularity waned somewhat. He is the poet's poet who became more widely read when he wrote at his most accessible.

6   Another outsider is Daniel Huws. Born in 1932, he has written but one book which was published in 1972. *Noth* was quietly received and Huws has published nothing since. However, he is an important poet of the period regardless of his tiny output. His poetry, praised by Ted Hughes in a rare book jacket blurb appearance, has the reticent innocence of de la Mare's work and is, in a way, a continuation of his type of verse. Huws writes with a simplistic form in which he reviews folk life and the plainer magic of common beings in a lyrical manner. Yet he is very competent technically and can handle metre and rhyme with ease and effectiveness. Sorrow is an integral part of Huw's work, too. Comparison with Edwin Muir's poetry is begged because of this and Huws comes off well against such a great poet as Muir:

> They pleaded with him, they gently urged
> 'The party's not yet over, come
> Just one more drink.' But right away home
> On twelve staggering legs he lurched.

> The front door slammed like a thunder of stones.
> So sound they slept, not a neighbour stirred.
> The air was close and he was tired.
> He took off his flesh and lay in his bones.

So ends the life and soul of the party, a man who seems happy but harbours an inner woe beyond all others'. One can mention Huws but briefly: his sole output is the one book. However, he has to be mentioned because he wrote poetry that was immediate in its impact and, had he continued to publish, he would have become a major figure at the centre of the stage. Instead, he inhabits the wings.

7   It is unusual for a poet to become an internationally famous author but this did occur, as has been mentioned elsewhere, in the case of D. M. Thomas, and riding with his prose success has come his poetry so that, by 1983, he has a wide following and his verse is published in the mass market place, brought out by Penguin Books. As a poet, Thomas was an outsider, someone who was not concerned with cliques and groups. Born in 1935, Thomas read English at Oxford and entered a career in teaching that came to an abrupt end when his college of education in Hereford was closed down and he was made redundant. Throughout his adult life he wrote verse that was forged with a strong awareness of his Cornish roots, the fantastical aspects of old religions and magics, his geographical environment and science fiction. Like many regional British writers, Thomas is more than conscious of his family's past and the histories of his area but he was to prove of wider appeal than the term 'regional' might imply. His semi-autobiographical poem, *The Shaft* (Arc brought it out in 1973), showed his potential to a greater degree than his previous two books published by Cape Goliard (*Two Voices* in 1968 and *Logan Stone* in 1971):

> Perhaps somewhere
> also, a wife, a son. Also perhaps
> a mistress. Certainly photos of two women
> and a boy share my desk with fool's gold. I am vague.
> Take home from the pub some little Cornish whore,
> strip tights, pants, go into that curious hole.
> I am a skilled opener of mines. Then
> a tiny tremor as of acute fatigue
> and the total infalling collapse.

Few poets could carry off such a conceit, a mine-shaft on a Cornish tin mine springing off into the privations and wonders of private life. Thomas has had this ability all of his poetic career. Much of his work, even up to his two major collections, published after his fame as a novelist erupted, is of this sort. His best collection, *Dreaming in Bronze* (Secker & Warburg, 1981), continues this Cornish attraction so that his poems, seen as a corpus, become a personalised saga of love, history and the inner workings of a commonplace but fortunate man. The sensual quality of Thomas's work – the eroticism in his poetry, the beauty and the love of women – has given it a power few have failed to notice. This quality, which is so over-used or over-played in the novels where it becomes almost overbearing, is subtle, touching and emotionally (occasionally physically) arousing in the poetry and it has brought Thomas many readers. Another aspect of his poetic success lies in the fact that he has kept clear of the literary mainstream and continues to write as he wants which is also what readers want. He writes and they understand.

8   Ted Walker's success lies in his being understood. His work is compared at times with Ted Hughes's earlier 'nature' poetry but this is only for want of a genre to stick him in. He is not a Hughesian writer at all but one who is set in his poetry in a world that involves nature as he sees it. Most of his poems are set in Sussex, where he makes a living from prose and playwriting as much as poetry. He has succeeded in keeping clear of the 'scene' and this has been his blessing for he has not been washed under by a tide of similar poets. He is an individual who regards poetry as lifeblood and he writes for an audience to accept him in his world. He is an outward-going poet, not one who is locked into his own confines, and he goes out to his readers, not requesting with artistic selfishness that they journey inwards to him.

His first book, *Fox on a Barn Door* (all of his books are published by Cape), appeared in 1965 and he published a new collection every three years up to *Burning the Ivy* in 1978. His poetry has been consistently powerful and he is unlike most other British writers in that his style is direct and uncompromising and not a little like the better American poetry of the period by such writers as Robert Bly, David Wagoner and William Stafford; indeed, Walker publishes much of his work in the USA being a regular contributor to *The New Yorker*. Perhaps it is his Americanistic stance that has led to his being shovelled aside by the poetry scene, for Walker, although his books have received major awards including the first Cholmondeley Award, has not been taken to the bosom of the poetry literati. This is, of course, to his benefit but it also shows the detrimental attitudes that can spring up in an art that is so incestuous. Having escaped the incest, however, Walker has survived probably better than most with his integrity intact. He was born in 1934 and studied modern languages at Cambridge where, like Ted Hughes, he fought against the rigours of academic training inasmuch as he did not allow these to destroy his art. Although not often called upon to do so, Walker is a powerful and fascinating poetry reader and the way out of the 1980s doldrums in British verse might well be found through him, for it is time that he was not so much revived as re-introduced to a new generation of poetry followers.

His poetry has wide range. 'Easter Poem', about finding a fox nailed to a barn door to dry out the pelt; shooting rooks; staying with disillusioned émigrés in the USA; creatures of the zodiac such as the archer:

Sunday morning. A public
park, behind the tennis court.

Behold the bourgeoise figure
practising toxophily.

She is as old as England.
Fibre-glass flexes. She aims.

Her green person is bedecked
with thongs. Inside that leathery

head are fletchings, fistmeles, nocks.

and his most famous poem, 'Pig Pig', based upon a fourteenth-century trial of a rich man's pig for murder in which the cruel social injustice of all ages is highlighted in a strong narrative poem amongst the best of the times. Walker is not concerned just with observing the world. He is intent upon commenting upon it, drawing attention to it (often from a socialist/humanist point of view) and explaining it. For this reason, he deserves a huge audience, and certainly his first book reprinted a number of times which is rare for a book of verse in Britain. That he does not have such a following into the 1980s is caused by the fact that he has not published a book of verse since 1978, concentrating instead on prose and television plays. If he was to re-appear in printed form, he might well cause a reversal in the trends towards moribundity that British poetry has followed after, roughly, the last Walker collection.

9   Leslie Norris is a Welsh poet and a close friend of Ted Walker; indeed, they are sometimes mentioned as a pair living outside the literary set-up and getting on with it. Norris began life as a schoolmaster and retired as a college principal lecturer: his university education was at a 'new' university and he escaped the pressures of the traditional establishments. His first book was *Finding Gold*, published by Chatto & Windus in 1968; at least, this was the first to gather major interest in his work. Born in 1921, Norris first published in 1941 and again in 1944 but seems to have become dormant in the interim years.

Norris is Welsh and his poetry illustrates the patriotism of the Welsh for Wales and 'all things Welsh' but this is not to suggest that Norris's work is narrow. Quite the opposite is true. He is a well-travelled man and his poetry looks at Italy, the USA, history, nature and Wales, personal relationships and memory. Indeed, memory is important for Norris in that his work relies upon the recreation of the past to enlighten the present. He is a keen reader of Edward Thomas's work and the sad and melancholic beauty of that poet's best writing often infiltrates that of Norris:

> Drugged all day, the summer
> Flagged in its heat, brutal
> Weather sullen as brass.
> There was no comfort in darkness.
> Hotter than breath we lay
>
> On beds too warm for moving,
> Near open windows. Full of
> Spaces the house was, walls
> Fretting for a brisk air.

Like Walker, Norris has had his share of literary prizes too but, regardless, he still finds his verse on the fringe of the main current because he has not allied himself to a group. In some respects, he might have done better to do so but in others, he is fortunate to have remained apart, retaining a distinct identity which is a common trait of many of the outsiders.

10 Ken Smith has, in the 1980s, seen a considerable and justified re-awakening of interest in his work due largely to the small press, Bloodaxe Books, reissuing and publishing a good deal of his material.

Smith has kept well clear of cliques and it has paid off in no uncertain terms, both in measure of artistic ability and success.

Born in 1938, Smith was first published in a Northern House pamphlet, *Eleven Poems*, in 1963 but it was his first book, *The Pity*, published by Cape in 1967 that gained him attention and caused him to share a Gregory Award with Ted Walker. It was to be his only full-length English collection for some years for Smith soon after moved to live in the USA where his second book, *Work, Distances/Poems*, was published by Swallow Press in Chicago in 1972. This book was to indicate a major talent at work, much of it influenced considerably by its being expatriate. In the last section of the book, Smith confronts his two poetically cultural halves and comes to grips with many themes and ideas central to trans-Atlantic poetry. In the mid-1970s, Smith returned to England and continued writing here, Arc Publications bringing out *Frontwards in a Backwards Movie* (1974), Bloodaxe Books doing *Tristan Crazy* (1978), Oasis Books *What I'm Doing Now* (1980) and Bloodaxe then returning to publish *Fox Running, abel baker charlie delta epic sonnets, Burned Books* and *The Poet Reclining: selected poems* between 1980 and 1983. These have all achieved considerable critical success and have sold very well indeed in Britain.

The poetry is not English. It has escaped the bounds of insularity and is not only universal in content but also wide in appeal. There is no indulgence or literary pandering in Smith's work; he speaks straight and true and all can understand him whether he is writing poems set in pubs (as in *abel baker . . .*) or on Dartmoor, on Mao Tse-tung's long march or of North American Indian folklore. His poetry is primal and basic, important for the discoveries that it makes of human action and interaction and the lyrical beauty with which it interprets the world upon which it looks:

> To Morden to Putney to Wandsworth
> to Beckenham Junction
> to Stockwell to Battersea Park
>
> Where I was anyone anywhere
> on hands and knees
> who would crawl to the horizon
> finding someone to say *yes* to

It is difficult to say just what it is of Smith's work that is the best. He has written to a consistently high standard throughout his career and he has not pandered either to his own or to literary fashions and whims. What is more, he has come close on a number of occasions to writing political verse: *Burned Books* is an ambitious collection of prose poems intermingled with free verse pieces which are about the burning of 'President Perdu's' library, and the parallels with Nixon, with modern society and with man's inner desire to self-destruct are evident and cleverly utilised in the sequence. Smith is known for his sequential work, too. *Fox Running* uses a period of breakdown to construct a series of poems about a poet lost in the metropolis of slums and poverty, seeking himself and a way out of his inner and outer states of destitution. This may sound selfish and narrow, but Smith is never that. He writes to people rather than for them and it is upon this that he must base a good deal of his success. It might also account for his having been outside in the poetic wilderness for many years, unheeded by editors and many of his peers alike. He is frankly too good and he must pose a threat to others. There is much jealousy on the part of the 'central', 'school-ish' poets for those who seemingly break the rules of obedience to education and self-interest in poetry.

11   Basil Bunting was born in 1900 and might seem markedly out

of place in this book but he is not for he came to prominence in the 1960s despite having been published first in the years prior to 1950. Fulcrum Press published *Briggflatts* in 1966 and Bunting's collected poems two years later. Although educated in London, Bunting is more a Northumbrian than a southerner and he became popular for a number of reasons: he was elderly and the poetry world, particularly that of the non-establishment poets, wanted a father figure; he was a poet of work that could easily be made into a cult and the 1960s was a time of cults; he wrote in dialect at times and that was unusual and fascinating and heightened his sense of regionality which was the 'in-thing' at the time with people thinking of Mersey music, Liverpool poetry and so on; he was a reclusive man and this added to his sage-like appeal to people who liked such attitudes of exclusivity; he wrote out of a mould. Or so many thought.

In truth, Bunting was a product of the pre-war years, so far as his poetry went. He wrote in a style very similar to the easier end of Eliot's output and comparisons between him and Eliot, Pound and the Poundian school are easily made:

> The view from the summit: sky bent over Kyoto,
> picnic villages, Fushimi and Toba:
> a very economical way of enjoying yourself.

His work is rich with esoteric reference, personal anecdote and private action and, in this, it is self-indulgent but it can be said to avoid the worst of that ilk for it does provide a wide entry for others to come in to it.

Briggflatts is Bunting's peak of verse. It is somewhat Joycean and does for Northumberland what Joyce did for Dublin but it does it to a higher standard. The poem, in five sections with a coda, is a lyrically magical voyage into Bunting's north, the history of it and its language and strangeness. The poem is without notes and it needs none which is unusual for such a narrowness of theme, and this is part of the praise Bunting earns – it lacks the need – though there is a glossary. It has to be heard in the correct dialect to be fully appreciated and, in this respect, it is a performance poem. On rare occasions in the 1960s, Bunting did read the poem but now his voice controlling it is retained on a long-playing record, issued by Bloodaxe Books. Even without the sound of the dialect, the lyrical beauty of the poem can be seen.

> My love is young but wise. Oak, applewood,
> her fire is banked with ashes till day.

> The fells reek of her hearth's scent,
> her girdle is greased with lard;
> hunger is stayed on her settle, lust in her bed.

Bunting is not a prolific poet. He published seven titles, some very slim. His lack of output may well have added to his popularity for he was and is regarded rightly as rare and somewhat unobtainable. This cachet of uniqueness was much prized and sought after in the 1960s, at a time of artistic explosion, and it must have done much to bring Bunting forward. His is the case of the poet resurrected after unjustly being put down.

12   Another poet whom one associates with the north-east of England is Douglas Dunn. Born in Scotland in 1942, he was first published in Faber's Poetry Introduction series, in the first volume, and was subsequently accepted into their list from which he has produced a number of books in addition to small press publications. He has lived for some years in Hull and is best described as a social poet, in that his main themes are the society and culture in which we live. His first book, *Terry Street* (1969), was a most impressive entry into the art. The poems were almost all about working-class life in Northern cities and comparison with the work of Philip Larkin was easily made. The poems did not seek to do more than expand upon the observation of the subject matter by way of emotive response to them. Imagery was stark and well chosen (recalcitrant motorbikes, frost-covered dog-shit describe winter; massed TV aerials like Chinese characters; women cooking and laundering in Terry Street), and the book had an impact upon all readers. It was easily understood. His second book, *The Happier Life* (1972), went further along the same lines. After that, though, the poems started to grow away from the popular mould and lines like

> Cartographical morass
> And the dissolve of speculation;
> Strabo in the poop
> Studying the periplum. . . .

started to replace such excellent poetry as

> They are my dancing girls, the wasted lives,
> The chorus girls who do not make good,
> Who are not given florist's shops or Schools of Dance
> By rich and randy admirers, or marry

A gullible Joe from Swindon or Goole,
But find themselves stiff and rotten at fifty. . . .

No one – possibly not even Larkin – has done better in describing the sad wrecks of women that inhabit dingy and morose northern industrial cities. Very sadly, Dunn has changed. His poetry is no longer about real life but the world of the academical, the man who looks at it all through strangers' lenses. In 1982, Dunn did depart from his later stream of poetry to write a long poem entitled 'Europa's Lover' and published by Bloodaxe Books; it was a look at Europe and its culture and, in parts, it is slickly clever but in others it is the old Dunn speaking through.

One might question why Dunn is an outsider when he is writing very much the kind of poetry that is the modern genre of self-conscious ideas and selfish catharsis. The answer lies in the fact that, in his earlier and best books, he was out of the ordinary and, in many ways, he is not a clique-er. He is an individual who has been swept along by the tide of boredom that has infiltrated British poetry by degrees throughout the 1970s and, as an example, he shows how a good poet can be wooed into providing for himself and his poet-friends rather than all and sundry. In Dunn one has talent abused.

13   Another outsider of considerable merit, but small following, is Harry Guest. Born in 1932, his first book came out when he was 30 but it was not until Anvil Press published *Arrangements* in 1968 that he was recognised. Subsequent recognition was gained by his appearing in number 16 of the Penguin Modern Poets series in 1970. Educated, like Ted Walker, in modern languages at Cambridge University, Guest took to schoolmastering for a living, a job he still holds, with an interlude as a lecturer in Yokohama National University in Japan. This post was of great importance, for Guest not only became fluent in Japanese and a translator and authority on post-war Japanese verse of which he edited a Pengiun selection, but he also broke with his roots to some extent and started to write in the 'vacuum' of the Far East: of course, it was not so much a vacuum as a totally new intellectual environment. It is of interest to see how many of the poets classed here as outsiders have had this ex-patriate or exiled experience and have written all the better for having escaped influences abounding on the home front. The wider the experience, the better the poet and, for a poet whose experience of life consists of England/school/university/educational job with poetry running through as a central string, there can be little to write about save what is gleaned from others in the class- or lecture room.

Guest did not suffer from his education but accepted it and added life to it. The result, so far as his poetry goes, is one of cosmopolitan originality in which one can see the heavy influences of oriental and North American contemporary poetry. Structure, attitudes towards subject matter, diction and language all show a knowledge of other poetic claims than the British. It is true to say that Guest has that ability to use his education's dustier corners in his poetry; Goethe, Mallarmé, various Japanese authors, Heyst and Zen writers are sprinkled through the earlier verse, but they are not the less readable for all that, for Guest makes allowances to the general reader and his poetry is clear and beautiful as a result, whilst still being coloured by the masters to which it relates. At his best, Harry Guest is a stunning writer whose poetic vision relates all things into a unit, perhaps because of his Japanese living, for poetry from that country must have infused him with this ability. Even his slightest lines, and he does write some very short poems or poem sections, show the inner light of his vision:

> Like birds that die
> robbing the day
> of movement

> Apples
> as hemispheres in the mud
> lend absence to the tree

> You're leaving my heart

In 1976 Anvil Press published *A House Against the Night* and since then Guest has published nothing with them except for a novella entitled *Days* which is, in truth, a short novel-length prose poem rather than a straight narrative. He has not, however, been idle and a number of small presses have produced booklets and pamphlets which show Guest to be moving in a direction parallel to his previous writings in accessibility, but changing in what he is writing about. *Elegies* (Pig Press, 1980), *The Emperor of Outer Space* (Pig Press, 1983) and *English Poems* (Words Press, 1976) show departures towards lighter yet more self-reflective poetry in which Guest seems to be taking stock of his inner self in the years after his fortieth birthday.

He is not a reader of his poetry. He seldom makes public appearances and is a private man who guards a talent that is rare in British verse. It is one in which truth prevails and experience is used to show others a new way of being. Never allied to any

other group of poets, Guest is a real loner and benefits from it.
14   From time to time, it happens that some poets are less well-
known as poets because they have first established themselves in
another literary sphere. One poet who has 'suffered' this fate,
and is an outsider partly because of this and partly because, like
the others, he has kept himself to himself in artistic terms, is Alan
Sillitoe.

Internationally famous as a novelist from 1958 and the
publication of *Saturday Night and Sunday Morning*, Sillitoe is
seldom thought of as a poet. Yet he is a fine one and has been
published in book form since 1960 when his first collection, *The
Rats and Other Poems*, appeared. This was followed in 1964 by *A
Falling Out of Love* and it was with this book that Sillitoe the poet
became known. Indeed, the book's appearance, right at the start
of the poetry boom years, places him as one of the first of the new
generation of realistic poets, for want of a better term. As in his
novels, where realism and social truth are paramount and are
reactions against the prose standards previously prevailing, his
poetry sought in keeping with his peers to take new stock of the
world. *Love in the Environs of Voronezh* appeared in 1968, as did
Shaman which indicated a split in Sillitoe's poetry. On the one
hand, he wrote poetry that was an extension of his outlook as a
novelist, and on the other he wrote magical, philosophical poems
about religious themes – not, it should be added, necessarily
Christian ones. This new trait developed and led to the 1979
publication of *Snow on the North Side of Lucifer*, a poem sequence
based upon the attempts of Lucifer to cast down God and
goodness fighting to prevent its destruction by evil. The poems
owe much to Ted Hughes's *Crow* sequence, but this does not
detract from them. They are not imitations or parodies, for
Lucifer is personified in modern, technological man who uses his
skills to destroy himself. The poem sequence is allegorical and, as
such, is uncommon in modern verse that has sought to be more
direct, as a general rule, in its commentary upon life. Interestingly, Sillitoe is not one of the main performance poets; a reading by
him, of either verse or prose, is a rare treat. However, the Lucifer
poems are written in such a way to make the oral reading of them
bring them alive and to hear Sillitoe's delivery of them is to give
them considerable dimension.

The 1970s saw two other books of verse appear from Sillitoe,
one of them his finest. *Barbarians* appeared in 1973 from a small
press and is an interesting book but not rich in the best of
Sillitoe's work. This is to be found in *Storm*, published in 1974.
Here one sees poetry that is very much in the mould of the
period, pieces that talk of the world and personal response to it

and its problems. The poems are personal, but universalised, and they have an immediacy that would have had great impact upon the reading public had the publishers gone all out to sell the book rather than see it as a pandering to one of their top prose writers. More than perhaps any other writer of the period, Sillitoe has suffered as a poet by the seemingly patronising manner of some publishers towards poetry. The book was not heavily marked and was not pushed. No use – or little – was made of Sillitoe's reputation as a novelist to plug this book. Subsequently, it was reviewed but forgotten and, to this day, it remains one of the lost treasures of poetry from the period.

In *Storm*, Sillitoe writes with feeling, poignancy and pathos about his responses to the world. His finest poem, bar those in the *Lucifer* set, is in this book, a poem that was typical of its times in that it takes a commonplace and uses it to comment upon the world. Called 'Alchemist', it is about the poet as a boy melting down lead soldiers in a pot on a gas ring, turning swords into ploughshares which were, in the final analysis, just cooling, hardening puddles of lead-death. The third verse of the poem encapsulates the power of the piece and the immense strength of Sillitoe's work at its best:

> The head sagged, sweating under a greater
> Heat than Waterloo or Alma.
> With tired feet he leaned against the side
> And lost an arm where no black grapeshot came.
> His useless knees gave way,
> A pool half spreading to his once proud groin,
> Waist and busby falling in, as sentry-go
> At such an India became too hard,
> And he lay down without pillow or blanket
> Never to get up and see home again.

Love is a major theme in Sillitoe's poetry and, in his handling of it, he is seen to be not only skilled at capturing the emotions but also of explaining these in terms of relationships and the human condition and he is thought by many to be one of the most important love poets of the post-D. H. Lawrence era.

Sillitoe is a major poet, yet because he is an outsider, one who has been seen to steer his own path, he has been unjustly ignored. Had his work appeared in, for example, the Penguin Modern Poets series, then his reputation as a poet would be justifiably much larger.

There are other outsider poets who have spurned the in-crowds and friendly societies who deserve a mention if only by name, in order that they might be looked at if not browsed over and pondered upon: one of these is Tony Harrison who was first published in 1964 and whose collection, *The Loiners*, won the Geoffrey Faber Memorial Prize in 1972. Published throughout his career by small presses, he has been taken on in the late 1970s by Bloodaxe Books who brought out *Continuous* in 1981 after a pair of pamphlets of which one, *U. S. Martial*, was a skilled retranslation from the Latin poet Martial via modern New York. Harrison is someone interested (to say the least) in the classics and he is known for his translations but, at the same time, he does not seek to be academical and he relates this work to the present. A namesake, Keith Harrison, is another: an attender at The Group, he published one book in 1972 (one of the last of the Macmillan list) after moving to the USA six years before. He is an outsider now by dint of geography as well as poetry. Keith Bosley is another who translates much but is a fine poet in his native language of English and who came to prominence in 1969 with a collection called *The Possibility of Angels*. His newest book, *Stations*, shows a considerable and quiet talent at work. Other names include John Cotton, Tony Connor, John Fuller, Ian Caws, John Cassidy . . . the list is not endless but it is lengthy.

These are poets who, without siding with others, took to exploring the world around themselves, their lives and their means of living and the reasons for it. They may have lost something by not belonging to a gathering like The Group, where artistic advance and personal development were more important than self-preservation and advertisement, but they benefited by keeping away from cliques. They sought to discover the poetic world on their own terms and their originality has enriched the art. For them, the expedition into the poetic jungles has paid off.

The poets who, in addition to Ted Hughes, have risen to the top since or during the early 1960s and stayed there, writing good poetry, are few, of course: statistically, there can't be a plethora of best poets. They are heard, read and considered for all that they offer – successful poetry, a large following, artistic integrity, dedication to their own talents and the ability to reach beyond the close-at-hand and mundane.

Excepting Hughes, these poets are Philip Larkin, Peter Redgrove and Seamus Heaney, Thom Gunn and (often omitted from the running) George Mackay Brown. In these six, Hughes having been mentioned previously, one has encapsulated the very best of British Isles verse.

All of these poets are treated to considerable critical attention and eyes are drawn to these studies for further information, for this is not the place for it. What is important here is to see how and why these men have given so much to British verse and could give a good deal more if allowed.

Philip Larkin is the elder statesman, a poet whose reputation rests upon but four books spread out over the post-war years at roughly the rate of one a decade. His poetry is amongst the most anthologised and most respected. It is characterised by human feeling, a cruel wit and a sense of self-deprecating shyness mingling with a strong desire to be outspoken and belligerent in a very quiet manner. From this, draw that Larkin is enigmatic not only as a poet but also as a man. He writes with a technical control that very few can equal and he has a natural ear for the cadences of the common language. He writes of common experience in such a way as to uplift it towards poetry and he is never short of his mark in that what he sets out to say he says with a force and clarity that many could do no better than strive at and pray they achieve by the half. The commonality of Larkin's poetry is what has made him so very popular. He is not airy-fairying his way over people's heads, but writing of what they know and giving it more depth:

> Once I am sure there's nothing going on
> I step inside, letting the door thud shut.
> Another church: matting, seats, and stone,
> And little books; sprawlings of flowers, cut
> For Sunday, brownish now; some brass and stuff
> Up at the holy end; the small neat organ;
> And a tense, musty, unignorable silence,
> Brewed God knows how long. Hatless, I take off
> My cycle-clips in awkward reverence. . . .

Not only that, but by the way he comments upon society with the eye of one who knows mankind intimately and, because we all know ourselves, we see our shapes and lives and worlds reflected in his work. His famous poem 'Sunny Prestatyn', about a resort poster on a hoarding, indicates superbly his skill. The poster carries a photo of a pretty girl upon the sands:

> She was slapped up one day in March.
> A couple of weeks, and her face
> Was snaggle-toothed and boss-eyed;
> Huge tits and a fissured crotch
> Were scored well in, and the space
> Between her legs held scrawls
> That set her fairly astride
> A tuberous cock and balls

Eventually, the girl is covered over with a poster advertising the fight against cancer. And this is what poetry should do: it should take life at all its levels and make it into what it is but is not seen to be. That is the poet's task and Larkin meets it, not always so flippantly. His poetry is moving and beautiful when he so desires it and in 'The Explosion' one sees this, the poem dealing with a mining explosion. On the way to the shift, one miner finds a nest of lark's eggs and shows them to his friends: at midday, there is an earth tremor:

> The dead go on before us, they
> Are sitting in God's house in comfort,
> We shall see them face to face –
>
> Plain as lettering in the chapels
> It was said, and for a second
> Wives saw men of the explosion
>
> Larger than in life they managed –
> Gold as on a coin, or walking
> Somehow from the sun towards them,
>
> One showing the eggs unbroken.

Philip Larkin is, despite the apparent obviousness of his poetry – no one can accuse him of obscurantism – suffering of late from the attention of the academic criticism writers. His position as an important poet is such that it is now seen to be necessary to issue interpretations of his work. A number of volumes have appeared which vivisect Larkin's poetry and analyse it as if it was a specimen for pathological study. This type of assessment, if it can be so called, simply insults the poet and his work. Is it important that Larkin's poem, 'Born Yesterday', is reminiscent of Yeats's 'A Prayer for my Daughter'? So what are G. S. Fraser and M. L. Rosenthal objecting to in the poem? Perhaps one of the more ridiculous statements to come out of such books is the following, which comments upon Larkin's mention of the seaside resort of Frinton in the poem, 'Mr Bleaney', about the last occupant of a bedsit, now deceased: 'This reference to Frinton is one of Larkin's rare slips, I think. Surely Frinton is a little too genteel for Bleaney? Stoke is more appropriate. Perhaps Larkin was attracted by the thin, flinty sound of its name' (David Timms in *Philip Larkin*, published in 1973). In that case, why not Bognor or Southsea, Torquay or Dover? What does it matter! And who cares? The poem stands and it is a superb one.

Not unlike Larkin in his uncompromisingly truthful poetic stance is George Mackay Brown, one of the few poets of talent to have come from Scotland in the period, although as truth will have it, he was writing in the mid-1950s and was discovered in the next decade. Born in 1921, he came late to poetry in book form but he must have had it in his blood from well before first printing. He was at Newbattle Abbey College when Edwin Muir was warden there and his poetry is not unlike Muir's earlier, earthier work. Like Muir, he comes from the Orkneys and he lives there still. And like Larkin, he is a success because he writes as others understand:

> Monday I found a boot –
> Rust and salt leather.
> I gave it back to the sea, to dance in.
>
> Tuesday a spar of timber worth thirty bob.
> Next winter
> It will be a chair, a coffin, a bed.
>
> Wednesday a half can of Swedish spirits.
> I tilted my head.
> The shore was cold with mermaids and angels.

Brown takes his readers into the familiar world and then shows them around the unfamiliarities of it. Or else he strengthens belief and understanding of the worlds in which we move. He gives a sense of order and well-being to the chaos of living. And he looks at the world with our eyes, but with different looks and that, too, is the poet's responsibility:

> The falcon on the weathered shield
>   Broke from his heraldic hover
>   To drift like a still question over
> The fecund quarterings of the field.
>
> Doves in that dappled countryside,
>   Monotones of round gray notes,
>   Took his bone circle in their throats,
> Shed a mild silence, bled, and died.

If it isn't the world of the everyday that captures people's minds, then it is the world of nature to which we all wish to be related, a move that has become strengthened by the years of technological advance; this has been part of George Mackay

Brown's success in that he writes of the wildness of his Orkney landscape. It has been most of Seamus Heaney's success.

Seamus Heaney was born in 1939 in Ulster and was educated at Queen's University, Belfast where he subsequently became a lecturer for a period. From there, he moved to teach at the University of California, and in recent years he has lived from his pen, living in a suburb of Dublin.

Without a doubt, Heaney is the most important Irish writer since W. B. Yeats and he has become the leading member of a loose-knit grouping of Irish poets that have sprung up around him since his first book, *Death of a Naturalist*, was published by Faber in 1966. He is much lauded and imitated but none of his followers match up to him for they do not, as a whole, have his skill with language, his particular brand of 'Irishness' or his poetic ability to get into what he writes about and feel it from the inside. Whereas he plumbs the core of his subject matter, the others merely observe theirs from a distance.

At first, Heaney's success lay in doing what Brown did so well – write in a charged and vital way about his personal landscape – and he did so within the conventions of traditional poetry. This trait of his has been the backbone of his writing ever since. Ireland is what Heaney draws upon for the mainstream of his life and he wrote, in his first two books, about it with a facile but brilliant pen:

> My father worked with a horse-plough,
> His shoulders globed like a full sail strung
> Between the shafts and the furrow.
> The horses strained at his clicking tongue.
>
> An expert. He would set the wing
> And fit the bright steel-pointed sock.
> The sod rolled over without breaking. . . .

Certainly, Heaney's earlier work was influenced by Ted Hughes's poetry (Heaney wrote of a trout in a particularly Hughesian manner as being 'a fat gun-barrel' slipping 'like butter down the throat of the river') and one wonders, too, how much of the lessons that The Group had received at the hands of Philip Hobsbaum had affected Heaney. Hobsbaum was, by the late 1960s, running a writers' group in Belfast where he too taught at the university in which Heaney was employed.

His second book, *Door into the Dark* (1969), established Heaney as a major poet. He was still writing primarily about the Ireland he knew as a boy and loved, an Ireland unaffected by politics and strife, at least on the surface. The poems took on the shape of thumb-nail sketches with poetic insight:

> Kelly's kept an unlicensed bull, well away
> From the road: you risked fine but had to pay
>
> The normal fee if cows were serviced there.
> Once I dragged a nervous Friesian on a tether
>
> Down a lane of alder, shaggy with catkin,
> Down to the shed the bull was kept in.
>
> I gave old Kelly the clammy silver, though why
> I could not guess. He grunted a curt 'Go by
>
> Get up on that gate'. And from my lofty station
> I watched the business-like conception.

Much of the diction in the book was unexciting. Heaney was not pushing at the barriers of language but simply letting it take its own simplistic course.

Wintering Out was published on 20 November 1972. It was a book that many looked forward to for Heaney had pleased not only the critics with his first offerings but also the public in whom he now had a following that was international. His style of direct description married to emotional response was appealing and much appreciated. Indeed, this was what poetry really was about – things that others could understand, not simply 'beautiful thoughts' from those who guarded them. He was a poet writing for people, not just poets.

The third collection was tightly controlled. The poems took on a primeval force, were terse and the diction was firmer and intense. The poems were still essentially Irish but they took on a deeper sense of creation and history. There was an innocence at play in the book that draws comparison with de la Mare's work, but there was alongside this a terrible awareness of the reality of life, a brutal comprehension:

> His real fear is gangrene.
> He wakes with his hand to the scar
> And they do their white magic
>
> Where he lies
> On cankered ground,

A scatter of maggots, busy
In the trench of his wound.

Whereas Heaney's earlier poetry had explained and emotional-
ised its subject, from his third book onwards it was to evoke the
material, bring its innermost structures and ideas forward in a
shamanistic spell of words that were so well picked as to be, at
times, breathtakingly good:

Fishermen at Ballyshannon
Netted an infant last night
Along with the salmon.
An illegitimate spawning,

A small one thrown back
To the waters. . . .

and the poem continues to describe the mother's thoughts and
actions as she casts her child to the waves, the poem ending:

Even Christ's palms, unhealed,
Smart and cannot fish there.

It was another three years before Heaney published his next
collection, *North*. With this volume, Heaney completed what he
had started in *Wintering Out*, an exorcism of writing in a mould
that was linked to traditions that tied him firmly, if not always
obviously, to Yeats and the poetry of Ireland. For the first time,
Heaney was an Irish poet in his own right with an originality of
expression and a desire to be himself without fetters, save those
that are inherent in Irish poetry – love of land and the way of the
land, interest in the archaic and historical past and a desire to
discover things that are deeply rooted in the consciousness and
can only be lit up by the process of poetry's divination. In a
lecture to the Royal Society of Literature in the years between the
third and fourth collection, Heaney spoke of his writing of poetry
as a 'somnambulist process of search and surrender', and
certainly his poetry was now just this, a process of allowing
poems, dreams and ideas to surface of their own accord, to burst
like miracle bubbles on the surface of the mind.

History was close to the fourth book. Heaney had come across
the bog people of Denmark and their relatives in Britain and, in
them, he could find a direct link with the past. The book, *North*,
contained a number of poems based upon these people, bodies
discovered in peat bogs where they had been ritually murdered to

the Mother Goddess in the late Iron Age; because of the nature of peat, many of the bodies were, apart from being dyed dark brown by the chemicals in their grave soil, perfectly preserved. Ireland has nineteen such graves discovered to date and this fired Heaney's imagination. At last, he had concrete links with the dead. The poems that ensued were moving, skilful reconstructions of the poetic responses – the human response – to the corpses, which sounds somewhat gruesome but is not:

> As if he had been poured
> tar, he lies
> on a pillow of turf
> and seems to weep
>
> the black river of himself.
> The grain of his wrists
> is like bog oak,
> the ball of his heel
>
> like a basalt egg.
> His instep has shrunk
> cold as a swan's foot
> or a wet swamp root.

Although one can see the influence of Ted Hughes's diction in this poem, it was a unique piece as were the others on the subject which were bolstered in the book by other poems about Ireland – the Viking finds in Dublin and the arrival of the Vikings prompted some good poems – and, for the first time, a long poem sequence of autobiographical material which looked at the Northern Irish troubles for the first time in Heaney's poetry:

> The muzzle of a sten-gun in my eye:
> 'What's your name, driver?'
>   'Seamus. . . .'
>   *Seamus?*
>
> They once read my letters at a roadblock
> And shone their torches on your hieroglyphs,
> 'Svelte dictions' in a very florid hand.
>
> Ulster was British, but with no rights on
> The English lyric: all around us, though
> We hadn't named it, the ministry of fear.

This sequence, *Singing School*, looked like setting a pattern for Heaney to follow, and four years later *Field Work*, his fifth book, appeared with poems in it that were based upon Ireland's terror. Now Heaney was writing with passion that was still rooted in the Irish history but also in the Irish present and he wrote in such a manner as to bring his poetry to new audiences for whom poems about the Vikings meant little, but poems about the troubles did:

> But my tentative art
> Has turned back watches too:
> He was blown to bits
> Out drinking in a curfew
> Others obeyed, three nights
> After they shot dead
> The thirteen men in Derry.
> PARAS THIRTEEN, the walls said,
> BOGSIDE NILL. That Wednesday
> Everybody held
> His breath and trembled.

Heaney's success lies in several facts: firstly, he is Irish at a time when publishers see it 'fashionable' so to be; secondly, he is a superb wordsmith and writes of the past with which people can relate if they think about it; thirdly, he writes of the present; fourthly, he is not a self-indulgent poet. Seamus Heaney writes for people, not for himself. He knows he has an audience and, whilst keeping his integrity, he writes for and to them, addressing them with emotions that they can appreciate and share. He has, with his attitudes towards history, Ireland and the present, hit upon a rich vein that appeals to many.

So it is with Thom Gunn, long self-exiled in California, though still to be considerably noticed as a British, not American, poet. His first collection, *Fighting Terms*, was published in 1954 by Fantasy Press: *The Sense of Movement* followed in 1957, then came *My Sad Captains* in 1961.

Gunn wrote with an urgency that was appropriate to the times. This gained him a few readers. What got him far more and was to extend his reputation were his poems that were about matters close to the common heart. Lorry drivers, 'rockers' in leather jackets, Elvis Presley, death and, in more recent books, homosexuality and drugs. His urgency is muted in the late 1970s and his writing is now more self-interpretative but not self-indulgent. He writes of his world, but he also writes of that of others. The result crosses the barrier between the poetry that is played close to the chest and is not open to the reader and that which is thoroughly in the light of readers' scrutiny. In this respect, Gunn is sailing close to the wind of being not for the good of poetry in that he narrows himself. On the other hand, the risks pay off. In 'San Francisco Streets', Gunn writes of a young man recently arrived in the sinful city, but quick to learn its ways:

> Later on Castro Street
>   You got new work
> Selling chic jewelry.
>   And as sales clerk
> You have at last attained
>   To middle class.
> (No one on Castro Street
>   Peddles his ass.)

Yet, though this might not get through to everyone, 'Elvis Presley' does. A poem that speaks of a public rock 'n' roll star, but also comments upon us and shows us to ourselves, is where poetry should be at and where Gunn is:

> Two minutes long it pitches through some bar:
> Unreeling from a corner box, the sigh
> Of this one, in his gangling finery
> And crawling sideburns, wielding a guitar.
>
> The limitations where he found success
> Are ground on which he, panting, stretches out
> In turn, promiscuously, by every note.
> Our idiosyncrasy and our likeness.

If Gunn plays it close, then Redgrove plays it even closer to the wind. It seems as if he throws all to that wind and sees how it comes down, writing as he will to please himself.

All poets write to some extent to please themselves: that is a fact that cannot be ignored. The point is, though, that they write for themselves as they see themselves through the eyes of others, at a distance. The more of a human the poet is, the more human his poetry will be. It stands to reason. A man who has nothing (or little) writes of nothing (or little). A complete man writes complete poetry. The trouble with so many poets is that they are lacking in human terms and, therefore, their poetry follows suit.

Peter Redgrove is not one of these. There are few men of such range of personality, human learning and understanding and zest for life. He is the most prolific poet of the last twenty years and one of the most enigmatic. He writes of everything.

Born in 1932, public school-educated and then on to Cambridge on a scholarship to read natural sciences (which degree he did not sit examination for), Redgrove is a man of massive erudition and charm. He verges on genius and has a mind like quicksilver which, luckily, he has not allowed to become blunted by educational establishments, the bane, as has been shown, of many a poet. His first book appeared in 1960 but it was not until this third in 1963 that he came to be shown to other than a poetic audience, although his second collection, *The Nature of Cold Weather*, was a Poetry Book Society choice in 1961. Redgrove has had great fortune in being with one publisher all along for his main trade collections, Routledge & Kegan Paul, and he owes much to this sense of security, but it must be said that the publisher, whilst doing much for Redgrove, has not maintained a poetry list as such which is an enormous shame for one could be built successfully upon association with Redgrove. Being able to relate to just one publisher has given the poet the freedom to exercise his own development and growth and Redgrove has done so growing not only in stature with time, but in artistic terms as well.

At first, Redgrove was a poet who dwelt in a world of mystery and fantasy. His poetry was always bent towards the inner ear and he wrote of strange, mythical subjects but not with the stand that, say, Yeats took in which the esotericism ultimately robbed the poetry of all meaning but to the creator. Redgrove's confidence at handling strange themes, that have formed the parapsychological side of his make-up before being imprinted on the page, linked to his awareness that the language was the message, has given his poetry a breadth few others even come near. In the title poem from his seventh full-length collection – Redgrove also has a gamut of small press titles under his literary belt – the poet demonstrates how he can take something very far removed from the common experience that this book has spent so much time stressing as being the main force in modern (and effective) poetry and make it into something all can grasp, most often not merely at a level of understanding but at a gut-reaction, emotional level, too. The poem 'Dr Faust's Sea-Spiral Spirit' starts:

I am frightened. It makes velvet feel too tall.
Its crest peers in at the library window and I cannot open
 the books,
They hug themselves shut like limpets months after it has
 gone.
The roses have learnt to thunder,
They spread petals like peals of red thunder echoing.

The sky looks like blue boxes of white powder being
     smashed by grey fists.

Accepting that modern man is an animal which is largely visually
orientated, it goes without saying that Redgrove's technicolour
imagery is well received. Being unique, Redgrove can also write
with a strange imagery and he is accepted with it:

> He seeds the rain-clouds with silver-salts,
> His little silvery aeroplane like flying Jesus,
> He steals my rain that should have fallen on my hills,
> It is cloud-rustling;
> He milks them all over his meadows.
>
> Who owns the 2,000 million tons of water
> Floating heavy as cathedrals in the skies of America?
> Jesus does, in his aeroplane.
>
> The rain begins.
> I zip up my fly and open my collar.

There are many who claim that this is the poetry of genius and so
it may be; time will be the judge of that, when one sees how long
the poetry will survive in the consciousness of men, charging it
up. Most probably this kind of poetry will last for it is universal
and it is not set in a period. Its lasting will be its affirmation of
genius, just as Ted Hughes's poetry will prove the same – genius has to be timeless.

Not all of Redgrove's output is as oddly surreal or imagist. A
goodly chunk of it fits in with the already stated premise that
good poetry is about things others can understand. For example,
his poem 'At the Edge of the Wood' goes:

> First, boys out of school went out of their way home
> To detonate the windows; at each smash
> Piping with delight and skipping with fright
> Of a ghost of the old man popping over his hedge,
> Shrieking and nodding from the gate.
> Then the game palled, since it was only the breaking of
>   silence.

This is clearly easy to understand. And, for Redgrove, it is one
of his more obvious poems, but in truth all of his work is
understandable. It requires not a knowledge shared, but an
emotion. Poetry must have an emotional response from the

audience members. Without that, it fails. What is more, that emotion has to be genuinely aroused positively by the poem, not as a negative response such as boredom or disinterest, as much emotions as hatred or love. Because he taps the subconscious, Redgrove is able to stir emotion. It is for this reason that he is so highly regarded by poets and read by readers.

There were those who criticised Redgrove for his esoteric imagist poetry, the surreal material that some found washing over their heads and, in common with all poets, Redgrove suffered at times at the hands of critics who were either apathetic to his work or ignorant of what lay behind it. Indeed, the standards of criticism in the period from 1964 have varied hugely from the intensely academic to the bluntly boring or personal. However, few have been so criticised, laughed at, castigated and ridiculed as the concrete poets.

Many would suggest that they have no place in a study such as this for they would claim the concrete poets to be not poets at all, but artists or musicians. Sound poetry – a branch of music in some ways and an offshoot of poetry in others – tends to be lumped into a whole with the concrete work and, for simplicity, this is done here although it is fair to add that this is for convenience.

Concrete and sound poetry is the very fringe of the art, the avant-garde in the extreme. It came to the fore in the late 1960s and was back underground in ten years. Its leading exponents gave 'recitals' with tape recorders, sound effects and their own mouths and the more visually orientated gave exhibitions. Some gave a hybrid of the two.

One cannot quote books to any great extent in this field, for there are not so many of them. There are magazines and tapes on cassette and 'poems' or 'pictures' in art galleries – there are even gardens of concrete poetry, but there are few books.

Both of the two facets of this genre were born of new directions in artistic appreciation. Concrete poetry was first seen in the early years of the century but it was not until the fast print, quick art revolution that the medium was ready for massive exploitation and expansion. As for sound poetry, the availability of the tape recorder made that possible. Without it, it would be a very narrow art form indeed.

Perhaps, as it is, concrete/sound poetry is narrow. It is neither one thing nor the other. It is poetry in that it uses words (or wordsounds); it is art in that it uses shape and texture . . . it is very much the mutant child of several artistic parents.

The main figures in the concrete poetry world were and are few. They have not achieved wide public acclaim and, in fact, have remained deliberately obscure in most cases, seeking only to please or relate to their peers and, in this respect, the art as they see it is very incestuous. They are not major poetry people but fringe activists who, thankfully, do not adversely affect the rest of the art. They are exclusive and seem to like things that way.

The best known, already mentioned earlier in this book, who came to prominence in the mid-1960s and, within a few years, was a leading force in The Poetry Society, was Bob Cobbing. Born in 1920, he founded the central pin of concrete poetry in Britain, a small publishing concern called Writers' Forum which has remained the most important concrete poetry outlet in Great Britain. He has written quite a number of publications and is available on record. His best-known publication is *Kurrirrurriri* (1967) but he is well represented in various anthologies of concrete poetry including *The Anthology of Concrete Poetry* published in 1967 when the art was on the rise, and now a very scarce book indeed. It is hard to reproduce concrete poems. They are visual and do not rely upon meaning very often. They certainly are not often quotable in lines. (It would be like showing just the bottom right quarter of Constable's *Haywain* as an example of the man's work.) However, a bit of one of Cobbing's poems, 'Alphabet of Fishes', gives a rough idea of his work:

askal		canker	
	barfas		dranick
ehoc		girrock	
	frango		hump

More visually orientated poems consisted of collages made of pictures, news cuttings, instant lettering sets, duplication machine smudges and blanked-out text. Some were simply black and white whilst others were multi-coloured. Some were printed, some lithographed and some hand-painted one-offs.

Other poets who became noted in this field included Thomas A. Clark, whose well-known poem 'Prayer Wheel' consisted of the phrase word *zen* repeated vertically five times thus:

z

z e n

n

There was also Dom S. Houedard, a Benedictine monk who was one of the most prolific of his poetic contemporaries and signed his work 'dsh'. With Houedard's poetry one sees a greater reliance upon visuals without words at all, letters taking on the command of shape and form. Alan Riddell was another concrete poet and one who, paradoxically, attended meetings of The Group where his work was discussed on more than one occasion: certainly, this shows the eclectic attitudes of the meetings and its members which made it such a potent and valuable force. Riddell was also one of the few concrete poets who published a book with a major publishing house rather than a small press. His volume, *Eclipse*, appeared in October 1972 from Calder & Boyars, a firm that published a number of books of or related to concrete work. Edwin Morgan was another poet with whom concrete poetry had more than a passing affair and his poetry, being nearer to verse than art, has survived and become, in the instance of a computer's Xmas card, famous and a stimulus in many a classroom. Indeed, of the whole concrete movement, Morgan is the one that has best survived, but it is important to note that he has done so on an ordinary poetical ticket rather than a way-out one.

Peter Finch, the editor/owner of *Second Aeon*, was another figure to whom concrete poetry owes much. After Bob Cobbing, he was the one who did the most to promote the art. His magazine contained some visual or concrete poetry in almost every issue and names such as Henri Chopin, Michael Gibbs, dsh, Peter Mayer and Ian Robinson were published alongside concrete work from other countries, even Japan where the art was 'big' due to the use of calligraphy where form had distinct, literate meaning. In 1972, Finch edited *Typewriter Poems* for his small press, a collection of poems that used the typewriter rather than additional collage or handwritten/illustrated material and in- cluded some poetry from Nicholas Zurbrugg, a noted exponent of the art who ran one of its major magazine outlets, *Stereo Headphones*. Peter Mayer subsequently edited *Alphabetical and Letter Poems*, a major anthology of the art which appeared from the Menard Press in 1978. This book shows the best of the concrete poetry. It is an entertaining but intelligent book and it shows that this kind of verse had its roots in tradition – the Psalms, Chaucer, Christopher Smart, Pope and Coleridge are all shown to have been on the edges of this fringe. The most authoritative book was published by Lorrimer Publishing in 1971; entitled *Mindplay*, it is the best introduction to concrete/sound poetry that there is.

The genre, though not dead now, is dormant and under- ground. Few new names have appeared and, as with any art, once interest has started to flag as it has in poetry in general then one can be sure that the outer reaches get burned first.

Concrete/sound poetry suffered before other forms. This is sad. Although it might be cranky, unserious and pretentious, it is nevertheless a part of the wide spectrum of poetry and to see one limb hacked off is sorrowful.

It is also true that when one limb falls, another rises. It is certainly the case – though unrelated – that as concrete poetry started to fade, the Irish limb started to build up.

Seamus Heaney, as has been stated, is the leader of the new Irish movement that has come about as Britain has become more aware of Ireland in the last fifteen years or so. To be more accurate, the poets might be better called the Ulsterman, for they are mostly from that province of Britain. However, because the Irish are one at base, regardless of political poles, it seems only right and just to see them as such rather than as adjuncts to Britain.

Heaney opened a floodgate of consciousness. His 'Irishness' struck home with many for he was writing from traditional sources and in a traditional framework of which many were curious and many others jealous. Publishers (notably Faber & Faber but others as well) began to bring out Irish poet after Irish poet: for some time in the 1970s it seemed as if one's background was all-important and some weak poets appeared on the scene. They did not last though and now a hard core remain who write from the security of their national position.

Alongside Heaney on the Faber list are Tom Paulin and Paul Muldoon. They are perhaps the most publicised of the Irish poets after Heaney because of the poetry list upon which they sit.

Tom Paulin first came to publication in book form through the Faber Poetry Introduction series in 1975 and his first full-length collection followed in 1977. Entitled *A State of Justice*, it was a good first collection but it did not merit the Poetry Book Society choice for the season nor did it warrant the ecstatic accolades that it received in the press. The poetry showed little excitement or originality and was not up to standards already set by many poets in the small press and magazine world. It was a bland book that had little new to say and it was over-promoted and over-praised. Roger Garfitt, reviewing the book in *The Times Literary Supplement*, hit the nail on the head in stating that the book showed its author's 'instinct in defining and developing an obsessive personal theme'. The poems are so inwardly obsessive as to be partly lost on outside readers. A second collection, *The Strange Museum*, showed more promise but the standard of the verse was still below par for the course in its year of publication, 1980. The poems in that book are more expansive and less self-obsessed, but they are still weak:

> A baggy gagman and a rubber duck,
> Some bits of eggshell on a dirty plate,
> The oilcloth with its scurf of crumbs,
> Spilt salt, dried yolk and greasy butter.
> A litter of newsprint and a stale joke.

So much for breakfast which, later in the poem, only 'the wisest bishop can call lovely'. His third book, *Liberty Tree*, shows things starting to happen. Politics, social comment (Irish), and life are portrayed and the poems come alive:

> We live:- dishonoured, in the shit. So What? it had to be.
>   This is the pits and yet we feed and sleep.
> Even here – penned in, watered and waiting for the chop
>   (just place your bets) – affairs take off,
> there's gossip, bitching and a pecking order.

but they are still secondhand, written away from experience or borrowing experiences – the above comes from a poem sub-headed 'after Chénier'. Paulin's poetic stance, of writing from reality's side but not too close to it, places him very much in the forefront of the direction British poetry is taking as the boom era dies. The poetry is now the medium and the message takes the hindmost. The cleverness isn't artful, merely hollow imitation of greater things.

Paul Muldoon was born in 1951 in County Armagh and was educated in Northern Ireland where he has worked for some years as a radio producer. Of the two young Faber Irish poets, he is the better by far, with four full-length collections under his belt along with a number of small press publications. From the start, he showed promise. In 1971, he printed and published a booklet entitled *Knowing My Place*, in which he showed his Ulsterman connections and love of the province. A year later, he appeared (like Paulin) in the Poetry Introduction series, and in 1973 Faber produced his first book, *New Weather*.

It was a sound first collection and received critical acclaim that was not misplaced. Alongside Heaney, it was obvious that here there was a poet in the true Irish sense – one with a command of language that was both poetical and yet down-to-earth and realistic, a poet with a sense of his national identity and the heritage to which he owed much and to which he paid more than lip service in his verse:

> I kept the whiskey in the caves
> Well up in the hills. It was never safe

234

To have it about the houses,
Always crawling with excise and police.

The people could still get the stuff
As often as they liked, and easily enough,
For those were still the days
When making whiskey broke nobody's laws.

The second collection, *Mules* (1977), showed that Muldoon's talent was firm and that he might even threaten Heaney's position as the top Ulster poet with poems that not only looked at Ireland but took on other cultures and material. A poem about a Japanese soldier from the last war, derivating from Bāsho's work, Paris and schoolday memories – this was the stuff of some of the verse, but the best was still that which was related to Ulster:

Once Duffy's Circus had shaken out its tent
In the big field near the Moy
God may as well have left Ireland
And gone up a tree. My father said so.

Why Brownlee Left, Muldoon's third book which was slimmer than the others and appeared in 1980, gained a Poetry Book Society choice listing and touched upon the quick of Ulster sentiment and politics, the hideous dilemma of the place. It was a book of poems that, when they did touch this vein, equalled some of Yeats's poetry of Ireland:

THE BOUNDARY COMMISSION

You remember that village where the border ran
Down the middle of the street,
With the butcher and baker in different states?
Today he remarked how a shower of rain

Had stopped so cleanly across Golightly's lane
It might have been a wall of glass
That had toppled over. He stood there, for ages,
To wonder which side, if any, he should be on.

A fourth collection, *Quoof*, published in 1983, continued along the same route.

When he is Irish, Muldoon is a fine poet, but at other times, his poetry tends towards the mundane in that it speaks of little and does it with nothing more than a skilled observer's eye. It is when

235

his emotions flow that his verse lifts and, in a nutshell, this is the problem of many young poets. They are too keen to simply see rather than feel their subject matter.

As a result of being published by such a prestigious firm, Paulin and Muldoon have tended to be regarded as the Irish duo, a sort of poetry band under the conductorship of Seamus Heaney and, adversely, this has pushed some of the others out of the light. They have sought publication with other firms or have been somehow overlooked on the same list, as has happened to the poetry of Richard Murphy who writes purely of the emotional background he feels and who is a far superior poet.

Born in Galway in 1927, Murphy started to publish in the 1950s but he came to prominence after 1964 with an outstanding book called *Sailing to an Island*, published by Faber. His poetry is lyrically beautiful, using as its background the histories of Murphy's life and the turmoil and gentle chaos of Ireland. 'The Cleggan Disaster', about a shipwrecking in 1927, shows Murphy at his best, describing and reconstructing events with clarity and pathos and interest. He feels for the doomed:

> Down the valleys of this lull, like a black cow
> In search of her calf, an upturned hull
> Wallowed towards them. Her stem had parted.
> All hands must have been lost. She hoved to his side
> And almost staved him. Were the men inside?
> Those who had thrown him their ropes from the quay?
> The one who had warned him about his crew?
> No help for them now. With his foot on her planks
> He fended her off. . . .

Murphy's success – and the success of the other Irish poets – lies in work that is timeless, like Ireland. Too much of the poetry of the 'new' Irish poets is quickly dated because it lacks emotional ties and it wants genuine attachment to the material on which it is based. When Muldoon, for example, is good, as in the poems quoted, he is so because he is dealing with an issue about which he feels compassion and for which he has an historical framework upon which to place it. Heaney's success lies in this direction, too.

One of the younger poets, Derek Mahon, also a Belfast man, is another example of poems based on Irishness being superb, but the rest hollow and shallow. Born in 1941, Mahon's first major collection, *Night Crossing* (Oxford University Press 1968), was a tour de force. Again, writing of matters Irish, on this occasion at the grave of Louis MacNeice, the poetry is true and fair:

Your ashes will not fly, however the rough winds burst
Through the wild brambles and the reticent trees.
All we may ask of you we have. The rest
Is not for publication, will not be heard.
Maquire, I believe, suggested a blackbird
And over your grave a phrase from Euripides.

Yet look at a poem about Bāsho – another instance of an Irish
poet looking to the classical Japanese: how much farther from
one's roots can one go? – and one sees Mahon at his weakest.
Snow is seen as '. . . falling/like leaves on the cold sea' and a
verse that mentions the burning of thousands of people in the
snow for heresy is but a statement. Poetry without emotion.

Many of the younger Irish poets have a problem. They accept
the label 'Irish' but they try to write outside that as well as in it.
Possibly they have a poetic identity crisis that cannot be
overcome, being aware of the pressures that are put upon them
because of their nationality as poets. Once someone is labelled, it
is hard to get shot of the tag or live up to it.

'Irish' implies Yeats, tradition, a certain historical and cultural
type, a specific beauty in language and form . . . and so on. And
the young poets of this category, when writing about matters
Irish, are good as often as not, capturing the emotive tenor of
their background. However, as soon as they move away from
this, most of them seem to flounder. Is this because they are
without the emotive response, that it is easier to understand the
problems of Ulster and its history, its beauty and its life than it is
to write into themselves a Japanese poet, a Scottish miner or an
Italian count, all personae one or other has touched upon? There
is a lot to be said for the fact that the Irish poets are too insular, if
they are in the new mould, too Irish, and cannot escape that
situation. (After all, Yeats had his faults too along these lines: his
Irish poems are gold, but his magical ones tend to be less than
silver.)

Surely the crux of the matter is one that strikes all the new
poets that have come to the fore since, say, 1974? That is, without
emotion there is no positive imagination and therefore no
positive poetry. Poets of the 1960s generation have not suffered,
by and large, from this restriction. They were people of an
expanding world and their visions went with it. These others are
of a restricting universe and they are shrinking with it. The
specialist era is back where, if one is a specialist, one shouldn't go
trying to do another's job. Irish poets must remain Irish or widen
their horizons. To do the latter is to break down attitudes and that
is not easy, for we live now in a world of attitudes and poles, and

the Ulster problem, apart from its social and political consequences, has had its poetical ones, too. It has caused a division of mentality and, once any art starts to split in such a way, it is doomed.

Of course, not all the Irish poets have been affected so adversely as Muldoon, Paulin and Mahon. Those who have avoided the problem have done so by not being Irish. Michael Longley, whose *No Continuing City* appeared in the late 1960s, is an example of the Irish poet who isn't. He writes on the broader spectrum of life and existing and even where Ireland does come into his work he writes of it in a dispassionate manner, keeping clear of all that it implies. He is not so much an Irish poet as a 1960s poet, one with vision and horizon. He is like Seamus Heaney. He uses his traditions to wider ends, seeking to write poetry, not Irish poetry. Unlike the younger of the breed, he is not bogged down by his background, the new attitudes towards verse being a slick treat of metaphors and the introverted look of modern versemakers.

Before leaving this area, two poets must be mentioned who are Irish and who write of the place with power, forceful emotion and reality. These two do not divorce themselves from but are married to the essence of Irish poetry in the Yeatsian frame. They are Eavan Boland and Paul Durcan.

Eavan Boland first published in her early twenties, in 1967, a book that appeared only in Eire but was well received. This book, *New Territory*, was followed in 1975 by *The War Horse*, published by Gollancz in their short-lived poetry list. Ms Boland is the essential Irish poet and certainly the best woman poet Ireland has seen for a long while. She does not let her muse wander but writes either directly of Ireland or in metaphor that relates the subject through emotion to her land. She is steeped in Irish history (as are all the poets) but has assimilated this and uses it to speak, not simply describe:

> 'Idle as trout in light Colonel Jones
> these Irish, give them no coins at all; their bones
> need toil, their characters no less.' Trevelyan's
> seal blooded the deal table. The Relief
> Committee deliberated: 'Might it be safe,
> Colonel, to give them roads, roads to force
> from nowhere, going nowhere of course?'

This is the opening section of a poem about the famine road, the degradation of the 'navvy' in his own land. This is gutsy poetry: put alongside Tom Paulin, the latter pales into insignificance.

So it is also with Paul Durcan's work. Published by the
Blackstaff Press which is based in Belfast and is the foremost
publisher of Irish books now operating in Ulster, Durcan writes
straight from the heart. For him there is no compromise. He feels
for his homeland and what he feels hurts at the pain and sings at
the joys. He writes straight from experience, covers nothing up
and is a poet of such force that it is truly terrible sometimes to
read his work. He places life in Ulster into context. He has tapped
the heart of the times and the people and he knows what he
thinks and feels. Poetry and Ireland run in his blood and he
writes of murders, love, injustice, humour. . . . He is the
complete poet, the man who encapsulates his world for others.
His poetry can be cruel. The opening lines of 'In Memory of
Those Murdered in the Dublin Massacre, May 1974' read:

> In the grime-ridden sunlight in the downtown Wimpy bar
> I think of all the crucial aeons – and of the labels
> That freedom fighters stick onto the lost destinies of
>   unborn children;
> The early morning sunlight carries in the whole street from
>   outside;
> The whole wide street from outside through the plate-glass
>   windows . . .

and it ends

> The aproned old woman who'd been sweeping the floor
> Has mop stuck in bucket, leaning on it;
> And she's trembling all over, like a flower in a breeze.
> She'd make a mighty fine explosion now, if you were to
>   blow her up;
> An explosion of petals, of aeons, and the waitresses too,
>   flying breasts and limbs,
> For a free Ireland.

On the other hand, his work can be beautiful and quiet:

> Often she used to linger on the sill of a window;
> Hands by her side and brown legs akimbo;
> In sun-red skirt and moon-black blazer;
> Looking toward our strange world wide-eyed.
>
> Our world was strange because it had no future;
> She was America-bound at summer's end.

She had no choice but to leave her home –
The girl with the keys to Perse's Cottage.

O Cait Killann, O Cait Killann,
You have gone with your keys from your own native place.
Yet here in this dark – El Greco eyes blaze back
From your Connemara postman's daughter's proudly
    mortal face.

This is the basic nerveline of what Irish poetry should be: a close, intense look at all that being Irish implies, one word rolling over a whole planet of national pride and knowledge. Muldoon, Paulin, Mahon . . . they play games as poets, write lines about things they see. Boland and, especially, Durcan see and then enter and think. Yeats's creed was to get inside the subject and write out through its eyes, as Heaney does, as Durcan does. The others just look on and poetry – and Irish poetry – is lessened for the action.

Before considering the poets who are all but destroying poetry, it is important to look at the poets many would say aren't poets. At least, at first sight, they seem not to be because their work doesn't feature in books. They are, of course, the music writers and as has been implied, their importance since the 1960s is immense. Large numbers of them have appeared, impinged themselves upon poets and public alike and then faded from view because of the transience of their art. The record lasts not as long as the book, for it is affected more readily by fashion. It has taken twenty years for Sylvia Plath to become out of literary fashion, but it takes only months for a rock music writer to vanish.

In the rock world, there are those who write rubbish – the do-do-rah-do/I love you school who are not writing art but gimmickry – but there are also those who write the real thing. As they are quite numerous only a few will be chosen for comment, as being typical or important.

The obvious leaders in the field are Paul McCartney and John Lennon, either together or apart. Few mourned Lennon's passing as a poet, but he was as much a poet as a singer and many of the rock writers are closer to poetry than the poets in that, like their early forebears a thousand years ago, they sing the words. This discipline demands a more conscious awareness of language and its cadences than many would readily admit to, especially the poets in their ivory towers of artistic conceit. Songwriters can teach poets a thing or two these days.

Songwriters have to write for the masses. They cannot afford to be arty. Or, at least, they couldn't before the Beatles. They have to write for those who listen. They do not regard the words as tools of the instrument of the voice, as early rock singers did, taking this attitude from jazz musicians for whom the mouth was as much another instrument as a conveyor of meaning. Those of the post-Beatles years are as concerned with meaning as poets and they have to use language as fully as possible, now involving art as a part of the process. Emotion is something they want to append to a neat tune and a skilful set of words. Music nowadays demands more than a pretty noise.

Of course, Americans have had more than their fair share of impact in this direction – Bob Dylan has perhaps influenced music and, through it poetry, more than any one other, but he doesn't count in a book that is concerned with British poetry.

A look at the songs of Lennon and McCartney, at least at the words of them, shows the criterion at work that should be the aim of contemporary poets – the use of everyday language to relay emotion, meaning and response to a circumstance or situation. In the seminal *Sergeant Pepper's Lonely Hearts Club Band* album, which had a massive impact upon both rock music and the more modern end of the poetry of the time, one finds moving poetry that works because of its attitude towards language. Much of this album has become somewhat clichéd over the years because it is so well known, but if one can try to see it with eyes fresh to the experience, one sees the superb standard of popular poetry that it holds:

> When I get older losing my hair,
> Many years from now,
> Will you still be sending me a Valentine
> Birthday greetings bottle of wine.
> If I'd been out till quarter to three
> Would you lock the door,
> Will you still need me, will you still feed me,
> When I'm sixty-four.

This is not sentimental waffle but sound emotive stuff that captures the imagination and successfully widens the listener's outlook. Few rock writers had ever written about such a topic and, for the everyman, it was revitalising to see such in music. After the moribund material that one saw coming from music from the end of the Second World War until the mid-1960s, this was new indeed. What is more, poetry off the vinyl record was doing the same thing. The popularisation of the arts – consider the theatre as well as literature, music and television, which was

241

now becoming an art medium in its own right – was working at all levels. Lennon and McCartney did not limit themselves to this kind of material only, though. They also wrote for the new artistry of the psychedelic mind, something that Brian Patten was looking to with his poems about dragons in the woodshed and those entitled 'Through the Tall Grass in Your Head' and 'Unisong', for example. The influence of the pop culture's psychedelia was not lost on poets and Lennon and McCartney gave it a huge boost with a song on the same album, entitled 'Lucy in the Sky with Diamonds':

> Picture yourself in a boat on a river,
> With tangerine trees and marmalade skies
> Somebody calls you, you answer quite slowly,
> A girl with kaleidoscope eyes.
> Cellophane flowers of yellow and green,
> Towering over your head.
> Look for the girl with the sun in her eyes,
> And she's gone.
> Lucy in the sky with diamonds. . . .

This kind of poetry, which was printed without a musical score on the jacket of the *Sergeant Pepper* album, was easily assimilated by the public, not because it was pandering to the usual abysmal tastes of that public but because the public was ready for it having been involved in the poetic revolution that had crept into the classroom, the advertising world and the arts in general which were, in the 1960s, impressing themselves upon people as never before. (In the late 1970s it is interesting to note that poetry had lost its immediacy with the public and, simultaneously, pop music had reverted – by and large – to the do-rah-de-run-ron variety that has 'beat' but precious little else. There are exceptions, of course, but they are gradually becoming fewer and fewer, just as in poetry the same is occurring.)

Once the break-up of the Beatles was announced, there was the chance that pop music would cease to be the same again, but this did not prove to be the case. Lennon and McCartney continued writing, but apart, and the results were as stunning as music and poetry as they had been when the duo were working and writing together. McCartney formed a new band to perform his own songs and Lennon, now residing in New York with his second wife, Yoko Ono, started to write poetry and music that was politically and socially aware and as outspoken as one would expect from such a man. A look at two songs from his best album, *Some Time In New York City*, shows the new awareness but still the consciousness of writing poetry that all could appreciate, an even more important point when one considers that John Lennon was trying to say something in his songs as well as simply rock his audience on. 'John Sinclair' carries the verse:

> If he'd been a soldier man
> Shooting gooks in Vietnam
> If he was the CIA
> Selling dope and making hay
> He'd be free, they'd let him be
> Breathing air, like you and me

and in the song, 'New York City', Lennon writes/sings about his experiences in the city which outlines the life of those days, to some extent. The writing is uncompromising and blunt: as poetry, it had to be and the musical score, though important, is secondary. It is the poetry that takes the upper hand:

> Standing on the corner
> Just me and Yoko Ono
> We was waiting for Jerry to land
> Up come a man with a guitar in his hand
> Singing, 'Have a marijuana if you can.'
> His name was David Peel
> And we found that he was real
> He sang 'The Pope smokes dope every day.'
> Up come a policeman shoved us up the street
> Singing, 'Power to the people today!'

This might not be great poetry and it might not be lasting poetry, but it is good poetry which talks plainly, speaks obviously, gives emotion and meaning and is for all to hear. That it has humour in it, anger (which is better shown by the musical score), double meanings and satire only adds to its overall effectiveness.

The point with this kind of poetry, that sets it apart and above the academically bent work, is that this is art as part of a social process, as part of a movement within the consciousness of many, not just a select few. It is perhaps in agreement with Marshall McLuhan's somewhat facile dictate that 'art is anything you can get away with', which is true, perhaps. But good art is not anything; it is something that has the spark of aesthetic pleasure about it or, bar that, the knack of changing the individual's outlook if even for a moment, from his own, usual, selfishly orientated frame of concern to an externalised one. Good poetry does this and bad doesn't. It is interesting to see that, in

1965, the singer Bob Dylan said that a poem was a naked person. That is no slight definition. It is the baring of emotion that makes a poem. This is also indicative of the new attitudes that poets took towards their art in the period from 1964 to roughly 1975: poetry was a business of opening the soul-doors and letting the truths show through – or variations on that. It might be that the doors opened upon a MacBeth narrative poem or a Ted Hughes *Crow* poem – it didn't and doesn't matter. The poem was but the medium in which the emotion that was there came out.

A host of other rock music writers have followed Lennon or risen with him: Pete Brown, writer of Cream's big hits, 'Sunshine of Your Love' (with Jack Bruce and the best of all guitarists in his field, Eric Clapton, of whom mention has been made), 'I Feel Free' and 'White Room'; Bernie Taupin, who wrote the lyrics for most if not all of Elton John's biggest hits including 'Goodbye Yellow Brick Road', 'Candle in the Wind', 'Rocket Man' and other songs such as 'All the Girls love Alice', 'Sweet Painted Lady' and the real rocker, 'Saturday Night's Alright for Fighting'; the unjustly lesser-known Ronnie Lane (of Slim Chance in recent years); Pete Townsend, the songwriter for The Who who wrote the rock operas *Tommy* and *Quadrophenia*, both of them stacked with good poetry set to contemporary music, and who has, in his solo albums, shown some remarkably fine poetry, either of his own invention or the reworking/adding to traditional songs – he has recorded 'North Country Girl' with the last two verses reading:

> See for me that her coat's pulled up close,
> And her beret frames her sweet pretty face.
> See that she's warm, and drink her a toast
> For I am exiled in a lonely place.
>
> Please let me know if she remembers me at all,
> A hundred times I've hoped and prayed
> That way up there near the Roman wall,
> She didn't suffer when the fall-out sprayed.

And there are many others. A listen-in to the more intelligent end of the hit parade uncovers them daily. They are poets who don't bother with books but aim straight at the record market. And they succeed. It is only now, half a century after the invention of the record and a quarter of a century after the start of the introduction of tape recorders into common folk's homes, that poetry publishers and poets are turning to the sound production of their art – Routledge & Kegan Paul brought out a recording of some of

Peter Redgrove's collection, *The Apple Broadcast*, in late 1981, and in 1983 Faber produced the first of a set of cassette tapes of their biggest or, in their eyes, most promising poets. In the small press, underground scene, tapes have been going around for ten years, but they are seldom obtainable except by the very keen members of the *cognoscenti*.

Before leaving rock music, there should be a mention of two songwriters/singers who stand out as being head and shoulders over the rest, certainly in so far as they stand for the possibilities of the new directions which rock music and poetry might take. Both have made it to the big time – Kate Bush and Sting, the singer/base player with the band, The Police.

Kate Bush, whose elder brother John was for some time a member of The Poets' Workshop, subsequently forming a poetry performance group (Sallaticum Poets) with Tony Buzan and Jeremy Cartland, came upon the music scene in early 1978, her first record reaching the top of the charts. She was unusual, to say the least: with a late teen, waif-like beauty, a voice that could reach notes opera singers would be glad to achieve and a mingling of dance with her music, she was unique. What was more, though, was the fact that her song – she writes all of her own material, rarely performing another's – was intelligent and based upon *Wuthering Heights*. This was but a beginning: to date, she has brought out four albums of her songs and the words of these songs become more and more poetically aware. Now she is not so much a singer who uses words but a poet who uses music. Her album *Never for Ever* is her best so far as her poetry goes. She writes with pathos, power and a deliberate consciousness of what the words do apart from the music. One of the best songs to come from Kate Bush is printed below in its complete form and, from this, one can see the expertise of the poet at work behind the magic of the music:

ARMY DREAMERS

Our little army boy
Is coming home from B.F.P.O.,
I've a bunch of purple flowers
To decorate a mammy's hero.
Mourning in the aerodrome,
The weather warmer, he is colder,
Four men in uniform to carry home
My little soldier.

(chorus)

245

What could he do? Should have been a rock star,
But he didn't have the money for a guitar.
What could he do? Should have been a politician,
But he never had a proper education.
What could he do? Should have been a father,
But he didn't even make it to his twenties.
What a waste,
Army Dreamers.

Tears o'er a tin box,
Oh Jesus Christ, he wasn't to know.
Like a chicken with a fox,
He cannot win the war with ego.
Give the kid the pick of pips,
And give him all your stripes and ribbons,
Now he's sitting in his hole,
He might as well have buttons and bows.

(chorus)

The techniques of poetry – ambiguity, emotion, metre and rhyme, 'message', accessible diction but undertones of meaning and drive – are all here. The song stands as words.

The success of this type of music does not lie in the listener's ability to get up and hop with it, nor does it lie in the abilities of the audience to sing along with it. Few ordinary mortals can even approach Kate Bush's vocal range. The success lies in the words. This is music that means something and the message, though not shallow, is easily grasped because it is not hidden in a mud of pretension.

This is also the successful aspect of much of the music to come from The Police, the material for which band comes from Sting, interestingly a schoolteacher before he saw the light that he would be able to teach far more from the vinyl than the blackboard. And he does. Unlike Kate Bush, The Police started writing and singing musically adept rubbish. A new attitude towards the part played by drums and a particularly metallic guitar sound gave them a wide following, but the words of their songs were most banal. But this changed with their fourth album, *Ghost in the Machine*. Now that band's music is socially orientated, critical and political. The music makes a good sound, but the words shake up the soul as well. What irony it is that poets think themselves often to be above such ordinariness as rock music, yet if they were to look they'd find that it was beating them at their own game. And, in this aspect, excelling them: there are very few political poets about in Britain these days. One song from the above-named album shows what is going on and the potential of both rock music and poetry – the former realising it and the latter letting it slip away. The song is 'Rehumanise Yourself'; some of its verses are:

> Policeman put on his uniform
> Likes to have a gun just to keep him warm
> Because violence here is a social norm.
>
> . . . . . .
>
> I work all day in the factory
> Building a machine that's not for me
> Must be a reason that I can't see.
>
> . . . . . .
>
> Billy's joined the National Front
> He always was a little runt
> He's got his hand in the air with the other cunts.

The refrain is 'You've got to humanise yourself.' This music is good poetry, but it is also excellent political comment of the kind all can appreciate at both political and emotional level.

The potency of rock music as poetry for the people cannot be in dispute and, thankfully, it is having its effect upon poets, though at present this is limited mostly to poets who are of the new vocality, the poets who write to be heard and seen, not merely read on the printed page. The leader of this new wave is a punk poet (for want of a better term) called John Cooper Clarke, already well known on a large pub/club circuit where he often rubs shoulders with rock musicians and the fringe of their worlds. His poetry is outrageous and frenetic rock without music, something that has come from the punk revolution that he has outlasted. His poetry is naive and bluntly plain and it lacks finesse to some extent, but it does speak to those who want to understand the immediacy of their own environment and not the introspective panorama of the lofty, etherial poets who are today's bad uns. Clarke writes – and this is typical of his work –

> roman catholic marxist leninist
> happily married to an eloquent feminist
> a lapsed atheist all my memories
> measure the multitude's density
> psycho citizens are my enemies
> crypto nazis and their remedies

keep the city silent as the cemetery's
architectural gothic immensity
a new name on the less-than-kosher list
the euro-communist/a gucci socialist

and this is better heard than seen, for the delivery is quick, patter-like and funny. Slick, too. Clarke is a performer.

This poetry isn't of the highest order, certainly, but it has a style of its own and it is successful in that people read it, hear it (on albums of the poet's work pressed by CBS), identify with it and enjoy it. It works.

Other poets that fit into this genre are growing in number: the better are Attila the Stockbroker, Seething Wells and a young poet from Glasgow, Liz Lochhead, who knocks the rest into a cocked hat. Her poetry is of social origins, in that she writes from the stand of the feminist, is funny, moving and yet gutsy. Yet there is one trouble: with the exception of Liz Lochhead, the rest are more or less imitations of John Cooper Clarke. Good imitations, certainly, but nevertheless of that secondhand quality. And this poses the problem that this kind of poetry which so many turn to is a dead end, one that cannot develop. Time will tell.

Having looked at the good poets who are furthering literature and the art of poetry and the poets who are not poets, so to speak, who are doing a likewise job in another medium, albeit one not that far removed from 'ordinary' verse, it is time to look at those who are doing harm to poetry.

Firstly, what harm is being done? The main harms are quite simple. These people are turning an audience away from verse by writing the kind of material that is not followed and is impermanent. It is not a matter of failing to get an audience in the first place, as with, for example, the work of Ezra Pound which has always been a minority audience poetry, but nevertheless is important in the overall scheme of the art. It is more a case of capturing an audience by one means or another and then turning it away, not just from the individual's work, but from others' as well, bringing poetry not so much into disrepute but into a limelight of apathy and disregard. Another aspect of the harm being done is the one that concerns a lowering of standards so that poetry becomes not an expressive art concerned with the basic emotions of humans but merely a slick and artfully devious entertainment in the weakest sense of the word: by this, I mean the lessening of integrity accepting that the basic integrity of poetry is that of showing humans to themselves, not just their outward leers but also their inner smiles. Next: the harm of having poetry laughed at. There are two kinds of laughing at poetry: the first is that of the laugh that finds fun and makes controversy and is the sort that appeared in the early 1970s when Bob Cobbing and others caused a fracas in The Poetry Society by going overboard for the avant-garde poetics – this laughter does good in the long run for it promotes discussion and a re-assessment of values; the second is the laughter of mockery which does not lead to controversy or discussion, but dismissal. And this is happening now.

Why are some poets doing this? The answer is twofold. They are hyping verse. They are seeing verse as a means of extending their own power bases, within literature or the 'world of the arts', using it merely as a stepping-stone to other things. In short, treating the art as a whore, to be used when the time is right then ignored.

As is often characteristic in the literary sphere, the poets who work towards a common aim often form a clique or semi-clique. The poets who graduated from The Group held sway for some years and still do, to some extent, in the upper echelons. It is fortunate for British poetry that they were of a high standard and that their aims were set upon advancing the art and not just their own sides of it. George MacBeth fits this category well: he held contemporary poetry broadcasting in his hand for many years and he could, quite easily, have done as he would with it. It is to his benefit, his honour and his deliberate catholicity of policy that he did not. The point is that he could have used his position to his own ends, in a very great way.

Poets who have come from a set section of the university world can be said to have held sway. Oxford and Cambridge poets still dominate the editorial posts in London and the number of them set up high in the poetic world is due to the in-crowding that goes on in this respect. An Oxbridge education has been, for thirty years, a sure entry into the poetic limelight for those who have wanted it. The Oxbridge syndrome is strengthening, too. A number of poets have come to the fore in the second half of the 1970s with the credentials of those two universities behind them and they are continuing the stranglehold already mentioned. The main figures seem to be Craig Raine, Andrew Motion and Blake Morrison, the latter actually being a graduate of Nottingham University and so, to some extent, an odd man out.

In themselves, they are pleasant people and their dedication cannot be questioned for they are working hard at the nucleus of the poetry atom. Craig Raine has risen through the ranks in a very short while to become poetry editor of Faber & Faber, one of the biggest and certainly most prestigious poetry publishers in

Britain, once guided by the likes of Eliot and de la Mare. Andrew Motion has come from winning £5000 for a single poem in the Arvon Foundation competition of 1980 to going straight into the editorship of *Poetry Review*, the country's oldest poetry journal, only to leave it after a few issues to become poetry editor at Chatto & Windus, a list formerly edited by D. J. Enright and C. Day Lewis: few could contradict the fact that, for a poet who had published at the time only one slim collection and a thick pamphlet as his major output, this is fame beyond all dreams. (Interestingly, at the age of 19, he did publish a very thin booklet from Norman Hidden's *Workshop New Poetry*; the small presses again foresaw the shape of things to come.) Along the way, Motion has picked up a few other little gems, too. He won the Newdigate Poetry Prize at Oxford (for thence he went), the Cholmondeley Award came his way for his first collection, *The Pleasure Steamers*, which was published by Carcanet, and he was awarded a Gregory Award on top of all this, in 1976. Blake Morrison, and here's a rub for one who has settled so high on poetry's perch, has not published a book of poems at all. He was included with six other poets in a Faber Introduction anthology in 1982, but that is that. (At the time of writing, his first collection is imminent from Motion's Chatto & Windus list.) Like Motion, he has however written a number of critical books, all of them aimed (it would seem) at the literary end of the undergraduate market. Motion's books are a study of Philip Larkin and a critical volume on Edward Thomas. Blake Morrison has done likewise for The Movement and Seamus Heaney. Both of these young men (Morrison born 1950, Motion 1952) have set themselves up as authorities both in poetry and matters poetical. This has come to a head with their collaboration in editing *The Penguin Book of Contemporary British Poetry*, a not-too-thick anthology of their immediate circle surrounded by a few others of like bent, not many of them either known to the public at large nor requested by them. The book was puffed as a collection of major poetry by reviewers in the establishment and of the poetry critics' club but it was seen for what it is by others. Most poets and many booksellers know that the book is grossly uncomprehensive, narrow in the range of poets chosen and not a little stilted. An introduction that might well serve as a good third-year under-graduate essay commences the book and attempts to justify its choice of contents and position. In truth, it does more harm than good for it gives to the mass audience a totally incorrect view of contemporary British poetry. Luckily, the public seem to sense this, even if they don't know it. The harm, though, lies in the fact that many see the book that should draw in the uninitiated through the far-reaching spread of such a popular paperback publisher as boring. It drives many away from what poetry can do and is doing these days in other fields.

Of all the reviews that covered this book, the most accurate and bluntly truthful was A. N. Wilson's article in the *Spectator*, of which he is literary editor. (Morrison holds a like post at the *Observer*.) Wilson knows the blinkered approach that the book holds: 'British poetry sounds as appetising as Traveller's Fare on British Rail', and the image that this produces, of a kind of curling sandwich poetry, is all too true. 'Major' can be a bleak adjective when used for some of the poets in the book, no matter how good they may be; it does make one wonder what word should be applied to Wordsworth, Coleridge and Chaucer. Perhaps Wilson's most damning comment is that much of the poetry in the book seems to be of a standard more usually taken for the poetry competitions in *New Statesman*, or at least the poetry that appears in that journal which has an intellectual readership and therefore wants only poetry of that ilk. That's fair enough, of course: but it doesn't mean that modern poetry is that and that alone.

The most terrible thing is that the poets in question have been set up by the editors of the Penguin book (in some instances not in keeping with their requests or liking) as the new pantheon of British poetry and indicators of the way forward. It is a direction that the editors seek to promote through their elevated positions as controllers of publishers' lists and they are, therefore, arbiters of taste and what they are presenting from their chairs of responsibility for the public to read (or ignore as fallacious) is largely boring. The work lacks verve. Seen alongside the poetry of Ted Hughes (who is not represented in the book which purports to contain the most important in contemporary British verse), this work is barely a wick guttering in a draught.

Boredom is more than an affliction. It is an infectious disease and once these poets spread it, poetry's had it. Their control of the art allied to their moribundity will wipe it out at major publishers' level. They have begun already. As the public at large mostly take poetry to be the words that come from the large London publishers, then they are going to see this, shrug their shoulders and pass on. To what? There are only the small press books left and they are hard to find in most bookshops. Poetry, it seems, is being 'safely tucked up for the night', to use Adrian Mitchell's words. But how long is the night to last? It will most likely be an Arctic one, for the new gods are but young and their altars are sturdy.

A look at the poetry of this triumvirate of poetic power has one anticipating work in the realms of the distinctly higher echelons of the art. In truth, one sees a versifying that is not only weak and lacking in force but also so poor as to make itself a mockery. (In the satirical magazine *Private Eye*, one finds a quotation from the poetry of Craig Raine taken – ironically, in the light of Wilson's comments – from the pages of the *New Statesman* and reprinted in the magazine's Pseuds' Corner column to which readers submit material that they consider to be fakey. The quotation in a spring 1983 issue reads:

> I dreamed your body was an instrument
> and this was the worn mouthpiece
> to which my breathing lips were bent.
>
> Each note pleased to love a little longer,
> longer, as though it was dying of hunger.
> I fed that famished mouth my ambergris.

Allowing for even some misprinting in the quotation, this is shoddy poetry and it sets the art up as something to be mocked in the most obvious of places – *Private Eye*'s popular pages. The poem is entitled 'Arsehole' and caused a stir when anti-pornography lobbyists attacked it. (That it is, in fact, a rather weak reworking of a poem written by Rimbaud and Verlaine in tandem appears to have been missed by them: hardly surprising, as Raine did not attribute the work as being related to their *Sonnet: To the Arsehole*.)

Firstly, though, a look at Blake Morrison's very small poetic output leaves the reader in a quandary as to how this can be hailed as not only impressive but important. His poetry, in common with that of his peers, lacks appeal of either popular or esoterically 'poetic' varieties. It has little life coming, it appears, from the pen of one steeped in the moribund. Style, diction and form are things of little import to Morrison who seems to write a deliberately laid-back type of poetry that appears both prosaic and prose-like:

> Somewhere a phone was ringing – perhaps for you.
> It crooned like a chance that would change the world,
> Though the room, when you got there, seemed
>   undisturbed,
> Dust and sunlight for a hundred years
> No noise had ever got under.
> It bothered you for a while, but friends came round,
> And the summer was a deep, deep blue
> That stretched over mountains and marram-grass
> And paved terraces with drinks at sunset.

Yet this is being regarded as a new poetry of position and relevance. If the following is an example of where poetry is heading, then it is for a period of unmitigated gloom.

> The Chancellor of Gifts is an elitist.
> You can't pretend he'll step out of the night
> with a gilt invitation-card or flowers.
> The brilliant words we wrote down in a dream
> aren't there beside our bedside after all.

Secondly, Andrew Motion: his work is better than Morrison's but that is a somewhat backhanded compliment. He writes in a similarly unattractive mode which the blurb of his very thin book, *Independence* (published by Salamander Press in 1981) states pompously as being – in this case – a narrative poem which is a 'story, and one that brings to a new sophistication, allusiveness and plangency the development of the narrative mode that has absorbed Andrew Motion since [his first collection] *The Pleasure Steamers*'. Well, that is one way of putting it. Another is to say that the poems ramble through narratives, semi-narratives or mini-narratives from which the reader is all but excluded from the start. The first lines in *The Pleasure Steamers* are

> Today your letter with its usual banter of strangeness
> – the forty years exile makes you write
> 'Napoli' now, without joking – until the postscript
> 'What would you say? Shall I come back?'

and the poem continues that way through three sections that draw no conclusion, either logically or artistically. In *Independence*, Motion is writing in the persona of one recalling his years in India and it does have some emotiveness to it (not emotion), but what there is is vicarious and secondhand. Motion wasn't born when the events in the historical basis of the book took place. He is merely reconstructing rather than constructing the past and its peoples. Once again, the poetry looks more like prose with a caesura erratically stuck in here and there either at whim or for some effect that doesn't seem to finally register. Certainly, the lines are not there to convey any sense of metrical direction:

> We were driving at once, my good right hand
> tight on the wheel, your left stretched
> over, changing the gears to MacFarlane.
> *Back here* – you said it teeth clenched
> as we stood in the dark porch

side by side for a moment,
our hands stretched clear in front,
You nodded towards them – *Symbols?*
Symbols? Balls, I said, and smiled
leading you in. *Nurse. Hello. Are you there?*

What is astonishing is that Blake Morrison has described Andrew
Motion as a potentially very important *lyric* poet. If you are a
member of the club, it seems anything goes. Certainly, in
Motion's work so far, there is not a shred to support this claim.
Perhaps it is that the potential has yet to indicate its potentiality.
Or is this simply a case of 'jobs for the (poetic) boys' – after all, if
one is in command, one can makes the rules, can't one?

Craig Raine is the same, but on a bigger scale. He has published
three books, is older, having been born in 1944, and whereas
Motion was only a student at Oxford, Raine was a student and
later a don – the academic bringing in his ways to the art. From
1979–80, Raine edited *Quarto*, a London literary journal that dealt
only with the major establishment issues and writers.

He is in many ways the doyen of the new poets which, with
those already commented upon, might extend to include James
Fenton (born 1949, educated at Oxford), Tom Paulin (born 1949,
Hull and Oxford Universities) Christopher Reid (born 1949,
Oxford), David Sweetman (born 1943) and Carol Rumens (born
1946; on the *Quarto* staff) amongst others. All write in a similar
manner and are all included in the Morrison/Motion Penguin
collection.

Bizarre and mostly ineffective imagery is one of Raine's
characteristic trademarks and is often unrelated to the subject
and seems to be added as an aside. Another characteristic is an
obtuseness that grates, making the poetry something that is
either totally lost on the reader or requires a reader's or listener's
guide before approaching the work. (Raine often provides this at
readings, but not in his books: quite often, the preamble far
exceeds the length and value of the poem it discusses.) From a
sequence of poems, *Anno Domini*, from Raine's first book, about
the life of a faith-healer, one has the following lines as the end of a
poem entitled 'Verdi's Requiem':

Twelve ordinary names

chiselled on stone.
Atwood, Anson, Tillotson, Calvert, –

names of the bones.
Gravel forces off their finger nails,

and the cabbage whites with caviar eyes
stare about this stony paradise.

Recorders, Jesu pie,
quod sum causa tuæ viae:

ne me perdas illa die.

And if that is not enough, consider a verse from the book's title poem, 'The Onion, Memory':

Tonight the arum lilies fold
back napkins monogrammed in gold,
crisp and laundered fresh.
Those crustaceous gladioli, on the sly,
reveal the crimson flower-flesh
inside their emerald armour plate.
The uncooked herrings blink a tearful eye.
The candles palpitate.
The Oistrakhs bow and scrape
in evening dress, on Emi-tape.

At least it rhymes. But is it good enough to merit such accolades as 'one of the most distinctive voices to have emerged in the past few years' (Blake Morrison in *The Times Literary Supplement*), 'an original and entertaining writer with a natural vein of sympathy and compassion' (Peter Porter in the *Observer*) and 'immensely talented' (John Carey in the *New Statesman*)?

A note to add: when I read and discussed the poem, 'The Onion Memory', with a group of postgraduate English students in Oxford in the summer of 1982, I received an almost blank response. They could say nothing, either of merit or de-merit. One stated simply that it was 'interesting, but . . . it seems too slight and has insufficient content in order to set itself up as a piece with any sense of direction. It goes nowhere.' One student asked me if I had written it in my student years. None could accept that it stood up to the puff the book received from John Osborne who wrote, in *Stone Ferry Review*, that 'for brilliance of figurative invention, 'The Onion Memory' is a book of poems unrivalled in this country since Sylvia Plath's *Ariel*.' No comment.

Those in position in this new wave of 'poetic sensibility' claim that what they are doing is introducing a new shift to that aspect of writing. In the introduction to the Penguin anthology mentioned above, the editors state that 'After a spell of lethargy, British poetry is once again undergoing a transition.' Too true, but at what a price! Artistry, skill with words, wonder, emotion and reality have gone. In their places stand slickeries, clevernesses and a poetry that has little of importance to the vast majority of those who would or might read it. A. N. Wilson struck the best chord in his review of this book and, through it, the whole of this new poetry and its makers, when he wrote that the editors' comments above are 'nonsense; but the sad thing is that no one will really mind if it is true or not. Very few people beyond the immediate circle of the 20 names in this book will have heard of these "British" poets. They are not much read because they're not much good, and no one will be reading them in 20 years' time.' This might be animus, but it is uncannily factual, alas! Where Wilson might be proven incorrect in his statement is in its closing comments. Those people may well still be around in the future decades because they are young and in positions of considerable authority over the whole poetry field.

The 'mafia' has taken over once again. British poetry has been set back a long, long way by this restrictive cartel. Gone is the freedom and the art; 'dormant' has become the key adjective to describe the situation poetry now finds itself in. It seems that lean years are ahead. The ketabolists are in control.

So are things of hope, in an age where standards are dropping and poetry is returning to the province of the academic (that is, narrow and self-indulgent) and the in-crowd, possible? The answer should be affirmative and is, but with reservations.

The lifeblood is still there, even if it is diluted by a group of poets who, with power on their side, are self-destructive and carry this attitude on to their art. There are poets who are writing serious, moving, skilful poetry and some of these are fortunate enough to have books placed with major publishers, although as has been shown, that is no guarantee of either a big readership or public attention. There are poets still writing who made the heydays. There are newer poets coming to the scene who uphold traditional standards and values but look upon these with a sense not of awe but of learning and progressing.

In the 1980s, however, matters do militate against these poets doing well. Public apathy has settled against poetry through the published efforts of the poor poets who have more attention. Public readings have dwindled considerably and the reading circuit that was so vibrant in the years 1966–73 has now all but disappeared. Small presses have also vanished in the face of real losses in readership and poetry lovers, as well as the recession causing costs of manufacture to soar. Small magazines, to an even greater extent than presses, have died a death, although there are signs that an upturn might occur in the mid-1980s. Costs, sales, distribution in print – all these can be recouped with ease. It is much harder to fight apathy and win back followers who have been driven away.

Poets seem to ignore the lesson that generations of writers have learnt: literature that lasts is for the masses, for thinking people and not for the writers themselves. Literature, to survive, must be totally unselfish. Modern British poetry is quite the opposite.

The lifeblood has support. Where small magazines have vanished, small 'recording studios' (for want of a better term) have come about: the technical advances in cassette home recording have brought out a new underground in tapes of poets reading their work. Ten years from now, the magic and excitement of the oral tradition, which set off the 1960s boom and which has been kept alive in no small part through the efforts and machinations of Horovitz and his *New Departures* capers and the like, may well return. The small presses that have survived are keeping alive the values of the art, are retaining for the future a gold-stock of followers who will, with luck, spread the gospel wide once more in the future. Those who are writing or publishing good poetry still see themselves as up against the barricades and fighting hard, and this gives them an added determination. Adversity can work marvels. There is still the hard core of good poets who will carry the tide – Hughes, MacBeth, Patten, Middleton, Redgrove . . . and they have others of younger years to help them such as Pete Morgan, Wes Magee, up-and-comers like Duncan Bush and Paul Hyland and many others who will do well if they can keep their heads above the pool of goo into which British poetry seems to have become swallowed. These poets, the next wave to hit the poetry beach, are writing for the world outside, not the confines of their own heads.

The way ahead seems plain. What poets must do is to overturn the moribund school that seems to be running the circus at present, avoid setting up power cliques and get on with writing, pressing to the boundaries of possibility what language and poetry can offer to everyone. What British insularity there is has to be actively worked against. After all, the best poetry works everywhere and through time. *Vide* Chaucer, Brecht, Wordsworth, Baudelaire, Catullus, D. H. Lawrence, Heine, Plath . . . these poets didn't write for their editors or a coterie of chums. They did not create for themselves alone. They wrote what people at large might share. They regarded poetry not as an academic game or some private activity. They saw it as distilled life, a purification of language and emotion, a means of exploring existence in a physical as well as mental framework. In short, to use modern coinage, they were *real*. And reality was their business, as it should be one of the first concerns of any true poet.

The times will change. Of that there is no doubt. Matters are constantly on the move, in a state of flux. The battle for poetry can be won once the battlefield is defined. As it now is.

INDEX

small presses, 35–42; expansion of, 43–59; *see also* magazine
Smart, Elizabeth, 73
Smith, John, 90
Smith, Ken, 47, 49, 55, 72, 210–11
Smith, Stevie, 94, 190–2
Snow on the North Side of Lucifer (Sillitoe), 193, 216–17
'Snowdrops' (MacBeth), 122
Snowing Globe, The (Scupham), 41
Snyder, Gary, 54
'Soliloquy at Potsdam' (Porter), 120
'Solstice' (Hooker), 168
Some Sweet Day (H. Williams), 157
Some Time in New York City (Lennon), 242–3
'Song of the Battery Hen' (Brock), 203
Song of Good Life, A (Brownjohn), 117
Songs a Thracian Taught Me (Beresford), 198
songwriters, 113–14, 240–7
sound poetry, 17–18, 230–1
South Bank Show, The (programme), 91, 103
Spark, Muriel, 61
Spender, Stephen, 94, 104
Spring Collection, The (P. Morgan), 103
Stafford, William, 185, 208
Stand (magazine), 55, 71–2
Starbuck, George, 172
State of Justice, A (Paulin), 233
State of Poetry Today, The (Hidden), 80
Stations (Bosley), 218
Stereo Headphones (magazine), 232
Stevenson, Anne, 98, 104, 195, 197
Sting, 245–7
Stones of Emptiness, The (Thwaite), 160
Storm (Sillitoe), 216–17
Strange Museum, The (Paulin), 233
Sugar Daddy (H. Williams), 156
'Sunday' (Hughes), 146
'Sunny Prestatyn' (Larkin), 219–20
'Sunshine of Your Love' (P. Brown), 244
Survivors (Peskett), 162
'Swaqk/Liverpool Soundpoem' (P. Brown), 141
'Sweet Painted Lady' (Taupin), 244
Sweetman, David, 254
Swinburne, Algernon Charles, 16–17
Sycamore Press, 42
'Symbols of the Sixties' (Brock), 203
Symptoms of Loss (H. Williams), 156
Szirtes, George, 39, 164

Tagore, Rabindranath, 61
Tarling, Alan, 38–9, 88
Tarn, Nathaniel, 96
Taupin, Bernie, 244
'Technicolour Dream, The' (P. Morgan), 202
television, 30, 91–2, 103–4
Tennant, Emma, 83
Tennyson, Alfred Lord, 3, 20
Terry Street (Dunn), 213
'That Morning' (Hughes), 151
Theory of Communication, A (Hobsbaum), 88
Thomas, D. M., 13, 39, 60, 90, 133, 197, 207–8
Thomas, Dylan, 20, 85–7, 110
Thomas, Edward, 210
Thomas, R. S., 44–5, 61–2, 64, 79
'Thought-Fox, The' (Hughes), 144
'Through the Tall Grass in Your Head' (Patten), 242
Thwaite, Anthony, 74, 158–61
Tigers (Adcock), 129–30
Tipton, David, 53
Title Deeds (Grubb), 128
'To a Slow Drum' (MacBeth), 122
Toczek, Nick, 82
Toddington Poetry, 101
Tom O'Bedlam's Beauties (Reading), 159–60
Tommy (Townsend), 244
Tomlinson, Charles, 96, 197
Tonight at Noon (Henri), 139–40
Torse 3 (Middleton), 175
Totleigh Barton, Devon, 24–5
Toulson, Shirley, 54, 130–1
Townsend, Pete, 244
Tractor (Hughes), 150
'training' for poets, 23–30
Travelling (Hamburger), 180
Travelling Behind Glass (Stevenson), 195
'Travelling Through the Dark' (Stafford), 185
Tribe, David, 88, 130–1
Trigram Press, 56
Tristan Crazy (K. Smith), 47
'Triumph of Time, The' (Swinburne), 16
Tropical Childhood, A (Lucie-Smith), 132
Turnbull, Gael, 83
Two Voices (D. M. Thomas), 207
Typewriter Poems (ed. Finch), 75, 232